Wisdom's Feast

Sophia in Study and Celebration

Susan Cady
Marian Ronan
Hal Taussig

1817

Harper & Row, Publishers, San Francisco
New York, Cambridge, Philadelphia, St. Louis,
London, Singapore, Sydney, Tokyo, Toronto

Library of Congress Cataloging-in-Publication Data
Cady, Susan.
    Wisdom's feast
Susan Cady, Marian Ronan, Hal Taussig.
    p.   cm.
    ISBN 0-06-254859-X
    1. Wisdom (Biblical character)   2. Wisdom (Biblical character)—
Prayer-books and devotions—English.   3. Wisdom—Biblical teaching.
4. Spirituality.   5. Femininity of God.   I. Ronan, Marian, 1947–
. II. Taussig, Hal.   III. Title.
BS580.W58C33   1989
220.6'4—dc19   88-45989
                                                                            CIP

89 90 91 92 93 HAD 10 9 8 7 6 5 4 3 2 1

*This book is dedicated to
Vivian Yoder,
feminist of heart as
well as head.*

Contents

Preface

She is strong and proud. She is creator and designer of all things. She promises to teach us about herself and the earth. Although she behaves quite playfully and with great abandon, her anger is also ready to scourge those who have ignored her. Human beings follow her, sometimes as students, sometimes as lovers, but she is also rumored to be the consort of a great God.

She reappears to us now with great promise out of the shadows of our own heritage. Her power and stature strike a deep chord in those who seek models of powerful womanhood. Her embrace of the entire creation mirrors the feminist/ecological spirituality of the past twenty years. Her important place in Judeo-Christian literature promises rootedness in the past and new images for the future as well.

This is Sophia or Wisdom. Those of us who have rediscovered her over the past fifteen years tend to call her Sophia, which is the transliteration of the Greek word for wisdom. Such a practice makes her sound more like the person she clearly is in the many biblical passages about her, passages that have been too often ignored.

As if her strong and evocative person weren't surprising enough, Sophia also turns out to have an important relationship to the figure of Jesus. So complex is this topic that we have explored it in two separate chapters, chapter 8, "Getting Acquainted with Sophia," and chapter 11, "Jesus and Sophia."

This book is an invitation to the reader to begin living with this amazing rediscovered goddess of the Bible who offers so much to contemporary spirituality. Most of the materials that follow are descriptions of activities and events focusing on this strong, female, and biblical figure. The Bible studies, rituals, liturgies, meditations, and sermons about Sophia in this book have emerged from a decade of exploration by men and women within and outside churches, people who wanted to learn what it might mean to live with Sophia.

We present this collection as a resource for others who wish to explore integrating Sophia into their own spirituality. We have not provided a rigid ideological frame through which one must pass in order to explore a living dialogue with her. Rather, we have recorded a number of religious/symbolic events and activities. In doing so, we hope that we have managed to reflect the breadth of human experience that went into the creation of these materials and the breadth of perspectives into which she can be integrated. We hope, likewise, that our manner of presentation will allow readers to enter into this venture of living with Sophia in an attitude of genuine exploration.

There are two ways to read this book. Of course, one's first thought is that a book is to be read from start to finish in a linear fashion. That is possible with this book, and may be the best way for some people who have never heard of Sophia.

But our preference as authors is that the reader—even the reader without prior acquaintance with Sophia—approach this book much like she or he would a cookbook. This book contains over fifty different events and activities about Sophia from many different points of view. It is very likely that reading some of the affective Bible studies, rituals, and worship services in part 2 of the book could engage the reader at a more personal level than the theoretical presentation of Sophia in part 1. We encourage readers to peruse the table of contents, especially the chapters in part 2 that contain all of the practical and affective work with Sophia, in order to find the best place to begin.

The rituals, affective Bible studies, and worship resources in part 2 have been the heart of the experience of Sophia for the authors. The spiritual poverty of our culture has much to do with the western and male-oriented preference for theory and abstraction over feeling and experience. We therefore can see a distinct disadvantage to reading this work from start (theory) to finish (practice).

Even for the reader who has not encountered Sophia at all prior to this book, starting with some of the introductory exercises in chapter 6 could be a more personal way of making her acquaintance.

A number of readers will want to begin with part 2 because that portion of the book can be used as a handbook for working with groups who are interested in Sophia. You may move from section to section, selecting studies, exercises, or rituals that are appropriate to your particular group situation. Each chapter in part 2 includes commentary and suggestions for selecting appropriate events and activities.

Some readers will note that most of part 1, except for chapter 4, has been previously published as a separate book, *Sophia: The Future of Feminist Spirituality*. In a number of the activities of part 2 the reader will be referred back to part 1 for a more extended theoretical discussion.

Wherever a reader may choose to begin, a number of assumptions permeate *Wisdom's Feast*. One concerns the role of affect in spirituality, while another has to do with approaches to Bible study that we have found most helpful.

The role of affect in spirituality is a matter of considerable importance in reflecting on the use of these resources. Research has long suggested that intellect cannot be separated from the emotions, nor can the body be split off from the spirit. We are whole people, and our spirituality must include all of who we are. Sophia cannot become a part of people's lives simply by being preached or talked about; people cannot integrate her through their rational processes alone. They need the opportunity to sing about her, paint their expressions of her, pray to her, meditate with her, move with her, and write about her. Sophia represents a shift of major proportions for most people in their image of God and their perception of reality. People need to use all of who they are as human beings to learn about her and to welcome her into their lives.

Because spirituality must include affect, we recommend that instructions accompanying Bible study material be followed carefully. Gaining information about Sophia as she appears in the various biblical texts is certainly a legitimate goal for participants in these studies. However, it is not the only possible goal; an equally important one, and perhaps more important in the long run, is the development of a spirituality that includes a vital relationship with this female goddess of the Bible. To change one's images of God requires more than information about biblical texts. One needs to live into these texts. Most of these Bible studies are designed to help a person do just that.[1]

The Bible studies in *Wisdom's Feast* are designed for use in groups. An individual can go through the questions and answer them on her or his own, but the real richness of discovery and depth of interaction with the texts takes place in a group setting. Ideally, a group should have at least eight people in it. The studies have been done effectively with as few as six participants, but the design is based on a Socratic style of questioning, which comes alive with a larger group.

The leader, in asking these questions, should continually remind those in the group that except in the case of strictly informational questions, there is no one right answer; rather, the goal is to generate as many answers as possible. Additionally, many of the questions invite individuals in the group to make deep connections between the text and their own experience. These questions are not easy to answer, so there may be long periods of silence. A leader must be patient and stick with the questions, rephrasing them if necessary. It is better to let a question go unanswered, letting the work of answering continue internally within each person, than it is to answer the question for the participants.

Because the questions are so important, it is absolutely necessary for the leader to meditate on them ahead of time, to answer them for herself or himself, and to be comfortable with them. This may mean changing phrasing or putting the question into one's own words. Invariably, a group will encounter times of discomfort in the face of particularly challenging questions; if the leader is at ease, she or he will be better able to help the group in these moments.

In addition to the questions, each study includes what is usually titled a "Closing Exercise." This is an opportunity for each person in the group to ground within herself or himself what has just been learned. The exercises are affective, using art, writing, meditation. They are crucial to the entire study, for they take place at the point where transformation in one's spiritual life begins to happen. Consequently, these exercises must not be dropped for want of time. The leader should anticipate that at least the last fifteen to twenty minutes of the study will be devoted to the closing exercise and should plan the rest of the study accordingly.

The activities in part 2 frequently refer to the great variety of biblical passages about Sophia, all of which are in the Appendix. The Appendix thus serves as a compendium of most of the major Sophia passages in the Bible.

Acknowledgments

Wisdom's Feast has been from the outset a collaborative effort on the part of its three authors. Because of the nature of the works presented here, however, many other individuals have been substantially involved in its development, and we take this opportunity to mention some of them.

We are indebted, first of all, to those who have taught us: to Burton Mack, for initially introducing Sophia as a figure to be taken seriously; to Walter Wink, who opened up the scriptures as a source of spiritual transformation; and to Janet Kalven, Eleanor Walker, and the other women belonging to the Grail movement who have over the years demonstrated that education is an adventure of the whole person.

We are also grateful for the institutions that have been home to us and have welcomed us. Calvary United Methodist Church in Philadelphia has been a deeply enriching congregation, with whom much of the work of this volume has been done. Without the Calvary context, much of the material in *Wisdom's Feast*—sermons, Bible studies, liturgies, and music—would not have come into being. Special thanks goes to the women of the Sophia Study Group at Calvary, with whom the Bible studies were used and developed and who provided a climate of receptivity within the congregation for continued experimentation with Sophia in worship. Our gratitude also to the Grail, whose members and associates have been warmly receptive to our work with Sophia, at Grailville in Loveland, Ohio, and at Cornwall-on-Hudson, New York; and to New York Theological Seminary where flexibility and support made the formulation of *Wisdom's Feast,* especially in its later stages, a lot more possible. Finally, First United Methodist Church of Germantown, in Philadelphia, Pennsylvania; the School of Theology at Claremont, California; Gladwyne Presbyterian Church, Gladwyne, Pennsylvania; and the Presbytery of Lansing, Michigan, all have been places in which we have learned as we taught, with people who have kept our excitement alive and growing.

The perspectives of others have been invaluable: Sylvia Sholar, whose enthusiasm for Sophia has lead to creative developments in women's spirituality; John Linsheid and Michele Bartlow, whose combination of excitement and caution regarding Jesus and Sophia has been helpful to explore; Karen King and Deirdre Good, who offered insights on Sophia from the gnostic perspective; Meg Root Bruck and Claudia Tscharner, who asked questions and made suggestions that opened up new ways of working with the texts; Cindy Hoffman and Marilyn Moyer, whose critical stance regarding the established church has pushed us into new territory; and William and Mary Louise Birmingham, whose wisdom, editorial experience, and unfailing humor were a great support throughout the process.

Many persons contributed to this volume through their own creative efforts: Gretchen Chapman, Anne-Marie Schaaf, Chip Coffman, Ray Henry, Lynn McMahon, Cherry Granrose, Ruth Woodlen, who collaborated in the design of a Sophia passion event; Heath Allen, who composed music for us; Alison Cheek, who willingly shared her Sophia eucharist; Pat Michaels, Rosemarie Greco and Marie Chiodo, who offered their musical compositions.

Finally, a special word of thanks and appreciation to Vivian Yoder, whose zeal for learning about Sophia was surpassed only by her zeal for word processing; without her, this book would still be stacks and stacks of unorganized raw material.

Part One

CHAPTER ONE

Spirituality, Feminism, and Sophia

For many of us, spirituality is something less than an everyday topic of conversation. The term itself conjures up a host of unfamiliar or unappealing associations—otherworldliness, disdain for the body, denial of pleasure, poverty, discipline. Such extreme behaviors, we're inclined to say, have little to do with ordinary people like us.

It can be perplexing, then, to realize that spirituality—no matter what terms people use to describe it—is becoming increasingly important in our time. Ordinary people, not monks or mystics, are engaging in practices which would once have seemed downright esoteric, whether T'ai chi, yoga, Zen, or more recent developments such as transcendental meditation or psychosynthesis. At the same time, political activists and workers for social change are beginning to recognize the need within themselves for sources of spiritual strength to sustain their efforts.

This contemporary turn toward spirituality is evident in many places. Centers of spirituality—creation centered spirituality, feminist spirituality, formative spirituality—have sprung up across the country,[1] while churches, retreat centers, and politically concerned religious groups are working toward the development of a spirituality for justice.[2] In addition, works on popular spirituality are being read widely,[3] and concern with the "spiritual" rather than the psychological is becoming a trend in some places.[4] Even allowing for a certain faddishness which seems inevitable in a media culture like ours, spirituality is clearly an important current topic, an indicator of a new turning toward the sacred in our time.

Feminists are prominent among those manifesting an active interest in spirituality. Because feminism has implications which reach far beyond the social and economic spheres, it both requires and implies the development of a new spirituality, one which enables the cultivation of nonhierarchical modes of human consciousness. In 1983–1984 seminars in feminist spirituality were conducted at the Women's Theological Center in Boston, at Union Theological Seminary in New York, and elsewhere. A graduate program in feminist spirituality has been established at Immaculate Heart College in Los Angeles, while Elisabeth Schüssler Fiorenza, Carol Ochs, Starhawk, and other feminist theologians and scholars are exploring its dimensions.[5] Feminist spirituality groups are developing around the country, not only among radical feminists, but also among more moderate feminists who recognize a need to cultivate their own spiritual gardens in a radically new way. So important is this emergence of feminist spirituality that it can be characterized as a major feminist development of the 1980s. At the same time, feminist spirituality can serve as a prototype of a number of new spiritualities arising across the contemporary religious spectrum.

Since this is the case, feminist spirituality is an exceptionally rewarding subject of study. An exploration of feminist spirituality will result in a deeper understanding of contemporary religious consciousness. It will also make clear that spirituality belongs to everyone, not simply to a religious elite. Such an exploration demonstrates the ways in which various religious traditions, especially Judaism and Christianity, are connected to the most crucial issues of our day.

The needs and possibilities of feminist spirituality lead us directly to Sophia, one of the great, unrecognized figures of the biblical tradition. It can almost seem that throughout these many centuries Sophia has been waiting in the wings for just this moment. The fit between her transforming power and the shape of feminist spirituality is nothing less than astounding.

TOWARD A DEFINITION

Spirituality has been defined as the actualization of the human capacity for self-transcendence.[6] Feminism is, however, a radical rethinking of the basic concepts with which we understand reality. When we use terms like "self" and "transcendence" within a feminist perspective, we must be prepared to understand them in a new way. In speaking of transcendence, for example, we do not mean "as opposed to immanence." We neither refer to the self in order to distinguish it from the other, nor speak of the spiritual in contrast to the physical. Instead, we struggle with these terms in an attempt to point toward a condition of basic oneness with reality which feminist spirituality both recognizes and strives to develop.

Since this is the case, it is easy to see why Carol Ochs, in her work on women and spirituality, understands spirituality as a conscious, deliberate transformation of the self to bring it into closer relationship with reality.[7] By foregoing the language of transcendence and emphasizing instead transformation and relationship, Ochs makes room for women's experience, especially mothering, in an understanding of human spirituality.

In not addressing the question of a specifically feminist spirituality, however, Ochs seems to imply that it is possible to move from the traditional, universal understanding of spirituality, which excludes most women's experience, to a new, genuinely universal definition which includes women's experience. This is, unfortunately, unrealistic. It is just too soon to be speaking about "human" spirituality. The classical western tradition has created a vision of reality which consciously and unconsciously excludes women, people of color, and the poor. Until a just and inclusive society has been achieved, it will be necessary to identify and foster the distinct aspects of feminist awareness (and black awareness, and campesino awareness, and so on) which are critical for human transformation. By moving too quickly to a universal language we run the risk of being sucked once again into an exclusive white male vision of reality.

THE PLACE OF EXPERIENCE
IN FEMINIST SPIRITUALITY

Given these qualifications, it is possible to make several basic assumptions about feminist spirituality. First of all, when we speak of feminist spirituality, it is our own spirituality we speak of, inasmuch as we are, whether male or female, in the process of becoming feminist. We are not concerned with the practices of some witches in Boston or San Francisco, unless, of course, some of us are those witches.

Another way of saying this is that our own experience is the authoritative reference point for this spirituality. Starting with women's experience is one of the basic tenets of feminism, and it is central to feminist spirituality as well. If we attempt to imitate some spirituality outside our ken, whether it be the spirituality of Archbishop Romero or Dorothy Day or Starhawk, we are involved in patriarchal spirituality. Feminist spirituality, on the other hand, is the experiencing, the cultivating, and the expressing of the unique spirit which is each one of us, an activity which is intimately involved with self-transformation, and with opening toward the other.

The first step toward appropriating this spirituality is to attend closely to our own feelings and responses to the world and to each other. This attention to our feelings and responses is the root of our connectedness with others and, as such, the root of our power to change the world. This is one of the central insights of Joanna Rogers Macy's book, *Despair and Personal Power in the Nuclear Age*. Openness to the environment and our response to it are at the very heart of our power to transform reality.[8]

Once the crucial role of experience in feminist spirituality has been established, some possibly inaccessible aspects of traditional spiritual practice may be opened to us. Prayer and ritual, for example, may be more understandable when we realize that each of them in its own way helps us to attend to our experience and thus enables us to be more profoundly aware of our connection with all beings.

All this notwithstanding, understanding the role of experience in feminist spirituality is no easy matter. Because women have been socialized to discount their feelings and responses, it seems almost impossible to overestimate the role of experience in feminist spirituality. On the other hand, one of the traditional pitfalls of spirituality has been, as Carol Ochs points out, to make experience the goal rather than the starting point, so that all too often supposedly enlightened persons are reduced to seeking after particular experiences and emotional states rather than seeking insight into the meaning of these experiences.[9] Thus Ochs emphasizes transformation as the essential component of spirituality. Yet because of the sexism which is intrinsic to their socialization, women have been all too ready to transform themselves, often before they have come to terms with who they actually are. And so self-transformation cannot be the essential component of an authentic feminist spirituality, though it has its appropriate place. Rather, it is the connectedness between all beings which is basic to feminist spirituality and which is the goal of the experiences and activities constituting feminist spirituality.

This connectedness is so basic, in fact, that feminist spirituality can be defined as the experiencing, the expressing and the effecting of the radical connectedness of all creation, and the radical equality of all human beings. Connectedness is the vision at the heart of feminist spirituality, a vision which informs and transforms our experiencing and our action so that we begin to treat reality in terms of our connection with it.

The second part of this definition, regarding the equality of all human beings, may appear to be redundant and unnecessary. Yet it is the present political reality, once again, which mandates this qualification. Religions traditionally oppressive of women and some theologians and philosophers who may be inactive in the concrete struggle for human liberation are still comfortable using a language of connectedness. Until women and people of color are fully accepted as equals within their own species, it will be difficult or even inappropriate for them to take as their first priority human oneness with all species or with the planet itself. Nonetheless, women, as nurturers and traditional tenders of the soil, have always intuited that basic oneness, and the emergence of feminist spirituality signals a conscious recognition of that reality.

This oneness is not fusion, but differentiated connectedness, a connectedness precisely because of our separation from one another.[10] In this sense, interdependence is the opposite of fusion. This distinction is crucial for women because women have been all too often unable to distinguish their own identities from the identities of those they serve or nurture—but this symbiosis is not what we mean by connectedness. Rather, we refer to a connection that becomes stronger the more we know that we are not identical to another being. It is a connection by virtue of our psychological separateness, by virtue of our ability to feel and to know and to imagine deeply about others. Thus the development of the self, learning to recognize our own feelings and to know what we want, is not in competition with the needs and feelings of others, but is rather essential for us to be in authentic communion with them. In other words, it is necessary to have a self before that self can be transformed, and thus the connectedness at the heart of reality is a differentiated connectedness. An image of great vitality which has proven useful for expressing this differentiated connectedness is the image of the web of life. Feminists and social activists are using this image in political and ritual events.[11]

THE SYMBOLS OF POWER

If a new vision of connectedness is basic to feminist spirituality, so is a new understanding of power. Instead of the old, patriarchal notion of power as power-over, domination, and control, feminist spirituality focuses on shared power—power with and power-among.[12] In fact, connectedness and shared power are virtual corollaries of one another—because we are in connection there is power among us. Unfortunately, experiences of shared power are rare whether in marriage, in the family, in church, in school, or in the workplace. Likewise, the symbols of shared power which would help us recognize this experience when it does occur are in short supply. One of the critical tasks facing feminist spirituality is to find or create, and then to disseminate, compelling and energizing images of shared power.

This will be no easy task. Inhabitants of the western world know all too well the symbols of power-over. Schooling in these symbols reaches back thousands of years, and clusters primarily around the figure of the hero. It is the hero who transcends material and social barriers, who discovers the mysteries of the universe and masters them, who launches himself from the earth into unknown realms. He is Ulysses, David, Solomon, Arthur, Roland, Michelangelo, Galileo, Voltaire, Einstein and Superman. The Enlightenment idea of progress is fueled by his image. The Christ-figure as well has served as a primary heroic symbol within the Church and western culture, placing progress, transcendence and domination close to the heart of classical western spirituality.

Yet the age of the hero, the age of transcendence and mastery, is drawing to a close. Some would say that it ended forty years ago, at Auschwitz and Hiroshima. The scientific and technological hero may have created and mastered new worlds, but in the process he has damaged the earth and basic human patterns so thoroughly that life itself is endangered. Classical western spirituality shares responsibility not only for the creative, developmental aspects of western culture, but also for its destructive, even its demonic components.[13] More and more, many of the glorious, triumphant symbols of the hero are being recognized for what they are, the symbols of patriarchal spirituality, of power-over: missiles, rifles, nuclear energy, fast cars, the thunder god in the sky, strip mining, deforestation, imperialism, the breaking of wills, forced obedience, expiation. We must come to terms with these symbols, with the shadow side of our past and present and with its power over us, in order to move beyond it to a situation of shared power and connectedness.

PATRIARCHAL SPIRITUALITY

Patriarchy is that interlocking system of oppressions—racial, sexual, political and economic—which aims to subjugate and control the earth, the poor, females, people of color, feeling and spontaneity. Patriarchal spirituality is the extension of that system into our hearts and minds. It is a demonic aspect of classical western spirituality,[14] a system of images, beliefs, and practices which has glorified and entrenched power-over in western culture and in Christianity. By patriarchal spirituality we mean everything that wars against our realization of connectedness with one another and the rest of reality, and, as a corollary of this, everything that wars against our experiencing and feeling deeply in our own bodies.

Another way of saying this is that patriarchy is what obstructs spirituality within us and outside of us. It is a token of the stranglehold patriarchy has on all of us that we actually understand ourselves in terms patriarchy has set, that is, in terms of disconnection, competition, control, domination, and in terms of exclusive dichotomies, the personal or the political, the sacred or the profane. Patriarchal thinking also assumes that the spiritual is separate from the political. For us, however, obstacles to the equality of persons in the political order are precisely those things which obstruct our spiritual development, and this is not meant metaphorically. The same mechanisms that stifle our connectedness with others in this society—drunks, the messy poor (not the ones we admire in El Salvador), rapists, neo-Nazis—stifle our connection with the part of ourselves that is like that person, and ultimately our spirits are diminished. If we could truly feel compassion for ourselves and for our fellow human beings, we would be forced to act on their behalf, because it would be on our own behalf. If we do not act politically, our spirituality is deficient, and, conversely, each step we take to truly empower our sisters and brothers will open us to more authentic experiences of the spirit within us.

Everyone to some degree understands reality in terms patriarchy has set; it is only collectively that we manage to have a steady vision of the equality and connectedness between us. Feminist spirituality is only just coming to be in us, our hearts and minds are being converted, our imaginations are being converted from a vision and practice of submission and domination to one of equality and connectedness. But we are all caught, to some degree, in patriarchy's stranglehold.

The process of breaking out of this stranglehold is lengthy and complex. On the one hand we are still in the grips of massive and relentless systems which rationalize and perpetuate oppression. Feminist scholarship and criticism aim to dismantle these systems, breaking them down into their underlying myths and symbols, demythologizing them, exorcising us. A second phase, one of remythologizing and symbol-building, must accompany this first phase in order for our hearts and minds to be eventually freed from domination. This second phase functions on the level of culture and imagination somewhat the way network building and the identification of role models has functioned for women seeking to build careers. We literally cannot imagine what we have no models and images for. In order to break out of patriarchy's stranglehold we must identify, appropriate, and share symbols of equality and connectedness. Here Sophia, that ancient and unrecognized biblical figure, can play a crucial role in the development of a new feminist cosmos of connectedness.

THE IMAGE OF THE GODDESS IN FEMINIST SPIRITUALITY

The Wicca movement is the goddess-centered stream within religious feminism. Wicca participants are sometimes organized into covens, and use spells, rituals, and chants as a means of coming into deeper contact with reality. Some people equate Wiccan spirituality with feminist spirituality. And there is no denying that Wicca has made a major contribution to feminist spirituality (in fact, to contemporary religious consciousness generally) by reintroducing the goddess as a symbol of immanence and radically connecting power. Some Wicca participants, too, have been deeply involved in various political actions, using Wiccan ritual to support resistance efforts.

Wiccan theory is at times flawed, however, by its use of the kind of dichotomies feminism is meant to oppose. In *Dreaming the Dark*, for example, Starhawk suggests a sort of we/they, good religion/bad religion split through her total identification of Judaism and Christianity with patriarchy, that is, with power-over, domination, control. She is careful to say that when she speaks of the goddess she is not proposing a new belief system. Some readers may question whether Starhawk's contrast of a one-dimensional version of Judaism and Christianity with a rather nuanced exploration of the "image of the Goddess" is entirely fair, however.[15] Such a contrast easily results in the identification of one particular religious tradition with shared power and connectedness, another with estrangement. This we/they dichotomizing weakens the connections between those of us who share the same religious universe.[16]

There is no denying that sexism is still a scandalous reality within Christianity and within other major world religions. This admission cannot block out, however, women of the past and of the present who stand with great integrity in the various religious traditions.[17] If feminist spirituality takes as its starting point women's own experience, some of us may choose to interact with our experience of the Christian or Jewish traditions by working to transform them rather than by separating ourselves from them. In fact, some of us refuse to be cut off from our religious heritages, choosing instead to become conscious subjects of our own religious development, and to have an impact on those traditions.

Our use of the image of the goddess in this transformation is critical. If the goddess becomes a strange, exotic figure, substantially lacking in historical context, if she is perceived as a mythic, romantic figure appealing primarily to alienated white middle-class women, she will be of little use in the struggle to develop a new consciousness of connectedness. Religious feminists must instead ask themselves: how can the image of the goddess become accessible to a broad range of women, women of color, white ethnic women, traditional professional women, women still involved in churches and local communities? We must find a way to mainstream the goddess into the universe within which women are actually living their lives. Or perhaps it is simply a question of recognizing that she has been there all along.

THE CASE FOR SOPHIA

Sophia arises in the midst of this discussion like a new moon emerging from the sea. Sophia is a female goddess-like figure appearing clearly in the scriptures of the Hebrew tradition, and less directly in the Christian Gospels and Epistles. Believed by some to be related to a number of Hellenistic goddesses, she has been much researched by scripture scholars and by Jungian psychologists as well.

Sophia is a real biblical person, then, a real part of the Jewish and Christian traditions, yet we have never learned to call her by her name and have never really acknowledged her dignity and worth. Many of us, of course, have come across various references to Wisdom in the Bible. Yet for some of the same reasons that women have been ignored and repressed within the biblical traditions, and for other reasons which we will soon discover, Sophia has never had the impact on us that she could have. The struggle to formulate a feminist spirituality, and our enormous need to find symbols of connectedness require that we now reconsider Sophia, in all her splendor and mystery.

Sophia has not gone entirely neglected, of course. She has been a subject of great interest to biblical scholars for some time, and in recent years a number of theologians have attempted to assess Sophia's place in contemporary religious consciousness.

Joan Chamberlain Engelsman, in *The Feminine Dimension of the Divine*, discusses Sophia in great detail. Using Jung's theory of the archetypes of the collective unconscious, in this case the archetype of the Great Mother, Engelsman examines Sophia in relation to the goddesses of the Hellenistic era, particularly Demeter, Persephone, Hecate, and Isis. It is

Engelsman's conclusion that although Sophia begins as a personified hypostasis of God, God's Wisdom, and continues as a creation of God carefully contained within monotheistic Judaism, she grows in importance until her power is similar to that of any Hellenistic goddess.[18] She even begins to rival Yahweh's power, in her demands for people to follow her and her promise of salvation to those who do.

Engelsman documents how Sophia's power as a divine figure was broken, using the Freudian concept of repression to describe Sophia's undoing. This repression begins with Philo, who substituted a personified, masculine Logos ("word" in Greek) for the feminine Sophia. Philo at first equated Logos with Sophia, then substitutes Logos for Sophia, until the masculine person of Logos has taken over most of Sophia's divine roles, including the firstborn image of God, the principle of order, and the intermediary between God and humanity.[19] Sophia's powers are limited and she is restricted to heaven, where she is described by Philo as "ever-virgin," "Maiden," "daughter of God," "first-born Mother."[20] Thus Philo effectively truncates her divine power.

Engelsman sees this process of repression continuing, with Christ replacing Sophia as personified Wisdom.[21] Paul identifies Christ with Sophia, and appropriates concepts and terminology of the Wisdom School to speak of Christ.[22] In Matthew, Jesus speaks Sophia's words, and he takes over her powers. Although the earlier Q tradition, which accords to Jesus the role of Sophia's messenger, is incorporated within the Gospel, this tradition is used to create "a Christology dependent on the Hellenistic understanding of Sophia, whose powers and attributes are now seen as incarnate in the man Jesus."[23] John transforms Sophialogy to Christology by transferring Sophia's power and attributes to the Logos, then identifying Christ as Logos incarnate.[24] Jesus' speeches in John's Gospel, both in style and symbolism ("I am . . . light, water, vine") evoke the style and symbolism of passages in Proverbs, Wisdom, and Ben Sirach (also called Ecclesiasticus) to describe Sophia.[25] In John as well, Jesus becomes Sophia incarnate. But, according to Engelsman, this transmutation of the feminine Sophia to the man Jesus is not the final repression of the feminine dimension of the divine in the Judeo-Christian traditions.

The final repression of Sophia comes several centuries later, during the Christological disputes of the third and fourth centuries. The early church continued to develop its understanding of Christ in ways similar to biblical Christology, assigning to Jesus attributes of Sophia and describing Jesus as the incarnation of Sophia. But Sophia had never developed fully as a divine person co-equal with Yahweh, due to the limitations imposed on her by Judaism's strict monotheism. Thus, if Jesus and Sophia were equivalent, Jesus' status was less than God the Father, which posed a threat to trinitarian doctrine. Consequently, the early church fathers, in their efforts to clarify Christ as equal to God the Father, abandoned references to Jesus as Sophia incarnate. At that point Sophia disappeared from western theological consideration.[26] Engelsman's conclusion is depressingly negative: Sophia reached her peak of power as a divine person in the Hellenistic era, only to be limited in her growth to full divine status by Jewish monotheism, replaced in Christianity by the male Jesus, and erased as a part of the Christological tradition by the church fathers.

Rosemary Radford Ruether addresses herself to Sophia in *Sexism and God-Talk,* and she also sees Sophia as the victim of patriarchy. Ruether traces the roots of the Sophia of the scriptures to the ancient near eastern goddess tradition, but notes that in Hebrew thought she has been limited to the status of an attribute of the male God rather than an autonomous female divine figure.[27] She describes the replacement of Sophia by Jesus in the Christian scriptures as Engelsman has done. Ruether notes, however, that this did not end speculation on a female aspect of God in the early church; the figure of the Holy Spirit picked up many of the traditions of Sophia and Hokmah (Spirit).[28] This female imagery of the Holy Spirit was not so much a heretical deviation of the early church, according to Ruether, as it was a view that was marginalized and repressed by western Christianity.[29]

Although she documents patriarchy's repression of the divine feminine, Ruether holds a negative view of Sophia's usefulness in resolving the exclusively male image of God that patriarchy has given us. She is troubled by a divine androgyny that ratifies "on the divine level the patriarchal split of the masculine and feminine."[30] This is especially troublesome when the feminine aspect of God is a secondary figure functioning as mediator which reinforces the subordinate position of females in the social order. "For feminists to appropriate the 'feminine' side of God within this patriarchal gender hierarchy is simply to reinforce the problem of gender stereotyping on the level of God-language."[31] Ruether's objection to Sophia as the answer to the need for a female divine figure is the same as the church fathers' objections to her as the primary model for Christology; she never developed in the scriptures as a fully independent divine figure, with co-equal status to Yahweh.

Elisabeth Schüssler Fiorenza, in her study of feminist biblical hermeneutics *In Memory of Her,* emphasizes the positive implications of Sophia's place within the Jewish and Christian traditions and thus her potential place in an authentic feminist spirituality. She begins by situating Sophia within the tradition of Jewish Wisdom theology which had developed during the third century, B.C.E. Unlike classical prophetic theology, Wisdom theology is not characterized by fear of the goddess—rather, it is inspired by a "positive attempt to speak in the language of its own culture, and to integrate elements of its 'goddess cult,' especially Isis worship, into Jewish monotheism."[32] Sophia is, in fact, the God of Israel expressed in the language and imagery of the goddess, according to Schüssler Fiorenza. Using a variety of titles and expressions, Wisdom theology attempts to describe Sophia as divine; it uses goddess language to speak of the "one God of Israel whose gracious goodness is divine Sophia."[33]

Schüssler Fiorenza shows that the early Palestinian Jesus movement used this Wisdom theology in its understanding of Jesus. For them, Jesus is

Sophia's messenger, and the earliest Christian theology is Sophialogy. This communal understanding, Schüssler Fiorenza suggests, is rooted in the biblical writers' understanding of Jesus as the prophet and child of Sophia. She supports this hypothesis by citing a number of Sophia texts spoken by Jesus. The message of Jesus as Sophia's envoy, moreover, is one of equality and inclusion for all Israel's outcasts and downtrodden: women, suffering, the poor. This proclamation was a political as well as a religious event, one which results in Jesus' death.[34]

While the early Jesus movement within Judaism accorded great significance to Jesus as the messenger and child of Sophia, a later stage of Christian evolution, the Christian missionary movement, saw Jesus as divine Sophia herself. Jesus, as Christ-Sophia, is enthroned as ruler of the whole cosmos, and this is the foundational myth of the Christian community. In addition, according to Schüssler Fiorenza, the early Christian missionary movement recognized the resurrected Jesus as Sophia-Spirit. Thus, in Schüssler Fiorenza's estimation, Sophia is at the very heart of the early Christian community's understanding of Jesus and of what we have come to call the Trinity.[35] Many Christian feminists have begun, without much fanfare, to speak of the Sophia-God of Jesus and of Jesus Sophia, giving us some indication of the possible significance of Schüssler Fiorenza's interpretation.

A number of the negative criticisms raised by Engelsman and Ruether cannot be denied. Much of the treatment of Sophia in the Bible and in the Christian tradition reinforces patriarchal values, making Sophia a potentially dangerous symbol of the divine. Too often she has played a mediating role, pointing toward God rather than to herself, and thus upholding male power. Because Sophia did not develop co-equal status with Yahweh, because her voice is not identified in the Christian scriptures, it has been easy to keep her secondary and derivative.

As Elisabeth Schüssler Fiorenza has shown, however, this is not all there is to say about Sophia. It is our thesis that Sophia, despite her flaws, can be developed into a powerful integrating figure for feminist spirituality, and that the biblical Sophia provides us with a starting point for that development. There are, for example, a few passages within the biblical material which point toward giving Sophia a fuller, co-equal status with God. These passages need to be highlighted and used to continue her development in our day when her full divine status can be seen as an asset rather than a threat.

We find one of these passages in Baruch 3. Sophia is hidden, with Yahweh in search of her; only after he finds her does creation begin. There is a hint here that Sophia is not derivative or secondary to Yahweh, but rather existed in her own right before creation—indeed, that Yahweh needed her to begin the creative process. As alternative reading of Proverbs 8:22 ("Yahweh created me") is "Yahweh acquired me," which also hints at her status as an autonomous divine figure. Again, in Wisdom 10, Sophia is depicted as the divine saving figure in history, guiding Noah to safety, calling Abraham, and leading Moses and the Hebrew people to safety through the sea. In fact, Sophia and God seem to be fully interchangeable, since halfway through the account of salvation history a male God replaces Sophia as the divine actor. Finally, since Sophia and Jesus were equated in the New Testament, it is possible to build on later Christological developments which affirmed Christ as co-equal with God the Father. If, through the Christological process in the early church, Christ took on equal status with God, and if Jesus is described as Sophia incarnate in the New Testament, then it follows that in our time Sophia can benefit from the earlier Christological development by also acquiring equal status with God.

Because of her ability to integrate much that has divided us, Sophia may become more and more central to feminist spirituality as feminist theology and practice continue to develop. It is fitting, then, to continue our pursuit of Sophia, to learn more of her history, to immerse ourselves in her imagery. For while we are forced, with Phyllis Trible,[36] to admit that the patriarchal stamp of scripture is permanent, we also understand that religious traditions have always, almost intuitively, found the language and symbolism needed for their own authentic evolution. At a time in history when our connections with one another and with the earth itself are threatened with destruction, we look with hope toward Sophia. By coming to know her and to love her, may we be enabled to move powerfully and decisively into a future of justice and communion for the earth and its inhabitants.

CHAPTER TWO

Sophia in the Hebrew Scriptures

It is tempting to greet this discussion of Sophia as she is portrayed in the Hebrew scriptures with irony, or even scorn. Our first inclination is to protest. Surely, we say, Wisdom is a minor figure in the scriptures. How can such a minor figure have any real importance in this exploration? How can a few obscure texts support a relationship between feminist spirituality and the Hebrew tradition?

A second glance brings us up short, however. There is more material on Sophia in the Hebrew scriptures than there is about almost any other figure. In all of these books only four persons have more written about them than Sophia. Only God (under various titles), Job, Moses, and David are treated in more depth.

There are more pages in the Hebrew scriptures about Sophia than about Abraham, Isaac, Jacob, Solomon, Isaiah, Sarah, Miriam, Adam, or Noah. But we do not know her. Churches and synagogues insure that children can recite the stories of Aaron or Joseph, but they never even allude to Sophia. Literature classes in schools and colleges examine the epics of Abraham or Solomon or even the story of Ruth, but Sophia, who stands taller than any of them, is ignored.

Western society has chosen to ignore Sophia throughout its history. In almost every case, she has been either repressed or used superficially. Sophia fit neither the dogmatic categories nor the models of human behavior which the Church developed. She was much too ambiguous and pliable to fit neatly into the discussions of humanity versus divinity which dominated the Church's thought for centuries. Since she was not clearly God and was so clearly not human, she was confusing to the dogmaticians, so they chose to repress or ignore her.[1]

Nor did Sophia act as society, especially the Church, wanted people to act. Sophia is proud, assertive, angry and threatening, creative, and energetic. Western society did not encourage such character traits among the general populace. Of course, such independence was especially discouraged in women. Thus Sophia was of no use to those in search of exemplary figures from the Bible.

Protestantism hardly knows her at all. The so-called champions of the Bible have lived in almost total ignorance of Sophia from the earliest days of the Reformation. For instance, even though she dominates the first nine chapters of the Book of Proverbs, Protestants think of that book exclusively in terms of the collection of sayings in the later chapters.

Catholicism also tended to leave Sophia out of the "Old Testament." Some of Roman Catholic tradition, however, noticed the presence of such a female figure and immediately used her as a prefiguring of the Virgin Mary.[2] This was a misreading of the Sophia texts. But a serious encounter with the figure of Sophia in the Hebrew scriptures was considerably less important than the more utilitarian purpose of underscoring the significance of Mary for the Church.

Once we notice that our initial impression of Sophia's minimal place in the "Old Testament" is not only incorrect, but also grossly mis-stated, several questions occur, rather quickly to us.

Who is she? If there is so much material about her, what does that material tell us?

What can we learn about her from between the lines? Is there research about her and the historical circumstances around the texts that describe her? Have biblical scholars of our time ignored her in the same measure as Church tradition? If not, what have they learned about her?

How is Sophia important in the Hebrew tradition? If there is so much material about her, she was clearly important in a number of expressions of the Jewish faith. What is Sophia's significance for the Hebrew traditions which called her forth?

Before considering these matters, it seems important to address ourselves to several prior questions of terminology. First of all, some may wonder about our use of the name "Sophia" throughout this exploration when the biblical translators invariably prefer "Wisdom." Sophia is, in fact, the Greek word for wisdom, or, rather, a transliteration of that word. Sophia immediately suggests a person rather than a concept, however, and this is precisely what the Bible intends. Use of the title "Wisdom" rather than the name "Sophia" contributes to further avoidance and repression of this unique biblical person, a practice we would like to see reversed. Thus the choice of Sophia.

The second problem of terminology has to do with references to the "Old Testament." We are well aware that Christian use of the term "Old Testament" is offensive to most Jews, and rightly so. But almost half of the Sophia material with which we are concerned in this chapter occurs in books found only in Roman Catholic editions of the Bible. The books of Ecclesiasticus (or Ben Sirach, as it is sometimes called), Baruch, and Wisdom belong to that set of works which are included in the Roman Catholic Bible but omitted from the Jewish and Protestant versions. Although these books are products of the Hebrew faith of their time, the existing texts are in Greek, and for the most part seem to have originated in the Greek-language circles of the Jewish people. This means that it is not entirely accurate to refer to these books as part of the Hebrew scriptures. The label "Old Testament" is more appropriate, since the texts are in the Catholic Bible, but our use of this label runs the risk of giving offense. Due to this rather complicated situation, we have chosen to talk about Sophia in the Hebrew scriptures and tradition, knowing that this stretches the labels a bit, or to refer to Sophia in the "Old Testament" with emphasis on the quotation marks.

SOPHIA AS CREATOR

Sophia is perhaps first of all the One at the heart of the creative act.

The book of Wisdom (7:25, 27) describes her this way: "She is a breath of the power of God . . . Although alone, she can do all. Herself unchanging, she makes all things new."

In Proverbs 8:27–31, Sophia speaks of her creating at the beginning:

When God set the heavens in place, I was present,
when God drew a ring on the surface of the deep,
when God fixed the clouds above,
when God fixed fast the wells of the deep,
when God assigned the sea its limits—
and the waters will not invade the land—
when God established the foundations of the earth,
I was by God's side, a master craftswoman,
Delighting God day after day,
ever at play by God's side,
at play everywhere in God's domain,
delighting to be with the children of humanity.

Sophia's presence at the beginning is also described in Ecclesiasticus 24:3–5:

I came forth from the mouth of the Most High,
and I covered the earth like mist.
I had my tent in the heights,
and my throne in a pillar of cloud.
Alone I encircled the vault of the sky,
and I walked on the bottom of the deeps.

But Sophia is not just Creator at the beginning. She is a part of the ongoing creative process. The author of the book of Wisdom talks about her in chapter 7:10–11 as the one in his life who is the source of all good things.

Her radiance never sleeps.
In her coming all good things came to me,
and at her hands riches not to be numbered.
All these I delighted in, since Sophia brings them,
but as yet I did not know she was their mother.

In the next chapter (8:34) this follower of Sophia describes further how the ongoing creative process happens through her:

She deploys her strength from one end of the earth to the other,
ordering all things for good . . .
Her closeness to God lends luster to her noble birth,
since the Lord of all has loved her.
Yes, she is an initiate in the mysteries of God's knowledge.
She makes choice of the works God is to do.

In Ecclesiasticus 1:14, this continuing presence in all that comes into being is illustrated in the following manner:

She was created with the faithful in their mother's womb.

It is fascinating to note the way in which the texts move Sophia's place in the creative process back and forth between Creator and created. Clearly the texts cited so far portray her as the One who makes all things new, orders existence itself, and decides what is to occur. But the text in Ecclesiasticus 1:14 describes Sophia's participation in the birth of people as being "created." In the same chapter (verse 4) "before all other things Sophia was created."

This ambiguity concerning Sophia's exact place in the creative process is reflected in the first part of the account of the "beginning" of the earth in Proverbs 8. The text itself is uncertain. Some translators choose to read in Proverbs 8:22, "God created me (Sophia) when God's purpose first unfolded." Others choose to read, "God acquired me (Sophia) when God's purpose first unfolded."

Heightening this ambiguity is a passage in Baruch (3:29–32) describing how God acquired Sophia:

Who has ever climbed the sky and caught her
to bring her down from the clouds? . . .
No one knows the way to her,
no one can discover the path she treads.
But the One who knows all knows her,
God has grasped her with God's own intellect,
God has set the earth firm forever
and filled it with four-footed beasts.

With Sophia in God's possession, the writer of Baruch implies, creation begins. Her presence is necessary to the creative process.

However one chooses to interpret this ambiguity, it is important to note that the creative process itself does not make a clear distinction between the Creator and the created. Often that which comes into being either seems to do so on its own or, on the other hand, as a part of the one which brought it into being. The Hebrew tradition which described Sophia at the heart of the creative process was aware of the ongoing nature of creation itself and of the ambiguity of that process.

Sophia's character throughout the scriptures will prove to be provocative and enigmatic. Yet, as we explore her other dimensions, it will be helpful to keep in touch with Sophia's central role in the creative process. Indeed, Sophia as creator can serve as a sort of touchstone for our further explorations.

SOPHIA AS WISDOM

Because she is at the heart of all things coming into being, Sophia is Wisdom itself. This, of course, is not an obvious connection for the twentieth century mind. But Sophia as creative and Sophia as wisdom are very closely associated for the biblical writers.

Before integrating this connection into our own understanding, it may help to sample the way the Hebrew traditional texts themselves talk about Sophia as wisdom. In Proverbs 4:1, 2, 5, 6, the sage writes:

> Listen my children, to a father's instruction;
> pay attention, and learn what clear perception is.
> What I am commending to you is sound doctrine:
> do not discard my teaching.
> Acquire Sophia, acquire perception;
> Never forget her, never deviate from my words.
> Do not desert her, she will keep you safe,
> love her, she will watch over you.

One notices in this typical injunction to associate with Sophia that she is, in fact, identical with "perception" itself or the "words" of the sage. Sophia is wisdom, both as content and process.

The relationship a person has to Sophia is virtually the same as their own relationship to the process of understanding. In Wisdom 6, relating to Sophia is pictured as the process of learning or knowing. For instance, in verse 13 it is said of her:

> Quick to anticipate those who desire her, she makes herself known to them.

This "making known" is described in verse 17 exactly in terms of the process of learning or gaining wisdom:

> Of her the most sure beginning is the desire for discipline, care for discipline means loving her.

Of course, all of this explanation of how a person can be the same as that which is learned and the process of learning itself would be easier, if the twentieth century knew of a person named Wisdom. That is, for the mind of the Hebrews, at the time of the composition of these "Old Testament" passages there was little difficulty in assuming that the name of learning itself was the name of a person. Sophia as a name meant learning.

But what does Sophia as wisdom have to do with Sophia at the heart of the creative process? Let's see if we can trace the logic of this association found in the texts.

As the One who is at the heart of the process of things coming into being, Sophia "pervades and permeates all things" (Wisdom 7:24). Therefore the way to encounter her is not, according to the texts, through any kind of piety or communal resolve. You do not encounter her by praying or by deciding. Rather, meeting Sophia requires disciplined study. The Sophia texts essentially say that disciplined study of all things (an earnest search for wisdom and understanding) leads to Sophia, the One who is at the heart of all that one studies. As Wisdom 6:12 and 16 proclaim

> By those who love her she is readily seen,
> and found by those who look for her . . .
> in every thought of theirs, she comes to meet them.

Disciplined study of all that comes into being (all that is created) results in a personal encounter with the One at the heart of the creative process.

This completes our overview of materials which deal with Sophia alone, in and by herself. But most of the texts about Sophia do not dwell on her alone. Just because she is wisdom itself, the great majority of the material about Sophia in the Hebrew scriptures has to do with her relationship to people. We see who she really is in the texts when we consult their portrait of her in relationship to humanity.

SOPHIA AS TEACHER

Sophia's relationship to people has mostly to do with whether or not they decide to be learners. Proverbs 1:20–22 shows this relationship from the point of view of Sophia herself:

> Sophia calls aloud in the streets,
> she raises her voice in the public squares;
> she calls out at the street corners,
> she delivers her message at the city gates,
> "You ignorant people, how much longer will you cling to your ignorance?
> How much longer will mockers revel in their mocking

and fools hold knowledge contemptible?
Pay attention to my warning:
now I will pour out my heart to you,
and tell you what I have to say."

Proverbs 8:1–11 fills out the picture from Sophia's side of the learning relationship:

> Does Sophia not call meanwhile?
> Does Discernment not lift up her voice?
> On the hilltop, on the road,
> at the crossways, she takes her stand;
> beside the gates of the city,
> at the approaches to the gates she cries aloud,
> "O people: I am calling you;
> my cry goes out to the children of humanity.
> You ignorant ones, study discretion;
> and you fools, come to your senses.
> Listen, I have serious things to tell you,
> and from my lips come honest words.
> My mouth proclaims the truth . . .
> All the words I say are right,
> nothing twisted in them, nothing false,
> all straightforward to the one who understands,
> honest to those who know what knowledge means.
> Accept my discipline rather than silver,
> knowledge in preference to gold.
> For wisdom is more precious than pearls,
> and nothing else is so worthy of desire."

In these passages and their companion texts, Sophia is the teacher. She is the one about whom the sage in Wisdom 9:10 says to God: "Send her forth from your throne of glory . . . to teach me what is pleasing to you, since she knows and understands everything." In this passage the connection between Sophia as Creator, wisdom, and teacher is also clear. She is the natural teacher since she knows everything, and she knows everything since she is the One who makes all things new.

It is difficult to avoid the impression that Sophia as teacher acts and talks as if she knows everything. There is no humility or shyness in this teacher. She is proud and assertive. Some readers are bound to think of her as arrogant. From the point of view of the texts, however, arrogance is impossible, for this teacher really does know everything.

Nevertheless there is an abiding impression of Sophia as impatient with the "children of humanity." The teacher is "intelligent, holy, unique, manifold, subtle, active, incisive, unsullied, lucid, invulnerable, benevolent, sharp, irresistible, steadfast, dependable, almighty, all-surveying, penetrating . . . , pure and most subtle. . . ." (Wisdom 7:22, 23). The human learners are "ignorant" (Proverbs 8:5), "unsure . . . , unstable," with a "perishable body" which "presses down the soul," for whom "this tent of clay weighs down the teeming mind" (Wisdom 9:14, 15). The texts therefore consistently portray Sophia as a teacher who must raise her voice and constantly enjoin her human pupils to have more discipline.

Now we come to one of the most curious twists in Sophia's character. She is regularly pictured in the texts as calling, crying out to, upbraiding, and berating her slow human pupils. Her main complaint is that they will not listen to her.

But what she has to say and teach is not found in the texts. Astonishingly, the passages never get around to Sophia's message to her human students. There is constant reference to her discipline, her wisdom, her commandments, and her teaching. But Sophia never teaches anything in the texts. She just urges people to accept her teaching.

One can conclude from this either of two things: Sophia has nothing to teach, or she herself is somehow what is to be learned. Since the first conclusion would bring an end to this entire investigation, let us explore the possibility that Sophia as contentless teacher is part of a more complex image.

Indeed, as soon as the texts begin to describe the learning relationship to which people are called by Sophia, Sophia is no longer just teacher. She becomes, instead, both teacher and that which is taught.

The one who learns successfully from Sophia is rewarded with prosperity and a full life. She is not only someone to listen to, she is someone to obtain or possess. As Sophia says in Proverbs 8:18, "With me are riches and honor, lasting wealth and justice." Ben Sirach says in Ecclesiasticus 1:17–20:

> She fills their whole house with their heart's desire,
> and their storerooms with her produce . . .
> The crown of Sophia makes peace and health flourish . . .
> The Lord has showered down learning and discernment with her
> and exalted the renown of those who hold her close.

In texts like Proverbs 4:5, 8 Sophia and her rewards become identical:

> Acquire Sophia, acquire perception . . .
> Hold her close, and she will make you great;
> embrace her, and she will be your pride.

In Wisdom 8:3, 5 the sage summarizes his quest for learning in terms of a decision to possess Sophia:

> I resolved to have her as my bride . . .
> If in this life wealth be a desirable possession,
> what is more wealthy than Sophia whose work is everywhere?

In these passages Sophia, the teacher, recedes into the background in favor of Sophia, the possession. Although it is almost always clear that by possessing Sophia one learns something, the ownership of Sophia (as one at that time possessed a bride or riches) dominates the imagery in at least half of the passages concerning the learning relationship to Sophia.

It is important to take note of this double imagery of Sophia in the learning relationship, because it indicates what is to be learned from Sophia. Since Sophia is both possession and teacher, her contentless injunctions to listen to her are not contradictory or pretentious. People are not just to learn from her, they are to learn her.

In twentieth century North America, learning from a person and possessing that person are two quite different matters. In the culture which produced the texts under consideration, there was no contradiction between the two: a woman was both a person to be learned from, and something to be possessed. Reprehensible as that may seem to us now, it does enable us to grasp Sophia as a particular kind of spiritual/intellectual commitment to learning. In a certain sense, learning and understanding may beckon to us, but there are other times when we appropriately take possession of them. What does it mean that the content of Sophia's teaching is Sophia herself? The constant call to discipline and knowledge along with the indication of worldly benefits to be gained from them make a case for learning itself. That is, relating to Sophia means learning. The commitment is not to a certain kind of knowledge or to a certain secret dogma. It is a commitment to the task of learning constantly. Sophia calls people to be learners. She can in this light be easily seen as that which is to be learned and the one who urges people to learn. She is, in fact, the learning process itself. She calls us to a life of seeking understanding of the world in which we live. Since she is the One who participates in bringing everything into being, she is the natural teacher and the natural content. Because there is always something more to learn and understand, she never stops calling people to herself.

It is devotion to this process of continual learning which promises so many rewards. The more human beings understand the world, the more success and contentment they will have, the Sophia texts seem to say.

At the conclusion of this section on Sophia as teacher of humanity and as content of what people need to learn, it is interesting to observe that Sophia at the heart of the learning process fits with Sophia at the heart of the creative process. When people learn something, something new comes into being. The learning process is a way that humans share in the creative process.

SOPHIA AS LOVER

In the passages about Sophia as teacher and wisdom, we have already encountered the metaphor of Sophia as lover. This image of Sophia grows directly out of passion for Sophia as the One who knows and creates all things. But the image itself gains so much momentum that in a number of texts it stands practically on its own without reference to the learning or creating processes.

For instance, in Ecclesiasticus 6:26–28 Ben Sirach urges his followers:

> Court her with all your soul,
> and with all your might keep her ways;
> go after her and seek her;
> she will reveal herself to you;
> once you hold her, do not let her go.
> For in the end you will find rest in her
> and she will take the form of joy for you.

Or in Wisdom 8:9, 16:

> I therefore determined to take her to share my life,
> knowing she would be my counselor in prosperity,
> my comfort in cares and sorrow. . . .
> When I go home I shall take my ease with her,
> for nothing is bitter in her company,
> when life is shared with her there is no pain,
> gladness only, and joy.

In Wisdom 8:2, 3 the love affair becomes more complicated:

> I fell in love with her beauty. [says the sage]
> Her closeness to God lends luster to her noble birth,
> since the Lord of All has loved her.

In other words here we have an allusion to Sophia as lover of "the Lord of All" and of the human sage. In fact the sage falls in love with her (and takes her as his bride) because the Lord of All has loved her. Very few of the Sophia texts dwell on the love affair between Sophia and the "Lord of All." But many of them seem to take this rather common theme in near eastern mythology[3] (the love affair, for instance, of the earth mother goddess and the father sky god, which results in the creation of life) as background. The scene in Proverbs 8 in which God and Sophia are creating, delighting, and playing together is certainly from this mold. Or, in Wisdom 9 when the sage pleads with God to "send her forth from your throne of glory," the implication is that Sophia and God are king and queen together.

But, as has already been said, the Hebrew scriptures concentrate on Sophia's relationship to humanity. So she is mainly pictured as the lover of human beings.

In Ecclesiasticus 4:11–18 she is lover, mother, and teacher:

> Sophia brings up her own children,
> and cares for those who seek her.
> Whoever loves her loves life,
> those who wait on her early will be filled with happiness.
> Whoever holds her close will inherit honor,
> and wherever they walk the Lord will bless them.

Those who serve Sophia minister to the Holy One,
and the Lord loves those who love her.
Whoever obeys her judges aright,
and whoever pays attention to her dwells secure.
If they trust themselves to Sophia, they will inherit her,
and their descendants will remain in possession of her;
for though Sophia takes them at first through winding ways,
bringing fear and faintness to them,
plaguing them with her discipline until she can trust them,
and testing them with her ordeals,
in the end Sophia will lead them back to the straight road,
and reveal her secrets to them.

The picture in this passage is more than the typical near eastern combination in which mother, lover, son, sister, and brother roles are assumed and transferred among the deities. Sophia's central call, the call to participate in and understand the world in which we live, is incorporated in this passage. It and all of the Sophia literature promise a life full of earthly joys in exchange for the discipline of going "at first through the winding ways." Relating to Sophia means involvement with the world. As the text summarizes the meaning of loving Sophia, "whoever loves her, loves life."

This overview of Sophia as lover is the final piece needed to gain a relatively clear picture of her in the existing "Old Testament" texts. She is at the heart of the creative process. Therefore she has much to teach humanity about the world, and she is someone to be loved.

Beyond this rather coherent portrait, the character of Sophia began to be elaborated in several different directions. Most of these developments of her character in the Hebrew tradition were broken off for reasons which require further investigation. Several others, however, while rather more straightforward, still deserve to be mentioned here briefly, since they round out our image of Sophia.

SOPHIA AS TREE OR PLANT

Perhaps because of Sophia's association with creation, or perhaps because a tree comes eventually to symbolize almost every major mythical figure, the Hebrew scriptures include a number of different images of Sophia as a tree or plant. The most striking of these is in Ecclesiasticus 24:12–19.

I have taken root in a privileged people,
in the Lord's property, in his inheritance.
I have grown tall as a cedar on Lebanon,
as a cypress on Mount Hermon;
I have grown tall as a palm in Engedi,
as the rose bushes of Jericho;
as a fine olive in the plain,
as a plane tree I have grown tall.

I have exhaled perfume like cinnamon and acacia,
I have breathed out a scent like choice myrrh,
like galbanum, onzcha and stacte,
like the smoke of incense in the tabernacle.
I have spread my branches like a terebinth,
and my branches are glorious and graceful.
I am like a vine putting out graceful shoots,
my blossoms bear the fruit of glory and wealth.
Approach me, you who desire me,
and take your fill of my fruits.

Likewise in Ecclesiasticus 1:16, 17 Sophia as tree provides out of her own abundance. "She intoxicates them with her fruits; she fills their whole house with their heart's desire, and their storerooms with her produce."

She provides more than her fruits; as tree, she provides shelter as well. In speaking of "one who meditates on Sophia," in Ecclesiasticus 14:20–27 the writer mixes metaphors to describe Sophia's sheltering presence; she is both tree and house:

He peeps in at her windows,
and listens at her doors;
He lodges close to her house,
and fixes his peg in her walls . . .
he sets his children in her shade,
and camps beneath her branches,
he is sheltered by her from the heat,
and in her glory he makes his home.

SOPHIA AS LAW

An indication of Sophia's importance to later Hebrew tradition is that in two of the later biblical books she is identified with the central institution of Hebrew faith, the Law itself.

Immediately following the Sophia tree monologue in Ecclesiasticus 24:23–25, Ben Sirach writes:

All this is no other than the book of the covenant of the Most High God, the Law that Moses enjoined on us, an inheritance for the communities of Jacob. This is what makes Sophia brim like the Pishon, like the Tigris in the season of fruit."

Similarly in the book of Baruch (3:37–4:2) after a long tribute to Sophia, the writer concludes:

God has grasped the whole way of knowledge,
and confided it to Jacob,
to Israel, God's well-beloved;
so causing Sophia to appear on earth

and move among humanity.
This is the book of the commandments of God,
the Law that stands forever;
those who keep her live,
those who desert her die.

This relationship of Sophia to the Law receives no further development in the canonical literature, that is, in the books designated by Jewish or Christian tradition as belonging to the Bible. As it stands in Baruch and Ecclesiasticus, it is more a sign that Sophia had gained major status in later Hebrew tradition than a clearly elaborated image.

SOPHIA IN HEBREW HISTORY

An unfinished project in the book of Wisdom can be understood in the same light. In chapters 10 and 11 of Wisdom, the writer retells the sacred history of the Hebrew people from Sophia's point of view. In this version of the stories of Adam and Eve, Cain and Abel, Noah, Abraham and Lot, Jacob, Joseph, and Moses, Sophia takes the place of God as the designer and controller of history.

For instance, here is what Wisdom 10:9–12 has to say about Jacob:

The virtuous man, fleeing from the anger of his brother,
was led by Sophia along straight paths.
She showed him the kingdom of God
and taught him the knowledge of holy things.
She brought him success in his toil
and gave him full return for his efforts;
She stood by him against grasping and oppressive men
and she made him rich.
She guarded him closely from his enemies
and saved him from the traps they set for him.
In an arduous struggle she awarded him the prize,
to teach him that piety is stronger than all.

This project is curious in several regards. The most curious is that it is broken off in the middle. In Wisdom 11:1 the story of salvation history describes how Sophia helps the "holy prophet" (Moses). But in verse 2 the story changes voice and the Exodus account proceeds with "You" as the guide to sacred history. And a few verses later it becomes clear that "You" has become once again the traditional Hebrew God. We are given no explanation for this abrupt discontinuation of sacred history told from Sophia's point of view.

It is also curious in that the writer's version of the stories differs from the versions in Genesis and Exodus. The Sophia story of the escape from Egypt includes this account in 10:17–19:

She herself was their shelter by day
and their starlight through the night.
She brought them across the Red Sea,
led them through that immensity of water,
while she swallowed their enemies in the waves,
then spat them out from the depths of the abyss.

The differences in this story are related to the change in divine figures. The pillar of cloud and fire imagery become shelter and starlight, images that are often associated with female mythic figures. Such is also the case with the sea and sea monsters. Sophia not only leads the Hebrews through the sea, but she becomes the sea (or sea monster) as well, swallowing the Egyptians and spitting them out.[4]

SOPHIA'S RELATIONSHIP TO GOD

From the material presented so far, it is rather clear who Sophia is to God. She is a co-creator with the Hebrew God, she is a heavenly queen, she is a messenger from God, and she is God's lover.

If we were contemporaries of the writers of the Hebrew scripture, this answer would probably suffice. Our problem is that thinking about God in the intervening twenty centuries or so has been dominated by a number of dogmatic considerations. Much of western theology has focused on the difference between God and humanity. The question, for instance, relative to Jesus and God has been whether Jesus was divine or human or both. Much of western theology also saw fit to emphasize the difference between God and humankind, thereby drawing a kind of sharp boundary on one side or the other of which every person falls.

For much of the biblical world this is not the case. In the biblical mentality, there exists a whole range of intermediary figures who are not quite God, but who are definitely not human. Sophia is one example of such a figure. But she is not the only one. The figure of the Child of Humanity ("Son of Man") who descends from heaven on the clouds in the books of Daniel and Enoch and in the Gospel of John, the Logos (or Word) in John 1, and angels are some other examples of this kind of intermediary person who is in some way divine, but not identical with the Hebrew God.

The question, "Is Sophia God?" will be posed by the reader in any case, even though the Hebrew tradition itself would not understand such a question. If one asks the question nonetheless, the answer will probably come out something like "Yes and no." One observation can be made, however, without such equivocation. The Hebrew tradition which we have been examining never goes to the trouble of saying no, while it does say yes in some rather poetic ways.

The root of this yes is repeated in many different Sophia texts. Perhaps the earliest is this one from Job 28:20–23:

But tell me where does Sophia come from?
Where is understanding to be found?
It is outside the knowledge of every living thing,
hidden from the birds in the sky.
Perdition and death can only say,
"We have heard reports of her."
God alone has traced her path
and found out where she lives.

Earlier in this chapter a number of the texts about Sophia creating were cited as well as those concerning her "pre-existence" with God at the beginning. Here is one of the explanations of the book of Wisdom (7:25–26) concerning Sophia and God:

For she is the breath of God's power
and a stream of pure glory of the Almighty.
This is why nothing polluted enters her.
For she radiates the everlasting light.
She mirrors God's energy completely,
and she images God's goodness.

The dogmatic status of the biblical Sophia then is clear. She is to all intents and purposes divine, creating, judging, and ruling just as God is.

If the sages, however, were asked directly whether Sophia was God, they would wisely sidestep the question in order to avoid conflict with those in Hebrew theological circles who insisted on God's uniqueness. They would avoid an unequivocal answer by using metaphors like "the breath of the power of God" or "the consort of the throne." This would in no way detract from their imaginative introduction of a new divine figure. It would only signal their political shrewdness.

SOPHIA SCHOLARSHIP

If dogmatic and systematic theologians have, like the Church itself, ignored or repressed Sophia, the same cannot be said for biblical scholars. Quite the contrary, and curious as it may seem, she has been a lively subject of biblical investigation through the twentieth century.[5] In fact, Sophia has played a major role in several arenas of biblical research in our time. A summary of biblical scholarship's chief findings and questions about Sophia and the literature we have been examining may help us to understand just how significant Sophia has come to be.

Biblical scholars agree that Sophia is a relatively late figure in the Bible. That is, the literature in which she is introduced is not nearly as old as much of the rest of the Hebrew scriptures. There is not agreement about when the first mention of Sophia occurred in Hebrew scripture. But the earliest possible dating would be in the middle of the fifth century B.C.E., at least five hundred years after some of the Hebrew tradition was developed. Most researchers place the majority of Sophia texts in the last 400 years before the common era.[6]

The lateness of the Sophia texts poses a major problem for Sophia researchers.[7] It means that Sophia seems to have appeared in Hebrew tradition without much precedent. Whereas almost all of the other near eastern civilizations have a long history of figures somewhat similar to Sophia,[8] Israel does not. In many near eastern locales it is possible to trace the development of female mythical figures from the early earth mother goddesses to relatively complex goddesses of the high civilizations. Sophia corresponds in many ways to some of these later goddesses (for instance, the later Isis in Egypt, who was also popular in later Greece). But Sophia as a Hebrew figure has no precedent or "ancestry." Researchers can find no source of Sophia within Hebrew tradition.

Where, then, did Sophia come from? Possibly she was "borrowed" from some of the nearby civilizations.[9] The problem is that unlike other such cases of borrowing, researchers have been unable to find a clear source outside Hebrew tradition. The Egyptian goddess Ma'at seems to be the closest to Sophia, but there are definite differences, and it is difficult to trace any direct dependence.

In point of fact, biblical scholarship has not at this time reached a consensus on how or why Sophia developed in the Hebrew scriptures. Theories range from her being a "construction" or "invention" of Hebrew theologians to her being the outbreak of the long suppressed female valence in Hebrew religion.[10] No one has been able to make a convincing case.

Biblical scholars have likewise been unable thus far to determine which segment of Hebrew society or culture was particularly dedicated to the study of Sophia.[11] As in the question of Sophia's origin, the more research done, the less clear the picture. Earlier in the century most researchers believed that there had been a kind of "wisdom school" in Israel similar to that in other near eastern cultures. Evidence suggests that such a "wisdom school," at least in those other cultures, comprised a group of philosophers centered in the court of the monarch, providing both counsel to the monarch and literature of a philosophical bent. But the more closely the Sophia literature is examined in the Israelite context, the less feasible it becomes to hypothesize such a setting for the texts.[12] The Sophia literature has too many characteristics which do not correspond to the concerns of such an elite group. And the socio-political history of Israel during the period under consideration seems to call into question the existence of such a group of philosophers. There was, for instance, really no king in Israel during most of this time.

Despite a lack of clarity in these matters, there is general agreement that Sophia's appearance and development has much to do with increasing contact between Israel and Greek civilization during the period we have been considering.[13] Of course, the fact that a good portion of the Sophia literature exists only in the Greek language (although definitely in some way a product of Hebrew culture) is a prime example of the influence Greek culture seems to have had on the situation in Israel. The emphasis on learning and philosophy ("love of wisdom/Sophia") in the Sophia texts must also have come to some extent from the Greek culture which was present in so much of the Mediterranean world. In addition, Greek culture and mythology also did not lack female figures of comparable stature to Sophia.

A final area of Sophia research in this century is concentrated on the relationship between Sophia and Jesus, and we will explore this relationship in chapter 3.

It is important also to note that this century of Sophia research has produced a significant negative conclusion. Although our exploration thus far has been able to detect a relative coherence to the "Old Testament" portrait of Sophia, it must be conceded that many of the texts themselves are fragmentary and unfinished. There is a definite incompleteness about Sophia in the Hebrew tradition. It is as if her development was cut off prematurely.[14] In fact, this is a basic conclusion of Sophia research.

For some reason Sophia was never fully elaborated. Clearly there was for some time much energy invested in her as a significant spiritual figure. This chapter has at least been able to correct the impression that Sophia is a minor character in the "Old Testament." The fact that the latest works in the canon about Sophia are expansive about her importance (identifying her with the Law and portraying her as the guiding force in history) indicates a growing momentum. The amount of Sophia material produced over a period of several hundred years speaks for her centrality in later Hebrew tradition. But the earliest texts about Sophia do not give a complete picture of her, those which come somewhat later seem somewhat unfocused, and the later ones do not complete their lines of thought about Sophia.

At this point, Sophia scholarship can only produce this negative conclusion concerning Sophia's unfinishedness. There are speculations about why she is not complete. Some scholars point to the sociopolitical turbulence in Israel (the Roman occupation, and then the destruction of the Temple), at the time when Sophia's development slowed, noting that the Sophia passages assume a relative stability in which disciplined study and reflection can take place.[15] Others suggest that Sophia may not have been able to stand as a figure on her own in Hebrew theology at that time.[16] Still others speculate that Hebrew monotheism censored her development.[17]

SOPHIA'S SIGNIFICANCE IN THE HEBREW TRADITION

If we attempt to set Sophia within the larger Hebrew scriptural tradition, she stands out. This is not to say that she is an aberration. But she is unique on several counts.

The Sophia texts in the "Old Testament" take care not to fly in the face of the constants of Hebrew faith. Monotheism is carefully protected through the subtle metaphoric phrasing of Sophia's relationship to the Hebrew God. The unique covenant of God with Israel is also respected. The book of Ecclesiasticus in particular makes the point that Sophia is within God's agreement with Israel.

But once this respect for the basics of the faith is noted, there are two major innovations which Sophia brings to Hebrew faith.

The first is the courageous call to intellectual and worldly integrity.[18] Sophia is a new kind of figure within the Hebrew world view. She encourages or rather demands reflection on the meaning of a wide variety of happenings in the world. In this she runs counter to the tendencies (particularly among the priestly class of Israel) in later Hebrew tradition to withdraw Hebrew faith into a nostalgia for the earlier, "holier" times. Sophia calls for humans to think about what is happening in their world. She promises that such disciplined reflection will be rewarded in this world. She makes this call in a way which relates such reflective worldliness to the Hebrew God.

Contextually it is good to note that this secularizing, intellectual tendency does not exist only in the Sophia texts, but also in the larger "wisdom traditions" of that time.[19] Other teachings besides those found in the Sophia material were produced by this tradition. It is also worth noting that the priestly class in Israel at this time was making a case for something of the opposite kind of stance. Many of the priests were calling upon Israel to resist outside (especially intellectual) influences, to place obedience to and participation in the cultic life of Israel above reflection on the broader historical happenings of the Mediterranean world, and to reconstitute as best they could the ancient Israelite culture.[20]

The second major innovation Sophia brings is her gender. This is no small matter in a tradition which defined itself by its monotheism in contrast to the worship of gods and goddesses in the surrounding cultures. That Sophia developed into a figure in her own right is noteworthy in itself; that she took on goddess-like qualities, calling people to herself in much the way that God does and even taking God's place as a saving figure in history, is even more remarkable. Of course her development was limited by monotheism; her final significance as a major female figure in late Judaism is already a matter of debate. As we have seen, some feminist theologians point to ways in which Sophia takes on many of the characteristics of patriarchal logocentric culture, while others understand her as at least implicitly positive in her impact.

But whether she has some patriarchal traits or not does not nullify the simple and rather astounding observation that the major spiritual figure of pre-Christian Judaism is female. Similarly, it remains remarkable that such a major figure evolved from a religious and theological heritage which has no other major female protagonists.

CHAPTER THREE

Sophia in the
Christian Scriptures

Who and where is Sophia in the New Testament?

According to a whole series of New Testament texts, Jesus is Sophia. The answer is at least as surprising as the question. But she is there in much of the New Testament. Our task is to uncover this Jesus Sophia.

In 1 Corinthians 1:23, 25 Paul writes, "We are preaching a crucified Christ . . . a Christ who is the power and the Sophia of God." A few verses later (30) he continues, "By God's action Jesus Christ has become our Sophia."[1] And then a few verses later (2:6–8),

> But still we have a Sophia to offer those who have reached maturity: not a philosophy of our age, it is true, still less of the masters of our age, which are coming to their end. The hidden Sophia of God which we teach in our mysteries is the Sophia that God predestined to be for our glory before the ages began. She is a Sophia that none of the masters of this age have ever known.

Once again we are confronted with a kind of presence of Sophia which does not correspond at all to our expectations. Who ever told us about Paul coming straight out and saying, "Jesus is our Sophia"?

And although this is perhaps the most dramatic New Testament affirmation that Jesus is Sophia, it is far from the only one. John's gospel portrait of Jesus is incomprehensible in its fullness without the recognition that text after text is proclaiming, "Jesus is Sophia." The Gospels of Matthew and Luke have Jesus speaking the words of Sophia as his own. And there are others.

The situation in the New Testament, however, is more complicated than in the "Old Testament." It is not simply a question of outlining a whole series of ignored passages. Sophia's presence in the New Testament is strong, but more convoluted. Understanding it therefore requires that we be introduced to the general study of Christology in the New Testament and the way this Christology influences the place of Jesus Sophia.

THE PLACE OF SOPHIA IN NEW TESTAMENT CHRISTOLOGY

Understanding the fullness of the identification of Jesus with Sophia in the New Testament requires an examination of the fundamental task of early church theologians—the attempt to find categories through which the significance of Jesus could be explained. That is, the many ways in which the New Testament writers identified Jesus with Sophia become clear only when their great adventure in seeking new language to explain Jesus is appreciated.

From its beginning to its end, the New Testament is a series of attempts to describe the significance the first disciples and the early churches saw in Jesus.[2] There is little systematic presentation of Jesus in the New Testament. Although some authors present some consistency within their particular works (e.g., Paul, John, Matthew), the New Testament collection itself exhibits a very wide variety of names and images by which the meaning of Jesus is explained. Jesus is everything from a lamb slaughtered every day since the world began (Revelation) to a learned rabbi (Matthew). He is a philosophical principle (the Logos in John) and an unsophisticated countryman (Mark). In some passages Jesus is the cosmic Lord (Paul). In others one dare not say too loudly that he has done anything unusual (Mark).

As we examine this variety of Christological expression in the New Testament, it becomes clear that although the titles, images, and categories used in describing Jesus do not contradict each other for the most part, they certainly do not form a system of meaning.[3] They are rather part of a lively and dispersed quest for language adequate to describe a new perception of reality. Sometimes the titles and categories seem almost intentionally not to fit together. In the synoptic gospel accounts of Peter's confession of faith, for example, in response to Peter's assertion that Jesus is the Messiah, Jesus instructs the disciple to tell no one. Then Jesus immediately refers to himself as the "Child of Humanity (Son of Man)"[4]—not a messianic figure in the old tradition—and says that he is going to suffer and die. Suffering and dying do not fit with either the Child of Humanity or Messiah titles.[5] In these cases the meaning sought is clearly a new one that requires standing old categories on their heads or juxtaposing them in vivid contrast to one another.[6] In other cases the passionate search for new language seems to have gone on in ignorance of the existence of other meaning categories in the early churches. The writers of the Johannine material, for example, use titles which appear nowhere else in the New Testament.[7] Images of Jesus as the true vine, the light of the world, the bread of life, or the word exist exclusively in New Testament works attributed to John.

One of the primary language problems in this Christological search of the early churches was Jesus' relationship to the traditional title of "Messiah." Was Jesus the Messiah? If, as his followers claimed, he was the most important human ever to have lived, he must have been the Messiah.[8] This seems to be the reasoning of many of the early Jewish disciples. The Messiah after all was the ultimate title of significance for human beings within the Hebrew worldview in which Jesus and his first followers lived.[9] So there was practically no way that the early churches could say that Jesus was not the Messiah. There were obvious problems with this assertion, however.

First of all, the Messiah was to be a king.[10] Jesus was certainly not a king. No matter what any particular early church knew or did not know about Jesus, there was no way that the historical evidence allowed them to see Jesus as king of any political entity.

Secondly, the Messiah was to establish a new reign of justice and peace for Israel. Again, it was clear to all that Jesus had not successfully established such a society. The most obvious problem in this regard was that Jesus had been executed as an enemy of Israel by the governmental powers. The claim that such a person had set up God's kingdom of peace and justice would have been perceived as very weak indeed. Jesus' death as a criminal did not fit well with the title of Israel's most powerful king.

These obvious problems with Jesus as Messiah were complicated by other more theological considerations. Much of the early church began to assert that Jesus had revealed God to them and for this reason needed to be considered divine.[11] This also did not fit with the traditional Messiah image.[12] For Judaism the Messiah is a human figure, at best a messenger from and a ruler for God; the Messiah is not divine. So any of Jesus' followers who considered him to be divine had either to change the Messiah concept or to seek another primary title for him while leaving the Messiah problems to rest quietly.

In this context of searching for new or revised categories we can begin to understand the New Testament association of Jesus and Sophia. Sophia, as a part of the Hebrew tradition, was never a messianic figure. Because of her divine qualities, she could not be the Messiah, who was to be human. She did have some of the same attributes as the Messiah. She was sent by God, and she was to change human society by her mission.

This similarity apparently evoked the interest of the early churches. And closer examination of Sophia by those early followers of Jesus revealed that she reflected Jesus' life in ways that the Messiah figure did not. She, like Jesus, was one who had failed. Jesus' crucifixion fits into the picture of Sophia calling vainly to humanity, and then going back to God without having visibly changed things. If one saw Jesus as Sophia, Jesus' lack of kingly success was no longer a problem but a confirmation of his divine calling. Similarly this association allowed those who saw Jesus as divine to do so without denying Jesus' fundamental mission. Sophia, like the Messiah, was to come to change humanity. The difference in the portraits in Hebrew tradition was that the Messiah succeeds and Sophia is often rejected.

This reflection on Sophia and Jesus in the early churches is not just an interesting sidelight. It is at the heart of almost all of the various New Testament Christologies. Almost every major New Testament portrait of Jesus depends on the implicit combination of the Messiah and Sophia figures. When a New Testament author such as the writer(s) of the Johannine material concentrates on Jesus as Messiah,[13] the Messiah figure itself is changed to include some of the crucial Sophia characteristics. The result, in John for instance, is a Messiah figure whose relationship to God depends on his pre-existent creative activity and foreknowledge of God. These are, of course, traits of Sophia, not of the Messiah.

What seems to have happened in general in New Testament Christianity is that Messiah was kept as a primary title for Jesus but was adapted at the same time.[14] This adaptation happened in two ways. Sometimes the New Testament writers used supplementary titles and images to expand the meaning of Jesus as Messiah. In these cases titles and images like Son of God, the vine, Sophia, Child of Humanity, the prophet, the light of the world, the Lord, and the lamb were used along with the messianic title to address the problems created by considering Jesus exclusively as the Jewish Messiah described in the Hebrew scriptures.

The other way in which the Messiah figure was adapted happened by lending Jesus, "the Messiah," character traits of other figures. In these cases Sophia was the primary donor to the Jesus Messiah figure.

JESUS AS SOPHIA IN PAUL

Although Paul is the New Testament author who most explicitly and dramatically proclaims Jesus to be Sophia in the above cited passages from 1 Corinthians, he is also one of the writers for whom the gnostic movement is most directly problematic.[15] The gnostic movement was made up of certain early Christian sects who believed that salvation was attainable only by those whose knowledge (gnosis) enabled them to transcend matter. They also believed that Christ did not have a body. Gnosticism was eventually considered a heresy by the early church. Gnosticism, as we shall soon see, was a major inhibiting factor in the New Testament proclamation of Jesus as Sophia.[16] So Paul's portrayal of Jesus as Sophia is explicit at times but generally inhibited.

One of Sophia's traits which Paul transfers directly to Jesus is Sophia's hidden, that is, yet-to-be-discovered, presence in all things which results from her participation in their coming into being. Paul acknowledges this trait of Sophia in 1 Corinthians 2:7: "The hidden Sophia of God which we teach in our mysteries is the Sophia of God predestined to be for our glory before the ages began." He says almost exactly the same thing of Jesus in Romans 16:25: "I proclaim Jesus Christ, the revelation of mystery kept secret for endless ages."

Paul takes this presence of Jesus Sophia in all things and applies it to the hope of the restoration of all things and persons in Jesus. For instance, in 1 Corinthians 15:23, 26, 51 he says:

> All people will be brought to life in Christ . . . everything is to be put under his feet . . . I will tell you something that has been secret: that we are not all going to die, but we shall be changed.

The secret presence of Sophia in all things is the basis of Paul's understanding of the new creation ("For anyone who is in Christ, there is a new creation"—1 Corinthians 5:17) and resurrection of all in Jesus.

JESUS AS SOPHIA IN JOHN

For the Hebrew scriptures examined in the last chapter, Sophia was, first of all, part of the creative process. She created the world with God. She was present in the birth of individuals. She was described as ordering all things and making them new.

With this central aspect of Sophia in mind, listen to the way the author of the Gospel according to John (1:1–3) introduces Jesus:

> In the beginning was the Word:
> and the Word was with God
> And the Word was God.
> He was with God in the beginning.
> Through him all things came to be,
> not one thing had its being but through him.

The description of Jesus as Word in John corresponds to the description of Sophia in the Hebrew scriptures. Later in this chapter we will consider why John, unlike Paul, does not speak directly of Sophia, since it is clearly Sophia to whom the text is referring. The name of this personage may now be the "Word,"[17] but she is the one we have studied in the Hebrew scriptures and come to know as Sophia. That the Hebrew scriptures do not attribute to the "Word of God" the Sophia-like characteristics John attributes to his Word only confirms this fact. What John has done is give Sophia a new name, and then proclaim that this pre-existent, co-creator is to be identified with Jesus. In short, Jesus is Sophia.

This identification of Jesus with Sophia is further underlined in the first chapter. The gospel echoes Ecclesiasticus's picture of Sophia (24:8) in which Sophia says:

Then the creator of all things instructed me . . .
"Pitch your tent in Jacob,
make Israel your inheritance."

John 1:14's version of this reads:

The Word was made flesh,
and pitched his tent among us.

This identification of Jesus Creator Incarnate with Sophia Creator Incarnate in John is nearly as dramatic as Paul's direct statement that Jesus is our Sophia. But John's portrait of Jesus as Sophia is far more thorough than Paul's. Paul occasionally borrows from Sophia in his description of Jesus. But John programmatically outlines the identification of Jesus as Sophia.

Perhaps most striking is John's portrait of Jesus as teacher. In the Gospel of John Jesus gives more teachings than anywhere else in the New Testament. The irony in this is remarkable. Although Jesus teaches at length, his main message is about himself. The central point of Jesus' teachings is that people should accept and believe in him. That is, Jesus as teacher borders on arrogance and contentlessness. Listen, for instance, to him in 8:23, 24:

You are from below;
I am from above.
You are of this world;
I am not of this world.
I have told you already: you will die in your sins.
Yes, if you do not believe that I am He,
you will die in your sins.

Or in 12:44–48:

Whoever believes in me
believes not in me
but in the one who sent me,
and whoever sees me,
sees the one who sent me.
I, the light, have come into the world,
so that whoever believes in me
need not stay in the dark any more.
If anyone hears my words and does not keep them faithfully,
it is not I who shall condemn them,
since I have not come to condemn the world,
but to save the world:
They who reject me and refuse my words
have their judge already:
the word itself that I have spoken
will be their judge on the last day.

This kind of teaching, which permeates the Gospel of John, reminds us strongly of Sophia as teacher.[18] She too had no real teaching except to commend herself to her followers. She did not hesitate to reprimand her listeners and to praise herself. The first verse of the oft-cited monologue in Ecclesiasticus 24 says so directly:

> Sophia speaks her own praises,
> In the midst of her people she glories in herself.

There is no other such proud figure excepting God in the Hebrew tradition. This model of self-proclaiming teacher which John uses to portray Jesus depends heavily on the "Old Testament" portrait of Sophia. The point in John, of course, is not just to record some similarities in style. It is to picture Jesus programmatically as the divine, pre-existent, co-creator whom we encountered in the Sophia texts.

The likeness goes further.

One of the main proclamations Jesus makes about himself in the Gospel of John is his closeness to God. It is because of Jesus' unique closeness to God that he is worthy of belief and allegiance. For instance in 5:19–22:

> I tell you most solemnly,
> the Son can do nothing by himself;
> he can only do what he sees the Father doing:
> and whatever the Father does the Son does too.
> For the Father loves the Son
> and shows him everything he does himself,
> and he will show him even greater things than these,
> works that will astonish you.
> Thus, as the Father raises the dead and gives them life,
> so the Son gives life to anyone he chooses;
> for the Father judges no one;
> he has entrusted all judgment to the Son.

Or in 10:37, 38:

> If I am not doing my Father's work,
> there is no need to believe in me;
> but if I am doing it,
> then even if you refuse to believe in me,
> at least believe in the work I do;
> then you will know for sure
> that the Father is in me and I am in the Father.

The many passages in the Gospel of John in which Jesus asserts his special closeness to God fit well in the larger picture of Sophia's closeness to God. For instance, the sage in Wisdom 8:3, 4 says:

> Her [Sophia's] closeness to God lends luster to her noble birth, since the Lord of All has loved her.

Yes, she is an initiate in the mysteries of God's knowledge, making choice of the works he is to do.

Or in Wisdom 9:9:

> With you [God] is Sophia, she who knows your works,
> she who was present when you made the world;
> she understands what is pleasing in your eyes
> and what agrees with your commandments.

In Ecclesiasticus 24:3, Sophia herself describes her relationship to God in this way:

> I came forth from the mouth of the most High.

Here, of course, we see not only how Jesus' closeness to God in John is like that of Sophia but also how Jesus as the Word in John is dependent on the picture of Sophia.

All of this also relates to another similarity between John's Jesus and Sophia. Both are sent by God to address the human situation. Both Jesus in John and Sophia in general are seen as special messengers to humanity because of their closeness to God. We have already reviewed these Sophia texts. Taking note of these similarities simply enables us to round out the Johannine picture of Jesus-Sophia.

In John 3:31–33 we read:

> The one who comes from heaven
> bears witness to the things he has seen and heard,
> even if his testimony is not accepted;
> though all who do accept his testimony
> are attesting the truthfulness of God,
> since the one whom God has sent
> speaks God's own words.

Here Jesus is the one sent from heaven to testify concerning God's message. Of the two biblical figures who descend from the heavens (the Child of Humanity/Son of Man and Sophia),[19] only Sophia comes to bring a message and to teach, as Jesus does in John.

This portrait of Jesus as Sophia, sent from God, is confirmed in John 7:28, 29, when Jesus cries out (we remember that Sophia's teaching is described as crying out in both Proverbs 1 and 8):

> Yes, you know me and you know where I came from.
> Yet I have not come of myself:
> No, there is one who sent me
> and I really come from him,
> and you do not know him.
> But I know him

because I have come from him
and it was he who sent me.

The ways in which John's Jesus mirrors Sophia in the Hebrew scriptures are too consistent to be either coincidental or insignificant.

Jesus in John takes his character from Sophia. The picture of Jesus in John as self-proclaiming teacher sent from heaven by God with whom he creates and communicates is the picture of Sophia.

JESUS AS SOPHIA IN THE SYNOPTIC GOSPELS

The Gospels of Matthew and Luke also present Jesus as Sophia in a manner that would have been experienced as quite dramatic by their original readers. Their presentation of Jesus as Sophia is on one level even more clear than John's. But Matthew and Luke both seem to have less interest in a general or programmatic presentation of Jesus as Sophia than John had.

Felix Christ, in a book published in 1970 entitled *Jesus Sophia: Die Sophia Christologie bei den Synoptikern* (literally *Jesus Sophia: The Sophia Christology in the Synoptics*) presents Jesus as Sophia in Matthew, Mark, and Luke. Christ demonstrates that the synoptics portray Jesus speaking words strikingly similar to those of Sophia, and this is the most dramatic discovery in Christ's study.

For instance, in Matthew 11:28–30, Jesus says,

Come to me, all you who labor and are overburdened, and I will give you rest. Shoulder my yoke and learn from me, for I am gentle and humble in heart, and you will find rest for your souls. Yes, my yoke is easy and my burden is light.

This is remarkably close to two passages in Ecclesiasticus. In Ecclesiasticus 51:26 Ben Sirach writes of Sophia, "Put your necks under her yoke, and let your souls receive instruction." And in Ecclesiasticus 6, "Give your shoulder to her yoke . . . For in the end you will find rest in her."

Immediately before the above cited example in Matthew, there is another striking example of Jesus speaking as Sophia. In Matthew 11:25–27, Jesus says:

I bless you, Father, Lord of heaven and earth, for hiding these things from the learned and the clever and revealing them to mere children. Yes, Father, for that is what it pleased you to do. Everything has been entrusted to me by my Father, just as no one knows the Father except the Son and those to whom the Son chooses to reveal him.

Such a saying is very similar to what the author of the Book of Wisdom (9:17–18) says of Sophia:

As for your [God's] intention, who could have learned it, had you not granted Sophia and sent your holy spirit from above? So have the paths of those on earth been straightened and people have been taught what pleases you, and have been saved by Sophia.

Ecclesiasticus 1:6, 8 also describes the secret sharing between God and Sophia:

For whom has the root of Sophia been uncovered? Her resourceful ways, who knows them? One only knows her. He is seated on the throne, it is the Lord.

Felix Christ shows how other sayings of Jesus in Matthew and Luke depend heavily on an understanding of Sophia. These texts include Matthew 11:16–19 (Luke 7:31–35), Luke 10:21f, Matthew 23:34–36 (Luke 11:49–51), and Matthew 23:37–39 (Luke 13:34f). He also examines in detail Matthew, Mark, and Luke's descriptions of Jesus as the carrier of wisdom.[20]

JESUS AS SOPHIA ELSEWHERE IN THE NEW TESTAMENT

We have already seen how Paul borrows from Sophia to describe Jesus as the one in whom a new creation occurs. This theme is carried further in several works of the Pauline school.[21]

For instance, in Colossians 1:15–17 an early church hymn about Jesus proclaims:

He is the image of the unseen God
and the first born of all creation,
for in him were created all things in heaven and on earth:
everything visible and invisible,
Thrones, Dominations, Sovereignties, Powers,
all things were created through him and for him.
Before anything was created, he existed,
and he holds all things in unity.

Here again Jesus is portrayed in the role of Sophia with God at the creation of all things. A number of students of this text believe that it could be a song to Sophia, which the early churches simply appropriated for their Jesus.[22]

Similarly we read in Ephesians 3:9–11:

Through all the ages this mystery has been kept hidden in God, the creator of everything. Why? So that the Sovereignties and Powers should learn only now, through the Church, how comprehensive God's Sophia really is, exactly according to the plan which he had had from all eternity in Christ Jesus our Lord.

Once again here it is Jesus who does the work of Sophia because he really is Sophia. Jesus is close to God in this text because as Sophia he has shared in the creation and planning of everything.

In the letter of James (3:13–17) Sophia appears in a less full manner, simply as the one from above:

> If there are any wise or learned ones among you, let them show it by their good lives, with humanity and wisdom in their actions. But if at heart you have the bitterness of jealousy, or a self-seeking ambition, never make any claims for yourself or cover up the truth with lies. Principles of that kind are not the Sophia that comes down from above. They are only earthly, animal, and devilish. Wherever you find jealousy and ambition, you find disharmony, and wicked things of every kind being done. Whereas the Sophia that comes down from above is essentially pure. She also makes for peace, and is kindly and considerate. She is full of compassion and shows herself by doing good. Nor is there any trace of partiality or hypocrisy in her.

Such a description of Sophia is reminiscent of Wisdom 7:22, 23:

> For within her is a spirit intelligent, holy, . . . unsullied, lucid, invulnerable, benevolent, sharp, irresistible, beneficent, loving to people . . . pure and most subtle . . . she is so pure, she pervades and permeates all things.

As we have already noted, Sophia plays such a large role in the New Testament's general search for and conceptualization of Jesus' character that there cannot be one straightforward collection of texts which effectively summarizes Sophia's role. However, the texts we have reviewed, taken from Paul, John, Matthew, Luke, the Pauline school, and James comprise the more explicit passages in which Jesus is Sophia.

THE NEW TESTAMENT'S RETICENCE CONCERNING SOPHIA

But one obvious question about Jesus as Sophia in the New Testament has not yet been addressed. If Sophia is such a fundamental figure for the understanding of Jesus in the early churches, why is this not said more often and more directly in the New Testament? Although it is clear that the New Testament incorporates Jesus Sophia in many implicit and some explicit ways, the material outlined so far certainly must be considered minor in comparison to the scope of the New Testament. After outlining all of the Jesus Sophia material in the New Testament we must finally admit that it is strangely unacknowledged and muted.

The answer to the question concerning Sophia's muted status in the

New Testament seems to lie mostly in a set of curious historical circumstances rather than in any implicit conflict between the figures of Sophia and Jesus. This view is supported by the refusal of New Testament authors to portray Sophia in any negative terms and by their mostly tacit acknowledgment of her in their descriptions of Jesus. Rather, Jesus Sophia, the largely unspoken basis for much of the New Testament's Christology and what might have become the centerpiece of Jesus' identification, was never accented in the New Testament itself because of the gnostic controversy in the early churches.[23]

Sophia's curious background status in the New Testament seems to be due to the way much of gnostic Christianity enthusiastically embraced her. Gnosticism and its forerunners were a part of the vibrant energy of the early churches. But the gnostic groups over the first two hundred years of the Christian era gradually became separated from the churches now considered "orthodox." This separation occurred because of several major theological controversies. These were not petty quarrels but fundamental disagreements about what life meant. In fact, so thoroughgoing were these differences that by the second century there was a lively conflict between the churches now represented by the New Testament tradition and the churches we call gnostic.[24]

The gnostic churches tended to downplay the humanity of Jesus and the crucifixion. Many of them rejected the notion that Jesus was human and that he died.[25] For them he was the divine redeemer and therefore could not die. They saw Jesus as the one who came to rescue humanity from a suffering world, not one who came into the world to suffer and die.

Without denying for the most part formulations about Jesus' divine origin, the churches represented in the New Testament held onto the humanity and crucifixion of Jesus. In fact, the gnostic controversy pushed many of them to formulate reasons why Jesus' humanity and death were crucial. They began to see it as a terrible misunderstanding not to proclaim Jesus as human and crucified.[26]

The gnostic churches developed a special liking for the Jesus-Sophia association.[27] Sophia fit well with their understanding of Jesus. Sophia was clearly a divine figure who came down from God with a special message. Since it was the knowledge of Jesus' message which, according to the gnostics, saved humanity rather than the crucifixion-resurrection event, the message-carrying Sophia was an especially appealing image of Jesus for them. Similarly the Sophia tradition of the Hebrews does not mention Sophia suffering or dying. Although that earlier tradition does not seem to reject such a possibility, it does not present suffering or dying as a part of Sophia's character. So the gnostic tendency to reject Jesus' suffering and death also matched the Hebrew scripture's picture of Sophia. The gnostics therefore began to proclaim Jesus more and more as Sophia.

It is against this background that the books were written and gathered into the collection we know as the New Testament. In this historical situation proclamation of Jesus as Sophia was practically tantamount to accepting the gnostic stance against Jesus' humanity and crucifixion. This, of course, put the New Testament churches in a perplexing situation. They clearly needed to acknowledge their debt to Sophia in understanding Jesus. What they said about Jesus was unintelligible without recognition of Jesus as Sophia. Without knowing who Sophia was, they could not have begun to revise the Jewish messianic figure and develop their own Christology related to Jesus. In fact, as we have already shown, Sophia is essential to all New Testament Christology.

On the other hand the New Testament churches could not proclaim Jesus as Sophia directly or develop the figure of Jesus Sophia further without being identified with the gnostic rejection of Jesus' humanity and crucifixion. Thus the gnostic controversy seems to have been the main reason for the New Testament's muted acknowledgment of Sophia. There are many other factors in explaining why Sophia was ignored after the New Testament writing. Many of these have to do with the Church's embracing of patriarchal world views and not exclusively with theological considerations. But the New Testament ambiguity relative to Jesus Sophia is for the most part understandable. What was a natural and imaginative development of the figure of Sophia in the early churches seems to have been intimidated, caricatured, and stunted by the gnostic controversy.

CONCLUSIONS

After this long, surprising, and sometime convoluted examination of Jesus as Sophia, what do we have to show for our labors? How are we to evaluate the significance of the New Testament's oblique, yet persistent, identification of Jesus with Sophia? Does this bond help us to understand Sophia's possible role as a figure for feminist spirituality? Or does it simply confound the issue?

The first conclusion to draw is the positive one. That is, the Jesus Sophia equation makes Sophia a significant figure for both biblical Judaism and biblical Christianity. Even though she is not so obviously present in the Christian scriptures, she is there in a very important manner. Although the way she is present in the New Testament raises a number of problems, the fact that she is thoroughly a part of the New Testament's portrait of Jesus makes her a figure to reckon with. Indeed, if we take into account Sophia's substantial presence in the Hebrew scriptures, her additional presence in the Christian scriptures makes her the third most discussed figure in the biblical traditions. Only Jesus and God are treated more thoroughly. Whatever final conclusions may be drawn concerning the way the New Testament relates Sophia to Jesus, there is no denying that the New Testament treatment of her confirms her as one of the most important figures in the Bible.

The second conclusion concerning Sophia is that she is a fundamentally ambiguous figure as presented in the New Testament material. Because of the muting of the early Christian discussion of Sophia, many basic questions about her must remain open from a New Testament perspective. The texts themselves simply will not yield the answers we need.

For instance, we must recognize that the "Jesus is Sophia" affirmations in the New Testament can be understood in two different ways. On the one hand, there is reason to believe that some of these New Testament affirmations adopt Sophia's character in order to strengthen the portrait of Jesus. In a certain sense Sophia disappears so that Jesus can have a stronger character. On the other hand, it is equally clear in some texts that associating Jesus with Sophia calls her forth again in a new and creative way. By saying "Jesus is Sophia," some New Testament texts seem to be expanding the space within which Sophia operates.

But the convoluted nature of the texts and the way in which the Jesus Sophia development was cut off make certain that the New Testament itself can yield no final verdict about whether Sophia's presence in the New Testament strengthens or weakens her as a figure in the biblical traditions. An honest judgment would probably be that she is both weakened and strengthened by her association with Jesus.

Similarly, Sophia's relationship to suffering and death remains unresolved in the New Testament. The question is posed cautiously.[28] Yet it is clearly a very important question for Sophia's future. We must explore Sophia's relationship to human suffering before she can come into her own as a central figure for feminist spirituality. But the New Testament treatment of Jesus as Sophia simply does not go far enough to answer that question.

It might have seemed more satisfying to be able to conclude this chapter with a resounding affirmation that Sophia really is at the heart of the New Testament message. We cannot, however, go that far. The quest for Sophia was by no means completed in the early Church. Yet the material we have reviewed demonstrates clearly that she is a substantial if hidden and unfinished presence in the New Testament. This presence of Sophia in the Christian scriptures as well as in the Hebrew tradition despite, or perhaps even because of, its unfinished nature, provides contemporary spirituality with a figure of great possibility. The image of Sophia may well contribute to the reintegration of the Jewish and Christian traditions into a larger, more functional and less patriarchal imaginative universe than anything we have so far experienced.

CHAPTER FOUR

Sophia and Her Sociohistorical Context

In Proverbs, immediately before the book's poetic description of Sophia as creator, we read the following:

> To Sophia say, "My sister!"
> Call Perception your dearest friend,
> to preserve you from the alien woman,
> from the stranger, with her wheedling words.
> From the window of her house
> she looked out on the street
> to see if among the men, young and callow,
> there was one young man who had no sense at all.
> And now he passes down the lane, and comes near her corner,
> reaching the path to her house
> at twilight when day is declining,
> at dead of night and in the dark.
> But look, the woman comes to meet him,
> dressed like a harlot,
> wrapped in a veil.
> She is loud and brazen;
> her feet cannot rest at home.
> Now in the street,
> now in the square,
> she is on the look-out at every corner.
> She catches hold of him, she kisses him,
> the bold-faced creature says to him, . . .
> "Come let us drink deep of love until the morning,
> and abandon ourselves to delight.
> For my husband is not at home,
> he has gone on a very long journey,
> taking his money bags with him;
> he will not be back until the moon is full."
> With her persistent coaxing she entices him,
> draws him on with her seductive patter.

Bemused, he follows her
like an ox being led to the slaughter. . . .
And now, my son, listen to me . . .
do not let your heart stray into her ways,
or wander into her paths;
she has done so many to death,
and the strongest have all been her victims.
Her house is one the way to Sheol,
and the descent to the courts of death.   (Proverbs 7:4–13, 18–22, 24–27)

How can this be? A stereotypical and sexist portrait of the "evil woman" at the heart of the book's salute to Sophia? The evil woman, who is contrasted to Sophia in chapters 5, 7, and 9 (note the metaphors of standing at the corner and of love which both figures have in common), is patriarchy's "bad girl." She is loud and brazen and bodily. She threatens the patriarchally dominated institution of marriage. She is, in fact, the "dark" side of patriarchy.

Such literature, even in its noblest moments of attempting to preserve marriage's sanctity, can be seen as nothing other than manipulation and vilification of women. It is classical, if not eloquent, in its projection onto women of the patriarchal alienation from and ambivalence about the body.

What is such a passage doing in direct relationship to our Sophia portrait? Is this not an indication that Sophia was an intrinsic part of an unredeemably patriarchal spirituality? To answer these questions, we must examine in some detail Sophia's relationship to the sociocultural setting(s) in which she emerged.

THE WISDOM TRADITION

Sophia is, as noted earlier, an important figure within a body of literature called "wisdom literature." Although this label has come under increasing scrutiny and critique by biblical scholars in the past twenty years, there is still a fair amount of agreement that the books of Proverbs, Job, Ecclesiastes, Baruch, and Wisdom are all of a similar type.[1] The term "wisdom literature" is still the preferred label for this type of literature. In addition, there is strong agreement that a number of sayings of Jesus in the New Testament and several Hebrew Psalms belong in this category.[2] R. Whybray has added Genesis 2 and 3, Deuteronomy, the Joseph story, Isaiah 1–3, Daniel, and other passages.[3] But Whybray's additions only highlight the growing fuzziness of the wisdom literature category as a whole.

What are the common characteristics of this literature? Biblical scholars have attempted to find common methods, common literary form, common views of humanity, and common life settings in the wisdom books with little success.[4] These books comprise an astounding diversity of topics, ways of writing, and situations. Scholars had expected to find a common point of departure rooted to some extent in a specific life situation, just as they had done with the priestly documents of Hebrew tradition. Within the priestly literature it has been possible to identify a social point of view (the class of priests), certain style and forms (for instance, rules and prayers), and to a certain extent a range of topics (mostly cultic). As a result scholars are able to investigate works like Genesis, identifying with some accuracy those places where the priestly writers made their contributions. Very little of this has been possible for the wisdom literature.

The existence of a common orientation is the most we can assert about the wisdom literature. This orientation brings two elements together: human experience and a theology of creation. First of all, wisdom tradition is concerned with the lessons and significance of human experience.[5] That is, this literature regularly expresses the significance and/or (un)desirability of various kinds of human experience. For instance, although the forms of discourse and opinion may vary in each case, both the aphorisms on spending money wisely in the Book of Proverbs and the skepticism of the "preacher" in Ecclesiastes are concerned with the lessons to be drawn from specific human actions. In another case, the wisdom books vary in their evaluation of marriage and the behavior recommended in marriage, but they share a common interest in this human experience. The wisdom tradition would appear to represent Israel's discovery of the ability to examine human experience critically and to state some general conclusions about the specific human experience which has been analyzed.[6]

Secondly, the literature concentrates on the relationship between Creator (God or Sophia) and creation. It is both the tie between Creator and creation and the difference between them which determine wisdom thought. Because of the Creator there is significance in creation. That is, to see God primarily as Creator makes it possible to consider values inherent in the experience of the created order. So commerce, art, marriage, education, and government as human experiences are to be evaluated and valued in terms of their relationship to the Creator. But creation theology, which seems in Israel to be by and large an innovation of the wisdom tradition, cuts both ways. Seeing God as Creator also separates him/her from the earth. As soon as we think of God in this way, creation and Creator are less a whole process. The core of Hebrew theology is about the history of Israel, not about the creation of the world. This theology tends to see God within the cosmos. But in creation theology God is moved outside.

This contribution made by the wisdom tradition was not incidental. The wisdom tradition developed during a time of great confusion in Israel. For several centuries it had been growing clearer and clearer that Israel was a pawn of larger states in the Mediterranean world, and the national consciousness was reeling from that recognition. The nation had been dominated, conquered, divided, exiled, and imperialized so thoroughly that only the most patriotic could think of Israel as a significant power. It seemed that the God of Israel had failed. So the God of Israel, under the wisdom tradition's guidance, was distanced from these dangerous developments by becoming the God of (and beyond) all creation.[7] Wisdom tradition helped the Hebrew God escape the fate of the nation by placing him/her beyond creation as the Creator of all.

Again the wisdom literature uses no single methodology, life situation, or series of forms to express the Creator/creation dynamic. We simply note that everything in the literature from the story of Job to the rather secular sayings about the good ruler concerns itself with this issue. All segments of life (not just those which have to do with what it means to be an Israelite) become the subjects of the wisdom literature because all of creation is now important. At the same time, wisdom literature becomes rather skeptical, as in Job and Ecclesiastes, because it is speaking from an awareness that the Creator can be separated from the chaotic and confusing situation within creation.

In this context the call to follow Sophia (Wisdom) is eminently understandable. She is the One who created all things with God, who permeates all things, and who rises above all things in her own (wise) being. Another way of putting this is that Sophia was the mythic figure developed in the wisdom literature to express its overarching concerns about creation and human experience. It is no accident that the first two categories we considered for Sophia (as Creator and as Wisdom) correspond roughly to the two common elements we have found in the wisdom literature as a whole. Most scholars believe that the wisdom tradition was a response to the new complex and subjugated situation the Israelite people faced in the centuries after the Babylonian exile. Seen in this light, Sophia was the mythic image for the learning disciplines of the wisdom tradition.[8]

For much of our century students of the wisdom literature have sought to identify the people who composed that literature. The results of this search will help us understand the relationship of Sophia to society, both in the Hellenistic age and in our own. An overview of this search for Sophia's authors will enable us to grasp more thoroughly Sophia's relationship to patriarchy. The investigation has developed along two major lines.

There has been much attention, first of all, to the question of what cultural influences in the near east spurred the development of the literature.[9] This has been an important question because since at least the 1920s clear influences from Egypt, Greece, and Israel have been noted. This first line of investigation has tried to sort out the ways these three (and possibly other) Mediterranean cultures mixed to produce the wisdom literature in Israel.

The second line of investigation has tried to identify the particular social settings of the writers. These studies have been less successful than those examining the cultural influences on the literature.[10]

In the past sixty years it has become clear that the Hebrew wisdom literature is connected to both the Greek and Egyptian cultures in ways more direct than perhaps any other portions of the Hebrew Bible. Exact parallels between Israelite and Egyptian literature have been shown definitively.[11] Most observers conclude from this that the Israelite literature was dependent on the Egyptian rather than the converse. Ties between Sophia and the Egyptian figures of Ma'at and Isis have been demonstrated, though her actual dependence on them is not necessarily clear.[12]

On the Greek side, the general cultural dominance of Greece throughout the Mediterranean after 400 B.C.E. makes it commonplace to note a number of Hellenistic influences on the development of the wisdom literature of Israel. These include the relationship of the mythologies of the wisdom and the Greek traditions, Greek modes of thinking and education which informed the Hebrew wisdom development, particular ideas such as "the immortality of the soul" which the wisdom literature seems to have borrowed from Greece, and wisdom references to Greek ritual.[13]

In other words, Israelite wisdom literature developed within an atmosphere of very strong cultural influence from the outside. The sociocultural situation of the wisdom tradition in Israel was an internationalized and cosmopolitan one, in which the continued independence of Israelite literature was hardly even thinkable. This is not to imply that Hebrew theology, ritual, and myth did not play important roles in the development of the wisdom literature.

Early in this century, as previously noted, it was thought that the wisdom literature was generated by a "school" of intellectuals at the court of the monarch (especially Solomon's). But this line of research rather quickly ran into a number of obstacles. Closer attention to the form and content of the wisdom literature tied the wisdom literature to later Hellenistic ideas and practices which existed in a situation unrelated to monarchy.[14]

Students of the wisdom literature have not rested, however, in their efforts to identify more exact social settings for the composition of this literature. In the last twenty years a number of probing studies have examined the specific forms of wisdom literature such as proverb, apodictic law, and admonition.[15] These studies have examined the larger functions of these forms of literature in the Near East, and from these have tried to identify a setting for their composition. The problem has been that each form seems to be coming from a distinctly different social setting. One seems to come from a school setting, another from an elite class, another from a clan. So instead of narrowing the social settings for the origins of the wisdom literature, these important studies have been unable to come to a focused conclusion. This has tended only to confirm earlier confusion, which stemmed from the realization that wisdom literature does not seem to be interested in any special social issues or to be written from any one point of view.

The complexity of results thus far suggests that it will be some time yet before scholars are able to talk clearly and comprehensively about the particular places within society where the wisdom literature was produced. For the moment we must content ourselves with having learned from the first line of investigation that the social settings of the wisdom literature was at the crossroads of several Mediterranean cultures.

There is a tendency to think of ancient literature, especially that which is sometimes called sacred, as having fallen from heaven. Such a tendency sometimes neglects the understanding of literature as coming from a particular social setting and from specific people, concentrating instead on the transcendent meaning of the words. Scholarship's difficulty in finding exact birthplaces for the wisdom literature could encourage such a reading of the texts. Since no real social context has been identified, perhaps the words did somehow fall from the sky, or so this sort of reasoning would have us think.

For the most part, contemporary wisdom scholarship has not yielded to this temptation. What we know now indicates that the wisdom literature represents a certain "intellectual tradition" within Israel.[16] This "intellectual tradition" which generated the wisdom literature must have been quite broadly based. Far from having its source in some otherworldly realm, the approach to thinking which generated the wisdom literature was the product of a fairly cosmopolitan society at the crossroads of the Near East. This way of thinking had penetrated a number of different social settings within Israel.

This is, of course, a partial answer. Further studies are needed to understand how this "intellectual tradition" of wisdom took shape within each of the social settings within Israel.

SOPHIA AS PART OF THE WISDOM TRADITION

Having described current attempts to situate the general phenomenon of wisdom literature within a social framework, we now need to ask specifically about the social context of Sophia's appearance in this literature.

Most students of the literature believe that Sophia is a later development of the wisdom tradition.[17] That is, the proverbs, stories, laws, and admonitions probably began to be written before Sophia was described. She does not seem to appear in the more ancient wisdom texts. To a certain extent then she evolved as the wisdom tradition became identifiable enough to need a symbolic figure. It is oversimplified to say that Sophia was the mythic or symbolic representative of the wisdom tradition. But there does seem to be a clear social need for such a figure in the later texts, and Sophia to a certain extent answers that need. It is too simple, however, to see Sophia merely as a figure chosen arbitrarily by the later wisdom writers to symbolize their work. To the contrary, there are strong indications that Sophia was an organic part of the social drama in later Israel.

We have already described this situation to some extent. The nation and culture of Israel were on the verge of disintegration. Just as the wisdom tradition can be seen in part as an attempt to understand the fate of Israel, so Sophia can be seen, in part at least, as an attempt to symbolize the Hebrew faith when the images of Israel and Yahweh were themselves no longer as evocative as they once were. Sophia was to a certain extent the wisdom literature's response to Yahweh's and Israel's endangered existence.[18]

But Israel's people were not just confused by the dismemberment of their culture and nation, they were also in turmoil because of their growing awareness of a complex and contradictory world. Residents of Israel during the Hellenistic ages in which Sophia evolved were confronted with much new information. The critical investigations of Greek philosophy and science were making themselves felt in Israel. New political systems were being introduced to an area which had previously modeled itself only on the monarchy. Trade expansion continued, bringing with it foreign wares and forcing new economic interdependency on Israel. This period was also characterized by a diversity of religious symbols moving freely throughout the Mediterranean area and interacting with one another.

In the midst of all this, the people of Israel required some new perspective or orientation to the world into which they had been catapulted.[19] Earlier in this chapter we saw that the wisdom literature itself was an attempt to come to terms with a more complex world. And in chapter 2 we noted that Sophia represented the human attempt to make sense of the created order. Now as we examine the social context for Sophia's emergence, we need note only that the figure of Sophia was a response to the increasingly complex social world the people of Israel were experiencing. She was herself understanding. She was also above, beyond, and in all that is. She was creator of more than Israel. She was, in fact, the symbol which represented the Hebrew people's attempt to relate to a new and larger world.

SOME CONTEMPORARY FEMINIST CONCERNS RELATIVE TO SOPHIA'S ORIGINAL SOCIAL CONTEXTS

Having reviewed the larger social context in which Sophia emerged, we return now to questions raised at the beginning of this chapter. Given the description of feminist spirituality with which we have been working, what is our evaluation of Sophia as we have come to understand her in her Hellenistic context? Did she represent the power men held over women at that time? Did she symbolize the connecting power in life which we have associated with feminist spirituality? Did she give voice to a specific spirituality, which we can understand, evaluate, and in some cases appropriate?

First of all, the obvious must be acknowledged. Sophia was not a symbol for the reemergence of women within Hellenistic society. There may have been some new female roles in the vigorous learning tradition which developed in Israel at that time. But Sophia was a lively image for that learning tradition itself in Israel and Judaism, not for the particular place of women within the learning enterprise or within Israel as a whole.

Similarly, we must admit that the society within which Sophia emerged was patriarchal. At certain points in the Sophia texts then, Sophia is part of an interlocking system of symbols which were used to confirm women's subordinate place in society. So although the "evil woman" texts of Proverbs may be seen from one perspective as a misdirected attempt to combat prostitution and to promote family life, they are also part of a symbolic world that ensured the oppression of all women. To contrast Sophia to the "evil woman," as Proverbs 1–9 does, makes Sophia into an oppressor of real women in that setting. Of course, it can be argued that the portrait of Sophia herself has just the opposite effect since she is such an authoritative female. But there is good reason to think that she served dual functions, both liberating and oppressing women in the particular social contexts of her emergence.

Third, Sophia's very appearance during the Hellenistic period as a response to a large sociocultural movement and consciousness can be important for our understanding of contemporary feminist spirituality. We have seen that to a large extent Sophia came into being because the wisdom tradition and Hebrew faith itself needed such a mythic figure to represent their response to the Hellenistic world. We have suggested that contemporary culture stands in analogous need of such a mythic figure who can express feminist spirituality's response to the problems and possibilities of our day.

There is, finally, an even more substantial connection between Sophia's original sociocultural setting and the concerns of feminist spirituality. Throughout this discussion we have stressed the distinctions between feminist spirituality's emphasis on connectedness and patriarchy's concern with abstraction, domination, and control. Feminist spirituality as we have portrayed it seeks to integrate human experience. It seeks connections before it seeks distinctions.

It was the drive to keep things connected that was at the heart of the wisdom tradition. In the face of threats to Israel's national consciousness and to its provincial view of the world, the wisdom tradition sought to create a new, more connected frame of reference. While groups within the priestly tradition in Israel and Judaism sought to separate and reisolate the Hebrew faith, the wisdom tradition was trying to integrate the Hebrew perspective into the larger picture. It is probably not accidental that the figure who imaged this effort to connect and integrate was Sophia herself. Although Sophia did not represent in any major way the reemergence of women in Hellenistic society, she was the primary symbol for the human connecting enterprise, an intrinsic component of feminist spirituality as we have understood it. Because Sophia symbolizes connectedness on a number of levels, she provides a promising starting point for the development of a powerful mythic figure at the heart of feminist spirituality. Whether she fulfills that promise will be determined by the ways in which she develops and is articulated in the future.

CHAPTER FIVE

Sophia and the Future of Feminist Spirituality

So now we have heard the story of Sophia—a female, not unlike many others, repressed, misrepresented, avoided, truncated, and struggling to emerge once again from her own problematic history. The more we understand about her, the more we will understand about ourselves, about all that is repressed within ourselves, about the parts of humanity and of creation that we are barely able to claim. Yet there is more than the past to be considered here. At a time when the future not simply of human beings but of the planet itself is at risk, and when connections between many of us are being weakened or destroyed, we must ask who Sophia is for us today, and what role she can play in the struggle for our survival.

As we have already seen, the evolution of a new feminist spirituality stands at the heart of the process of human transformation. We must create and express a vision of connectedness in order to move beyond the unequal power relations that are tearing our world apart. Yet the symbol systems with which we understand reality are often essentially patriarchal. We lack alternative images with which to transform ourselves and creation. In too many cases the great religions of the world have built up rather than dismantled our vision of inequality and disconnection. The angry father God in heaven raining down punishment upon disobedient children reinforces destructive human behavior. But traditional religion still exerts a great influence on many hearts and minds.

Sophia bridges the gap between feminist spirituality's need for transforming images and the demand of the biblical traditions that such images be congruent with their history and experience. Sophia can serve as the image, the "role model" at the heart of feminist spirituality, symbolizing as she does the connectedness between all beings. Her real presence within Judaism and Christianity, however, makes her a legitimate object of devotion for all but the most antifemale of the traditional denominations.

Furthermore, as the female figure within the biblical faiths, Sophia integrates many of the advantages of the goddess into Jewish monotheism and New Testament Christology. Sophia can, in fact, become a major connection between feminists and traditional churchgoers, between Christian, Jewish, and goddess-centered feminists, between historical and mythological worldviews, between the image of the hero and the image of the oppressed in history, art, and literature. Because she is such an important integrator her significance can hardly be overestimated.

THE DANGERS OF CO-OPTATION

Yet precisely because Sophia is such a powerful figure, she runs the risk of being co-opted by those who wish to use her power for their own ends. Some scholars believe that the development of Sophia by the wisdom school was simply the patriarchal manipulation of the image of the Near Eastern goddess. From this perspective the unacknowledged use of Sophia's words in the New Testament portrayal of Jesus, and the later pirating of her image for use in Roman ecclesiology and Mariology, simply completed this process of co-optation.[1]

We have good reason to fear that this co-optation of Sophia will be repeated. Three possibilities come to mind. First of all, Sophia can be used by some as an apology for a return to the Bible. Others may attempt to make her the only focus of feminist spirituality, rather than one significant figure in a universe of discourse so rich and promising that an entire range of symbolic possibilities will necessarily emerge. A further danger involves the portrayal of Sophia as a "white Christian goddess," one who will strengthen rather than help to heal the dichotomies of race and class that exist in our society and in the women's movement.

Sophia's fate in the Bible and in the postbiblical periods makes it difficult to use her to justify a nostalgic or apologetic return to the Bible. As we emphasize in the fourth chapter, Sophia was not only cut off in her biblical development, she was also misrepresented in the medieval and patristic periods, and in the Kabbala. Even if she were a fully developed biblical figure, biblical scholarship and new understandings of feminist historical reconstruction[2] would discourage any attempt at nondevelopmental, apologetic uses of Sophia. Nevertheless, it seems important to restate that Sophia is a mythic figure whose place within feminist spirituality is strengthened by, but by no means limited to, her roots in the Bible. Study and worship materials already being used experimentally in churches and retreat centers affirm that Sophia is a figure who offers a wide range of exciting possibilities for future developments in spirituality.

An attempt to make Sophia into an exclusive symbol within feminist spirituality—a kind of Sophiolatry, if you will—seems as unlikely as the use of Sophia as an apology for a return to the Bible. Sophia's presence in the wisdom literature and in the Christian scriptures witnesses to a greater richness and diversity of god-symbols within the Jewish and Christian traditions than we had been led to expect. Yet the centrality of a few symbols of the divine in the past cannot help influencing the structure of the western religious imagination.

Although Sophia is able to speak powerfully to some of us, and possibly to many of us at different times in our lives, feminist spirituality requires a symbol system of considerable nuance and diversity if it is to begin to communicate adequately the equality and connectedness of all beings.[3]

Moreover, there are times in the process of spiritual development when all language and symbols become inadequate and the person is faced with a situation of helplessness and impasse which cannot be avoided or denied. Constance Fitzgerald has suggested that this experience of dark night and impasse may be especially critical in the religious development of women who are coming to terms with the violence and domination of patriarchy, and their expression in the language and symbols of the Christian tradition.[4] Such religious development is an intensely personal process, and no mythic figure, not even one with Sophia's power and integrating capacity, can necessarily counteract the loss which is the hallmark of such a process. Sophia will speak to many for whom the central symbols of the traditions are no longer meaningful. Honoring one's own experience is basic to an authentic feminist spirituality, however, far more basic than the ability to relate to a particular symbol or set of symbols. This applies to Sophia just as it applies to God the Father.

The third danger confronting Sophia is that she will be used, unwittingly, to strengthen the domination of whites in the church and within feminism. Delores S. Williams has reminded us that "the divine as goddess is a concern emphasized in *white* feminist theology. . . . There is not yet enough data in from Afro-American Christian feminists, and from other Christian feminists of color to support this notion." Until things change, she assures us, data about black women's (and black Christian feminists') understanding of God will remain too meager for feminist theologians to come to solid conclusions about points of commonality.[5] Similarly, Joan Martin, a black Presbyterian pastor points out that the categories used by white feminist theologians are not authentic to the experience of black women.[6]

These criticisms can be applied to the feminist spirituality which we are describing and to the central role proposed for Sophia as a figure who can heal the dichotomies that are tearing humanity apart, not the least of which are the divisions of race and class. The spirituality we propose has been formulated by white, middle-class feminists, and many—but not all—of those who have explored the Sophia materials with us have been white middle-class people as well. However, our decision to propose Sophia as an alternative to the goddess as a focus for feminist spirituality emerges at least partially out of our respect for those who remain deeply loyal to the biblical tradition, many of them women of color as well as white women of several classes.

A further consideration qualifies our discussion of Sophia as a figure who can express and strengthen the connections between different races and classes. Sophia is unfinished. She is a female mythic figure who was truncated and suppressed at a number of different times in her history. For better and for worse, then, she is not a fully developed symbol which can be plugged neatly into a feminist spirituality. She is instead a female figure of considerable promise, rooted in the biblical traditions, yet requiring extensive development if that promise is to be fulfilled. This cannot happen if Sophia becomes a white goddess. Rather, the figure of Sophia must integrate and express the experience of the poor and people of color, especially the women in these groups. Such a development will require the involvement of all races and classes, not simply white middle-class feminists, if it is to come about. Later in this chapter we discuss the essential role which the literature and music being developed by women of color must play in the evolution of Sophia's image in our time.

If Sophia is to play the role within feminist spirituality which we envision for her, these possibilities of co-optation cannot be overlooked. Despite these dangers, the figure of Sophia offers possibilities for connection and transformation which may prove invaluable to us. Let's turn our attention, then, to the various connections which Sophia embodies. For as we struggle to understand each of these instances of connectedness, we may begin to overcome the alienation within our hearts and minds, and the transformation which feminist spirituality promises can begin within us.

SOPHIA CONNECTIONS

One of the most important connections embodied by Sophia is that of the creator and the created. As we have seen in Proverbs 8, Sophia was there at the beginning, a master craftswoman, and an ongoing part of the creative process. No sharp division exists between Sophia as creator, and Sophia herself created by God.

By bridging the supposed gap between creator and creation, Sophia provides exactly the image needed to make us aware of our own collective power, not as God's puppets, but as co-creators—or potential destroyers—of this planet. Sophia's continuing creativity, too, helps to keep before us the renewal of the earth, in birth, death, and resurrection. As we touch down again and again into the creative process, in parenting, in gardening, in politics and resistance, in the arts, in sport, in prayer and ritual, we fill out Sophia's image as creator and created in our own lives.

Because of the manner in which she is portrayed in the Wisdom literature, Sophia bridges the gap between creator and created fairly easily. Because of the complexity of her history in Judaism and in Christianity, her ability to make and be the connection between other dichotomies, between earth and heaven, transcendence and immanence, is more complex, yet no less critical for feminist spirituality. The split between these qualities, which is characteristic of western consciousness—the obsession with power-over, the identification of transcendence with God, and immanence with the earth—is integral to our planetary crisis.

In some ways, Sophia can be identified with heaven and the transcendent side of these divisions. Certainly in many of the "Old Testament" passages Sophia is a heavenly figure, identified closely with Yahweh. The gnostics picked up on this spiritual Sophia, and used her in their efforts to "transcend" the physical.

Sophia, however, is also (as Yahweh is) clearly bound to the earth in many passages. It would be incorrect to see her only as a heavenly figure. In addition, females have been traditionally identified with the underside of these dichotomies—with the earth, with immanence, with feeling. Symbols which are associated with the female run the risk of being devalued,[7] of being identified with the weak and the physical—even a heretofore strongly "spiritual" symbol like Sophia. Fear of this process, of the devaluation of Christ and the priesthood through their identification with the female, is most likely at the heart of the Roman Catholic resistance to women's ordination.

The Jesus-Sophia connection is crucial in the reintegration of these dichotomies by Sophia. Jesus has served as a major symbol of the reintegration of earth and heaven throughout Christian history. If the early church fathers in their attempt to establish the divinity of Christ felt the need to abandon earlier Christian references to Jesus as Sophia incarnate, in so doing they deprived Sophia at that time of the opportunity of being identified with God incarnate. We now propose to reverse the process of repression. Let us, in the service of overcoming dichotomies which could destroy us, emphasize once again the identification of Jesus with Sophia. In so doing we will liberate Sophia as the incarnate one and initiate the healing of ancient wounds.

By anchoring our understanding of Sophia firmly in that of Jesus, we are further justified in recognizing her as the connection between earth and heaven. The Jungians, in fact, describe Sophia as the one who binds humanity to the earth. This is a peculiarly alienated way to speak of our relationship to the earth, however. Human beings, like other living and nonliving things, have in fact come from the earth, and their embodiedness is the root of their ability to think and feel. Thomas Berry understands human beings as the earth becoming conscious of itself,[8] and we can take that understanding a step further by understanding Jesus as the fullest expression of that earth consciousness. It is not the incarnate Sophia's role to bind or reconnect us to the earth but to help us recognize that our understanding of ourselves as separate from the earth is a delusion. The incarnate Sophia, as a female figure, is peculiarly suited to helping us envision ourselves as we truly are, earth beings.

Along the same lines we can use the image of Sophia to integrate the notions of transcendence and immanence within the Western imagination. Once again the Jesus-Sophia connection is basic here. Divine Sophia, by becoming one with the earth in incarnation and suffering, skews the tendency to identify the transcendent with the male and the hero, and to identify the immanent with the female, nature, victims, and the endlessly returning mother-goddess. Sophia becomes instead the connection between them all.

As wisdom, Sophia incarnates other crucial connections. In the second chapter we came to understand that Sophia's wisdom and understanding are closely related to her role in the creative process. Disciplined study of all that is results in a direct encounter with Sophia, the one at the heart of the creative process. This understanding of the relationship between being and knowing brings to mind the image of the interactive web of life. As members of this nerve net—jewels in the net of Indra, Joanna Macy calls us—"we cannot avoid feeling and thinking about, and responding to these other beings, any more than a hand can avoid reacting when it touches a hot stove."[9]

Sophia as wisdom and understanding is analogous to the web of life. She reintegrates some of our most deeply entrenched dichotomies, the division between thinking and feeling, between reflection and action, between the learner and that which is learned. Sophia is the very personification of interactive learning, as distinguished from alienated, manipulative learning. As wisdom, Sophia symbolizes God, humanity, and the earth as colearners.

SOPHIA AND WOMEN'S IDENTITY

Sophia brings power. She has power to share, and this power is especially available to women. Women who incorporate Sophia's symbolism within themselves can experience an extraordinary affirmation of every aspect of their being. Through Sophia women can claim power as their right, exercise it creatively, share it, and be sustained by it. They can be strong and independent in ways that are not possible within an exclusively male symbol system.

Why does a female rather than a male mythic figure make so much difference? A woman whose only symbol for God is male may be able to pray to him and be comforted and strengthened by him, but there is a level which is beyond her reach: she can never identify with him. She may believe that she is created in his image but what does it mean to be like someone who is called "Father"? Only by denying her own sexuality or by placing it in a sphere which is totally out of reach, beyond sexual identification, can she relate as one who is created in the image of a male god. She can never have the experience that is open to every male in our society: to have her sexual identity affirmed by God, and to identify directly with "him."

The exclusively male religious symbol system has served to reinforce male domination at every level of society. To be a white male in this society is to be able to claim power. To be female is to be powerless or, at best, to have one's claim to power held suspect. Geraldine Ferraro's bid for the vice presidency and the reaction of men and women alike to her attempt is a good example of the difficulty women have in legitimizing their right to power. Women at every level experience this same struggle, whether in the fight to gain equal pay for work on the job or in the attempt to equalize household tasks at home. And what makes this struggle so difficult—in fact, unthinkable for some women—is that male domination of society appears to be a part of the divine plan ordered and maintained by God.

What is it like to live with this kind of subordination? Living on the margins of power can make women experience themselves as shadows, semipersons who lack thoughts, feelings and gifts of their own. Life on the margin is spent smiling, when shouting is more to the point, and learning how to manipulate those with real power. It is a life of rage, expressed sometimes in child abuse, but more often unexpressed, except in depression or psychosis. It is a life of invisibility, a life which accepts battering and sexual abuse as one's due. Every woman in this society has experienced the life of powerlessness to some degree. It is this life which Sophia can transform.

Sophia offers divine female power, a power needed to balance that which is generated by the present male symbol system. Through Sophia women can affirm their own female identity, and can claim full participation in this society as a legitimate right. Sophia brings women strength and nurture for the struggle, and upholds them in the midst of difficulty. She unlocks the power which has been accessible only through male symbols of the divine and shares it with those who have been shut out.

Sophia makes her power available in a number of ways, but perhaps most important among these are the role models she provides for women. In the "Old Testament" and in the Christian scriptures Sophia presents women with a variety of models which they can claim for their own growth. As creator, as respected nurturer, and as a strong, angry, assertive, and sometime prophetic woman, Sophia provides women with alternatives to the traditional behaviors into which many of them were socialized.

First of all, Sophia is full of creative power. She who was with God at the beginning, before creation (Proverbs 8, Baruch 3), who herself is the mother of all good things (Wisdom 7:12), is the source of newness and growth. Women can claim their own creative power—their procreative power in all its wonder and mystery, but also the power that is theirs to bring into being new ideas, new projects, new ways of working and being together. Patriarchal society has attempted to keep women's creativity tied to home and children. By identifying with the one who took a playful part in the creation, women can imagine new and larger arenas in which their creativity can flourish.

Sophia is also a strong, assertive female who is proud of herself. In Ecclesiasticus 24:1 Sophia is described in this way:

Sophia speaks her own praises,
in the midst of her people she glories in herself.

What would it be like for women to begin to emulate her, finding aspects of themselves that are worthy of praise, and glorying in what they find in one another? What power would be present in women who were truly proud, who were not hindered by feelings of inadequacy, but calmly asserted themselves as strong, able, and deserving of respect?

At times Sophia's assertiveness takes the form of prophetic anger. She calls aloud in the streets (Proverbs 1 and 8), shouting out warnings of disaster to those who are foolish enough to ignore her. Following her lead, women are free to voice their anger and impatience with those who wrong them, and who wrong the rest of creation. In claiming their anger and directing it at those people and institutions who have sought to keep them invisible and powerless, women can open untapped stores of energy and vitality within themselves. Anger redirected brings with it the possibility of real change in this society and in women's lives.

Sophia is also the warm, nurturing one. "A tree of life for those who hold her fast" (Proverbs 3:18), she provides shelter and nourishment. The role of nurturer is a familiar one for the majority of women. Yet nurturing has been devalued because it is considered a female activity, and because women themselves are devalued in this society. Sophia, however, is a powerful, divine figure who, in addition to creating and ordering the world and empowering leaders to rule, also provides comfort, shelter and nourishment. Sophia's divine status demands respect for the work that women do to enhance life and promote growth.

What happens to women when they become aware of Sophia's divine power within themselves? Reality is changed or, rather, their perception of reality is changed. No longer can women be relegated to the periphery, for in identifying with the divine Sophia they move to the center. They move from seeing themselves as subordinate to seeing themselves as full human beings. This change in perception is gained from knowing Sophia's reality within themselves, not from any significant change in the situation in which they find themselves. But this change in their perception of themselves alters their relationship to their situation and empowers them to find ways to move to the center within that situation. It alters their entire notion of the divine plan, and makes possible their full participation within society.

This means that women begin to value their own thoughts, feelings, and experiences. Through Sophia's presence in their lives what they think becomes important, what they feel becomes legitimate, what they experience becomes real. They refuse to be silent and invisible; they risk asserting themselves in the world around them; they challenge the status quo that renders them subordinate.

Perhaps the most important aspect of this change is that women will be able to affirm their own bodies, will celebrate themselves as female. In Sophia the female body, so long debased and viewed as evil, becomes the source and center of divine power, of creativity and life. With this new way of relating to their bodies, women will no longer tolerate beating, abuse, and rape. Such affronts to the female body will no longer be seen as the inevitable consequences of inferiority and evil but as an outrageous affront to the very center of divine reality, and they will not be tolerated.

What we are describing here is the process of consciousness-raising, a process which has been experienced to some extent by many women in the last twenty years. Consciousness-raising has gone on with little reference to the divine, except when the divine has been recognized as a pseudo-justification for women's oppression. We propose that the female power which is utilized, encountered and released in consciousness-raising be given a divine name. That power within women is Sophia, who "permeates all things" (Wisdom 7:24).

This power has, of course, never really been lost. Over the centuries, sometimes with great struggle, women have gained access to the power within them. And in our own day we have experienced a new manifestation of this power, through the liberation of women and other oppressed peoples of the world. Yet the resurrection of Sophia provides us with a direct, emphatic entrée into that power. The woman who finds God within herself and loves her fiercely can now call her by her name, and the struggle will never be the same again.

SOPHIA UNFINISHED

We noted earlier that the portrait of Sophia is unfinished. Both in the Hebrew scriptures and in the New Testament, she is cut off or disguised so that her image is never fully formed. Rather, like someone who has lost a parent or sibling early in life, we attempt to reconstruct her, but we can never find her in her entirety.

In some ways, Sophia's incompleteness is a tragedy. Who knows the impact she might have had if she had developed fully? If she had grown to her full stature, attitudes toward women might be far different.

On the other hand, Sophia's unfinishedness, like our own, makes further development possible. At the very least, her foreshortened quality makes unlikely blind, obsequious imitation of her. Instead, as members of a community of equals, we are called to flesh out her image, to work toward completing Sophia in our own lives. So we can never say of Sophia, as certain romantic believers sometimes say of Jesus, "Oh, if I had only lived then, if only I had seen Sophia as she actually was, how much easier it would be for me to believe."[10] Instead, as we confront this mysterious figure who is sometimes like a cedar of Lebanon and sometimes like the mist, the question we must ask is—how does Sophia address us now? What claim does she make on us in our day to day existence?

SOPHIA AND SUFFERING

The absence of suffering and death in the story of Sophia presents us with another gap, and quite a serious one, in our portrait of her. Except insofar as she is identified with Jesus, the biblical Sophia does not suffer and die. We have seen how this situation appealed to the gnostics, and how the resultant portrayal of Sophia drove her underground in the New Testament. This only serves to reinforce our wariness. How can a figure devoid of suffering play a role within the feminist spirituality?

The way human beings understand and integrate suffering and death tells us a great deal about their vision of reality. Our responses to suffering are of a piece with our acceptance or rejection of the earth and of the body. Our ability to feel and to express our feelings and to act on them is basic to our spirituality. It is one of the foundational mechanisms by which human beings are connected to one another and to the rest of creation, and as such it is central to feminist spirituality.

Within a feminist spirituality the struggle against suffering and oppression requires not only commitment and energy, but also the collective recognition that suffering and injustice exist and that we human beings are responsible for them. When groups and societies recognize the existence of suffering and oppression, social transformation, whether reform or revolution, begins. Conversely, denial is intrinsic to personal and political repression. In individuals lives human growth and transformation depend upon the acknowledgment and processing of experiences of suffering. A person frees herself from past hurt by recognizing it, by expressing that pain to herself and others, and by acting in whatever way is possible. Dorothee Sölle describes the affliction of certain factory workers and concentration camp inmates, suggesting that the worst kind of suffering is that which has no expression at all—"the suffering that can find no language" she calls it.[11] In the cosmos of connectedness toward which we are moving, groups and individuals will be able to acknowledge their own experience of pain and to assume responsibility for the pain they have caused others.

Myths and symbols function to incorporate understandings of reality into our individual and collective awareness, and they serve this function in relation to our understanding of suffering and death as well as other aspects of the human condition. A Sophia who does not suffer is limited in her ability to function within a feminist spirituality. In her history thus far Sophia is more a symbol of creation than of the passion, and this is in some ways a genuine strength. Yet the absence of suffering and death within the Sophia story also gives her a certain disembodied quality which is less than helpful in our attempt to express the connectedness of all things.

Sophia's unfinished quality may help us here. All mythic and symbolic figures evolve and develop over time, and so it is worthwhile to consider the ways in which suffering and death can become part of the Sophia story—ways in which Sophia can develop in our time, and with our assistance. Possibilities here include associating Sophia with Jesus' passion and death—in effect, imaginatively experiencing the passion, death, and resurrection of Sophia. We can also come to terms with the suffering of Sophia by recognizing the silencing and repression of Sophia in biblical and postbiblical times as strikingly similar to the suffering of many women throughout history.

THE PASSION AND DEATH OF SOPHIA

In the first instance we propose that Sophia assume the story of Jesus' passion and death. In an earlier chapter we saw that the sayings of Sophia and those of Jesus have become one in many of the Christian scriptures. And we noticed that Jesus assumes Sophia's role as creator in the Pauline and Johannine descriptions of him. In this same spirit, in response to the needs of the contemporary community, Jesus' suffering and death can become Sophia's own.

It is possible to imagine a number of different ways of introducing the passion and death of Sophia to our collective religious consciousness.[12] One approach involves inserting Sophia, literally and directly, into the passion story and then noting the effect this transformation has on us. The use of the image of Sophia in a variety of representations of the passion—in hymns, in visual works such as crucifixes and stations of the cross, and in litanies and prayers—can also help us to imagine her in the role of sufferer as well as playful creator. The cross supporting a female corpus provides us with an example of this sort. The uproar which greets this kind of expression is an all too discouraging example of the distance between the contemporary Christian imagination and the connectedness toward which feminist spirituality is pointing.

There is, of course, a temptation to discount this kind of experimentation as faddish and ineffective manipulation of the tradition. Such dismissals suggest a romanticized understanding of the formulation of the Christian scriptures. Similar "manipulations" constituted the methodology for the drawing of the portrait of Jesus in the Gospels, as we have seen in our examination of the incorporation of the Sophia texts by the Gospel writers. Yet the results have sustained our spirits and our imaginations for centuries.

This creation of the passion and death of Sophia will make many new connections possible. In some sense, what we propose is not far removed from the black community's use of the image of a black Jesus during the liberation struggles, an image which reinforced a sense of potency and worth within the black community. Sophia's presence in the Jewish and Christian scriptures, and particularly her close identification with Jesus in the Gospels, doubly justifies such an association. For a very long time now Jesus' death has enabled individuals to acknowledge and process suffering in their own lives; the passion and death of Sophia can enable her to take on people's suffering in a similar way. Jesus' crucifixion and death likewise symbolize his solidarity with the poor and the oppressed, and Sophia's passion can become a symbol of collective struggle as well. Finally, just as Jesus on the cross has become a symbol of a new kind of kingdom, Sophia on the cross can represent a new creation which integrates many apparent dichotomies and contradictions, even the dichotomy of life over suffering and death.

In order for this endeavor to succeed, it must be both playful and experiential. In a certain sense we are allowing ourselves to vandalize the well-loved story of Jesus' betrayal, trial, crucifixion, and burial. The last fifty years of scholarship regarding the biblical accounts of Jesus' passion encourage us in our daring, however. Scholars have made it clear that the historical basis for all four of the Gospel accounts of the passion is extremely shaky.[13] Rather, the Gospel writers seem to have constructed the passion narratives so as to conform to certain "Old Testament" references. Telling the passion story with Sophia as the main character does not necessarily clash with the story as it is told in the Gospels, then, and we would even argue that such an undertaking corresponds quite closely to the spirit of the writing of the Gospels.[14]

SOPHIA'S SUFFERING AND THE ANONYMITY OF THE OPPRESSED

Conscious recognition of the injustices done to Sophia during the biblical and postbiblical period can also help us come to know the suffering Sophia. We have already noted, of course, the large volume of Sophia material in the Hebrew tradition, and in the Christian scriptures, and the extent to which many Jews and Christians are unaware of these materials. And those who have been aware of Sophia within the biblical traditions have most often thought of her as "Wisdom," a concept having no personal or mythical dimensions. Her real power has been effectively negated because she has remained an outsider, invisible, hidden, and unknown. In the Christian scriptures she is literally invisible, incorporated within the figure of Jesus and unidentified there, while in the Hebrew wisdom literature, especially in the book of Proverbs, she lashes out at all those who have ignored her. Finally, during the patristic and medieval periods Sophia is folded into the figures of Mary and holy mother Church, unnamed, misrepresented, and misunderstood, emerging only occasionally in an uncensored work of art and in the Eastern Orthodox tradition.

This suppression of an important female mythic figure, and the attendant loss of her power, corresponds to the reality of the lives of many women. For the most part, women have been invisible, particularly in Western civilization. Their achievements have either gone unrecognized or have been taken for granted. Women are not heard. They struggle for recognition and are dismissed with a nod or a pat on the head. Like Sophia, they are outsiders, invisible in their own communities. Finally, and most tragically of all, many women have become invisible to themselves, unable to act or to think as anyone other than the daughter, the wife, or the mother of someone else.

This experience of marginality is true not only of women. It is just as true of all whose histories have been obliterated by their oppressors. This includes blacks who have lost their African heritage, native peoples under various forms of colonialism whose culture has been undermined, and the poor who have been denied pride in the past and hope for the future.

For those who have lived on the margins of life, Sophia's particular kind of suffering, the suffering of invisibility, anonymity, and repression can be a strong and poignant means of identification. Claiming Sophia may enable many to objectify their marginality, and gain the power to speak out about their situation. She who was herself hidden and kept invisible speaks powerfully to those who ignore her. Through the power and the anger of Sophia, those who have been made invisible can claim their own anger, refuse to be silenced, and begin to experience the power which comes from that process.

SOPHIA AND STRUGGLE

Twice in the past the development of Sophia's image within the history of God's people has been abruptly cut off. Today her presence is growing once again, but she has no more guarantee of flourishing now than she had in Hellenistic Judaism or in early Christian times. How can we foster Sophia's development in our day and extend her image into the future of God's people?

Our most important task is to recognize and celebrate Sophia's presence among the poor and the oppressed. Because Jesus-Sophia lived among us and suffered and died and this death was not the final triumph of evil, the lives of third world people, inmates in prisons and asylums, lesbians and gays, people afflicted with diseases, the handicapped, children—all are Sophia's reality in our day. And their suffering is not the final triumph of evil. As we draw closer to them, as we learn to recognize the oppressed in our sisters and brothers, and the oppressed (as well as the oppressor) within ourselves, Sophia's outline will become clearer to us, and she will influence our actions.

Sophia incarnate is particularly recognizable in the art, literature, and music of Third World people, and especially in the work of women of color. The art of black, Asian, and Hispanic women has already led some of us to an awareness of connectedness which would otherwise be inaccessible to us. Audre Lorde, Barbara Smith, Cherrie Moraga, Toni Cade Bambara, June Jordan, Alice Walker, Maxine Hong Kingston, Michelle Cliff, Paula Gunn Allen, Fay Chiang, Bernice Johnson Reagon and other women of color give expression to Sophia in innumerable ways. It may be that the coming to speech of the community of women in our time, especially as it has been expressed in the work of women of color is so powerful, and of such revelatory force that it can be compared to the coming to speech of the early Christian community around the figure of Jesus. Each encounter with their work will enflesh Sophia in our imaginations and will bring those of us who are white and middle class into some kind of contact, no matter how limited, with people who are an important manifestation of Sophia in our time.

Beyond this, in order really to come to know Sophia, those who are white and middle class must become involved in their everyday lives with the poor, with people of color, with the oppressed. This involvement will have nothing to do with any assistance which the privileged can provide the oppressed. It is a question, rather, of the need of white, middle-class people to have their imaginations radically expanded, so that they can begin to understand what equality and connectedness can possibly mean. All of this is Sophia's work, in us and in society.

The final task of enfleshing Sophia in ourselves and in our world involves acting unambiguously for justice. For it is in our practice finally that we will find and fully express the vision of radical connectedness which we have been exploring. Of course we also find Sophia in prayer and meditation and Bible study and literature and music. But these must inform and shape our action, our slow, steady trudging toward justice, or they are devalued. Without a clearly expressed commitment to justice in the world, there can be no feminist spirituality. A Sophia who does not drive us to action on behalf of others becomes a travesty, one more image shoring up the old patriarchal spirituality which divides religion from politics, and the self from the society. It is always, of course, a temptation to slide back into this disconnected spirituality, this piety without struggle. But Sophia calls out to us when we are tempted. Her vision will surely keep us moving. May she be for all of us the strength, the courage, the splendid arrogance with which together we will undertake the transformation of society.

Part Two

CHAPTER SIX

Getting Acquainted with Sophia

Most people think of a movie star when they hear the word *Sophia,* and most think of books or owls when they hear the word *Wisdom.* Although the Bible contains more material about Sophia than about any other figure except Jesus and God, she is unknown to the great majority of people. Even those who are relatively well versed in the Bible and in the Jewish and Christian traditions often do not know who she is.

In our experience, Sophia has been introduced to groups of people in one of two ways. Some groups set aside a single session of two to four hours. Other groups prefer a series of four to six sessions. This chapter delineates several ways of approaching each possibility. At the end of the chapter you will also find several celebrations and a sermon appropriate for introductory sessions and suggested uses of these materials.

Three different presentations have proven effective in a single-session introduction; two of these emphasize an affective learning style, while the third uses a more theoretical approach. The choice among these three will be based on the group's makeup and history. If the group is comfortable with participatory and expressive styles, then we recommend the first or third presentation. If the group resists such expressive approaches, the more theoretical presentation, which is the second one in this chapter, will be more appropriate. The first presentation, "A Tree of Life for Those Who Hold Her Fast," is an especially apt introduction for a group interested in women's concerns.

An hour and a half is the minimum length of time needed for one of these introductory sessions. The material is too new and the questions raised too varied for a shorter period. We have found, in fact, that a Sophia introduction of less than ninety minutes can do more harm than good, even causing confusion and antipathy in the group. On the other hand, if three hours are available, it is possible to combine the first two presentations, making for a stronger balance of expressive and intellectual elements in the introductory sessions.

The one topic that cannot possibly be considered in a single introductory session is that of Sophia in the New Testament. We strongly recommend that group leaders avoid introducing New Testament material on Sophia during an introductory session and that all questions about the relationship between Jesus and Sophia be carefully deferred to a later date. If questions about Jesus and Sophia are raised in a one-session introduction, simply acknowledge the importance of such questions and say that in a course or series on Sophia it's possible to consider these questions in some depth. Chapter 3 of *Sophia* provides a good introduction to the treatment of Sophia in the Christian scriptures.

SINGLE-SESSION INTRODUCTIONS TO SOPHIA

❧ The Tree of Life for Those Who Hold Her Fast: A Bible Study

---

Materials Needed: Sheets of white paper for everyone, crayons, watercolors, colored pencils, and/or colored chalk.

Opening Exercise:

Close your eyes. Picture your favorite tree. Watch it change; watch it grow or change with the seasons. Observe the life around it. Notice what is near it. Watch the tree in relationship to its surroundings. See how it is affected. Notice how the tree affects what is near it.

Scripture Reading: Read these passages together: Ecclesiasticus 14:20–27; Ecclesiasticus 24:1–22. (These and all major scriptures concerning Sophia may be found in the Appendix.)

Questions: In the group, consider the following questions:

- What are the characteristics of Sophia as tree/plant in these passages? Name as many as you can.

- What do these characteristics contribute to your picture of Sophia? What is she like?

- Often you will find that Sophia plays a connecting role; what kind of connections does she make? What does she connect in Ecclesiasticus 24?

- Look at trees/plants in relation to their environment—the earth, the sky, animals, humanity, etc. How are trees/plants connectors? What roles do they play?

- What does Sophia as tree/plant connect for you? What relationship do you have to her? What else do trees/plants provide?

- Recall references to trees/plants in the New Testament. How are tree/plant images used in the New Testament? Compare them to the tree/plant images used to describe Sophia.

- In Ecclesiasticus 14, how is Sophia described? What is she here?

- What kind of person is this human being in chapter 14? Describe someone you know who is like this person.

- How does the person in chapter 14 approach Sophia? Describe the relationship to her. How does it change?

- What does this human get from the relationship to Sophia? What do you need or want that Sophia has? What would you need to do to get it?

- Describe what making your home in Sophia's tree/house would be like. If living in her tree/house were an active image for you, how would it affect the way you lived? What would change?

Closing Exercise:

Think again of a tree or plant. Imagine this tree or plant as a way of encountering Sophia.

Invite people to find a free space in the room to participate in a guided movement exercise. They may choose to face the wall so that they don't feel inhibited.

Imagine yourself as a seed on the Sophia tree/plant. Let yourself move, however that might happen, to a new place, to plant yourself in the earth. . . . Let yourself burrow deep into the earth . . . into the darkness. . . . Begin to put down roots . . . deeper . . . in all directions. . . . Enjoy the warmth of the earth. . . . Push up to meet the sun. . . . Face the light and the warmth. . . . Continue to grow. . . . Put out branches, leaves. . . . If your plant blossoms, put out blossoms . . . and fruit. . . . Feel the breeze. . . . Notice other plants or animals nearby. . . . Enjoy yourself. . . . Take a deep breath. . . . And come back with the others.

After the movement, each person is asked to draw a picture of herself or himself as a tree or plant.

After you have drawn the picture and reflected, take a pencil and write as many statements about the tree/plant as you can. Begin each statement with the words, "I am, do, enjoy, etc."

The group then comes back together and each person shares as much of their picture and statements as they want.

&. A Survey of Sophia's Texts: A Bible Study

Since this exercise has very few affective components and can be done alone, it is unlike almost all the other Bible studies in this book.

Materials Needed: Paper and pencils, scripture for all.
Scripture Reading: Each person in the group should read silently Ecclesiasticus 24:1–29. (See Appendix)
Questions: This portion of the study should be limited to fifteen minutes at most. The leader asks the following questions, mostly as preparation for the more intensive examination of the text that follows in the next part of the study.

- What are the main events in this passage?
- Divide the passage into major segments according to subject matter.

(The leader should make sure that the group is aware of the different sections of the passage. They are: Sophia introducing herself, Sophia's search for a place to live, Sophia as a tree or plant, Sophia as the Law.)

- If, after reading this passage, you had to put your initial feelings about Sophia into five words or less, what would they be?

Scripture Reading: Now the leader begins an extensive exercise in which the group rereads the passage from Ecclesiasticus 24. To begin, the leader directs the group back to Ecclesiasticus 24:1, 2 and then asks them to read Proverbs 8:1–21. (See Appendix)
Questions:

- What is Sophia like here?
- Have you ever met someone like this?
- Have you ever dreamed of someone like this?
- How do you feel about Sophia's pride and self-assurance in these passages?

Scripture Reading: The leader asks the group to reread the following scriptures: Ecclesiasticus 24:3–6; and then Baruch 3:29–31; Proverbs 8:22–31; and Wisdom 9:9–11. (See Appendix).
Questions:

- Describe Sophia in these passages. What is her main activity?
- In the Proverbs 8 passage, how does the work of creation seem to be divided up between Sophia and God?

(As the group becomes aware that Sophia is playing more and God is "working" more, the leader should remind them of the essential role of play in the creative process.)

- Is Sophia more human or more divine in these passages?

(Some of the group may begin to ask questions about Sophia's relationship to God. At this juncture, the leader should simply say that a direct consideration of these questions is included in the next section of the study.)
Scripture Reading: Reread, in this order: Ecclesiasticus 24:7–12; Proverbs 8:22 and 30; Wisdom 7:24–8:4 and 9:4. (See Appendix)
Questions:

- How would you describe Sophia's relationship to God in each of these passages?

(It is important that the group realize at this point that the relationship is described quite differently in each passage. In some of the passages she is subservient to him, in some he is subservient to her, in some she is essentially alone, and in some they are partners. The group should be discouraged from attempting a synthesis of these passages.)

- Which picture of the relationship between God and Sophia do you prefer?

(This question is for individuals to answer. The group itself does not need to decide on a preference.)
Scripture Reading: Reread Ecclesiasticus 24:7–12; Wisdom 10:1–11:3. (See Appendix)
Questions:

- How does Sophia relate to life on earth in these passages?
- How does Sophia strike you, as she is depicted in the stories of Adam through Moses?

(See "Sophia and History," page 81, for additional directions on some likely reactions to these questions.)
Scripture Reading: Reread Ecclesiasticus 24:13–22. Then read Ecclesiasticus 14:25–27; Proverbs 3:18. (See Appendix)
Questions:

- Is the picture of Sophia in Ecclesiasticus 24:13–22 of a person or a tree? (The leader should be aware that the answer is "both.")

- What kind of person can be compared to a tree?

Scripture Reading: Reread Ecclesiasticus 24:19–22. Then read Wisdom 6:12–17. (See Appendix)
Questions:

- What does one receive when one approaches Sophia?
- What social role does she seem to have in Wisdom 6?
- In these texts, what is an approach to Sophia like?

Scripture Reading: Now again read briefly Ecclesiasticus 24:19–22. Then read Wisdom 7:22–30. (See Appendix)
Questions:

- What does Sophia have to offer?
- To whom would you compare Sophia in the Wisdom 7 passage?
- How does Sophia carry her greatness?

Scripture Reading: Reread Ecclesiasticus 24:23–29. Then read Baruch 4:1–4. (See Appendix)
Questions:

- With what is Sophia associated here?
- How does this make the Law seem to you?

Closing Exercise: The leader invites the group to review briefly all the material they have read on Sophia. She or he asks each person to list four characteristics of Sophia that seem central to her person. After everyone has listed these characteristics, each then thinks of a person with whom to compare Sophia. This could be a real human being, a mythical character, or someone else in the Bible. Each person then reports back to the group concerning the individual to whom they have compared Sophia.

৯৶ Sophia Through Role Play: A Bible Study

Introducing Sophia through role play requires a group of fifteen or more people. Since the activity centers around role playing, some openness to expressive and participatory exercises is needed. But it can certainly be done by those who have no previous role-playing experience.

Materials Needed: Paper and pencils for all, assigned scriptures for each group.
Opening Exercise: Divide the group into five different subgroups. Each

group should be in a space sufficiently separate to allow movement and talking without interference between the groups. Each group should be assigned one of the following passages, which are to be read in silence.

Scripture Reading: (See Appendix)

Group 1: Proverbs 8:1–21.

Group 2: Proverbs 8:22–31.

Group 3: Wisdom 10:1–11:3.

Group 4: Ecclesiasticus 24:1–21.

Group 5: Wisdom 7:22–8:1.

Questions: Each group should discuss the following questions about the assigned passage. The leader emphasizes the need for everyone in each small group to speak.

- What is Sophia like in this passage?
- How do you feel about her?

Role Play: After the small groups have had approximately fifteen minutes to read the passage and discuss the questions, the leader of the larger group should instruct each small group to prepare a role play of their passage for the rest of the groups. In the role play words from the assigned passage are not to be used; rather, the role play itself should communicate to the audience the kind of person Sophia is without the passage being read aloud. Fifteen to twenty minutes should be sufficient for planning and rehearsing, after which the leader calls the groups back together to present their role plays. After each group presentation, ask the entire group to give impressions of what kind of person this Sophia is. Allow the presenting group to make any explanations it wishes in response to the group's comments.

Closing Exercise: Ask each person to take a few moments to identify one characteristic of Sophia presented in the role plays that she or he has a very strong feeling about. The leader should explain that the feeling may be positive or negative. After several minutes of reflection, the leader asks everyone to tell the group about that particular aspect of Sophia.

INTRODUCTORY COURSES ON SOPHIA

The way one organizes a four- to six-session introductory course on Sophia depends, to a large extent, on the kind of people who will participate in the course. A series for women and men, for instance, will probably be somewhat different than a course for women only. A church group generally has different needs than a women's spirituality group. And the ease with which the persons concerned participate in expressive exercises as well as their intellectual interests need to be considered as the exact content of the course is determined.

The ideal course, rather than covering prescribed content, is compatible with the needs and abilities of a particular group of people. Once this principle is established, however, experience also suggests that activities that encourage participation and help people to experience and express their feelings are much to be preferred to purely cognitive activities and should therefore be included in the course whenever possible. Although it is true that some groups have limited toleration for affective activities, at least initially, leaders should encourage groups to be as open to these exercises as possible.

The reason for this bias toward affective activities is simple. In our estimation, Sophia is important primarily because of her potential impact on personal and collective spirituality. (See chapter 1, "Spirituality, Feminism and Sophia.") Affect is a major component of spirituality. A purely theoretical treatment of Sophia is not an effective approach to the development of spirituality; we might compare it to an understanding of lovemaking that is mostly anatomical. The second portion of this chapter contains, therefore, several study units that are primarily affective and participatory in character.

Here are some of the ways an introductory course could be organized.

Course A

Session 1: A Tree of Life for Those Who Hold Her Fast: A Bible Study (see 74 to 75).

Session 2: Introducing Sophia Through Role Play (see 78 to 79).

Session 3: Sophia and Christology (see 84 to 88).

Session 4: Sophia Walking on the Water (see 152 to 154).

Course B

Session 1: A Tree of Life for Those Who Hold Her Fast: A Bible Study (see 74 to 75).

Session 2: Raising Her Voice: A Bible Study (see 107 to 109).

Session 3: Sophia as Teacher and Lover (see 82 to 84).

Session 4: Sophia and History: A Bible Study (see 81 to 82).

Session 5: Sophia Walking on the Water: A Bible Study (see 152 to 154).

Course C

Session 1: Introducing Sophia Through Role Play (see 78 to 79).

Session 2: Sophia and Christology (see 84 to 88).

Session 3: Sophia Walking on the Water: A Bible Study (see 152 to 154).

Session 4: Sophia and the Woman with a Hemorrhage: A Bible Study (see 113 to 116).

Course D

A group could read together part 1 of this book, covering one chapter during each session. This is recommended only for groups who are adamant in their resistance to more affective and participatory approaches.

These introductory units of study and celebration can be used in the ways just outlined or in ways appropriate to the particularities of one's setting.

🕿 Sophia and History: A Bible Study

The text for this study retells the story of the people of early Israel with Sophia, rather than God, as the main actor and protagonist. But then, suddenly, in the middle of the story, the traditional male Hebrew God appears and reassumes his central role in the remainder of the story. Few scholarly attempts have been made to explain why this new story of Sophia in history begins and why it is suddenly cut off. The text clearly provides us with a strong yet incomplete attempt to reimage God in history.

Groups working with this text, and women's groups in particular, frequently need to be encouraged to come to terms with the content of the story and to raise whatever objections occur to them regarding the particular way the story is told. Specifically, Sophia's rescue of the men in the first part of Israel's story often triggers memories for many women of having rescued and cared for a series of men who went on to achieve credit or recognition. Although we present this text as a basically positive experiment about reimaging God within the wisdom literature, many participants may be unable to appreciate the horizons it opens up unless they have the opportunity to react to the female-rescuer dimensions of the passage. Often these questions are raised most easily in the first "Questions" section.

Materials Needed: Several sheets of paper and a pen or pencil, and scriptures for each participant.

Scripture Reading: The group reads in silence Wisdom 10:1–11:2. (See Appendix)

Questions: The group, with the guidance of the leader, discusses these questions for fifteen to twenty-five minutes.

- What does Sophia do in this passage?
- Who are the various individuals that she is helping?

(The group should go through each portion of the passage and identify the biblical figure Sophia is relating to.)

- Do any of these stories sound different from stories about the same characters in other parts of the Bible?
- Where is God in this passage?
- Who does Sophia remind you of in this passage?

Exercise: Each individual will need several sheets of paper. The leader gives instructions for a writing period of twenty to thirty minutes:

> The passage in Wisdom 10 showed Sophia in charge of history. Take time now to see how this story might continue. You may write about one of two stories. Either continue the story of Sophia in biblical times or write the story of another historical period from the point of view of Sophia's engagement in that time. For the first option, you may want to continue with stories of Miriam, David, Solomon, and/or Isaiah. Rewrite them from the perspective of Wisdom 10. How would they sound if Sophia were active in history? For the second option, you may wish to think about Sophia in a particular period of history such as the twentieth century, the Middle Ages, or the Age of Reason.

Closing Exercise: Everyone returns to the full group, and time is given for each person to read her or his Sophia history.

🕊 Sophia as Teacher and Lover: A Bible Study

In the texts for this study, motifs of teacher and lover intertwine. The study requires the participation of at least seven people.

Materials Needed: Photocopied parts for each participant in role play, paper, and pen or pencil for each participant.

Opening Exercise: The leader asks members of the group to think of their favorite teacher.

> Recall how she or he looked and talked. Remember what you liked about him or her and how you felt in her or his presence.

Then the leader asks each person to think of someone whom they have loved intensely. Allow a few, although not too many, minutes for each person to recall that person.

Role Play: Assign each of the seven parts below to a participant. Everyone in the room should have a part. The leader asks everyone to look at his or her part and to practice it. In particular, each person should be encouraged to practice putting feeling and expression into the part he or she will read.

After three to five minutes the leader convenes the group and begins the role play. The parts should be played with as much drama and expression as possible, although melodrama is not encouraged. If the group is large enough that several people have the same part, let several people take turns reading the parts. (See Appendix for passages)

SOPHIA: Ecclesiasticus 24:19–22.
STUDENT A: Ecclesiasticus 51:13–22.
STUDENT B: Proverbs 4:5–9.
SOPHIA: Proverbs 1:22–27.
STUDENT C:

    Sophia I loved and searched for from my youth;
    I resolved to have her as my bride,
    I fell in love with her beauty.
    She enhances her noble birth by sharing God's life,
    for the Master of All has always loved her.
    Indeed, she shares the secrets of God's knowledge,
    and she chooses what he will do.
    If in this life wealth is a desirable possession,
    what is more wealthy than Sophia whose work is everywhere?
    By means of her, immortality will be mine,
    I shall leave an everlasting memory to my successors.
    I shall govern peoples, and nations will be subject to me;
    When I go home I shall take my ease with her,
    for nothing is bitter in her company,
    when life is shared with her there is no pain,
    nothing but pleasure and joy.
    Having meditated on all this,
    and having come to the conclusion
    that immortality resides in kinship with Wisdom,
    noble contentment in her friendship,
    inexhaustible riches in her activities,
    understanding in cultivating her society,
    and renown in conversing with her,
    I went by all ways, seeking how to get her.

                (Wisdom 8:2–5, 13, 14, 16–18)

STUDENT D: Ecclesiasticus 6:9–22, 24–31.
SOPHIA: Proverbs 8:6–21.
STUDENT E: Wisdom 6:12–17.
STUDENT F:

    To love her is to love life;
    To rise early for her sake is to be filled with joy.
    The one who attains her will win recognition;
    At first she will lead you by devious ways,
    filling you with craven fears.
    Her discipline will be a torment to you
    and her decrees a hard test
    until you trust her with all your heart.
    Then she will come straight back to you again and gladden you
    and reveal her secrets to you.   (Ecclesiasticus 4:12, 13a, 17–18)

Questions: People should be seated again and discuss the following questions.

- When you were watching Sophia, what was your impression of her?
- What was your impression of those with whom she spoke?
- When you were playing Sophia, how did it feel?
- When you were playing those who were speaking with Sophia, what did you feel about her?
- When you were playing those who were speaking with Sophia, how did you feel?
- Would you like to learn from this Sophia? What would the advantages and disadvantages of learning from her be?
- Could you love this Sophia? What would loving her be like?

The leader should make sure that the different persons who played the same roles have a chance to speak. It is likely that different persons will not have experienced the roles in the same manner.

Closing Exercise: Each person should take a piece of paper and write a letter to Sophia. The letter may be to Sophia as lover, as potential lover, as teacher, or as potential teacher. About ten minutes should be allowed for the writing of these letters. The group should then be reconvened, and people may read what they wrote. The reading aloud of one's letter is, of course, optional.

?❧ Sophia and Christology: A Bible Study

This unit of study demonstrates and illustrates the connection between Sophia and many aspects of Jesus in the Christian scriptures. It provides a participatory way of working through the materials in chapter 3, "Sophia in the Christian Scriptures." Chapter 9, "Jesus and Sophia," further discusses the relationship of Sophia to Jesus, and a study session leader may want to explore that chapter for further background on the implications of the Jesus-Sophia relationship. Several of the proposed introductory course outlines include Bible study activities taken from that chapter. But in each case it is necessary for those who want to explore the Sophia-Jesus connection first to work through the materials in the following study. This study assumes that participants have had some introduction to Sophia in the Hebrew scriptures.

The following study uses a group reading and discussion format.

Materials Needed: Blackboard or several large sheets of paper, chalk or markers.

Opening Exercise: Using a blackboard or several large sheets of paper visible to the entire group, the leader asks participants to list attributes of the messiah. As members of the group call out these attributes, the leader records them. At some point early in this exercise the leader reminds the group that the word *Messiah* is the Hebrew word translated into Greek as "Christ." (The leader needs to know the following concerning the messiah: *Messiah* means "anointed one," which refers to the anointing of a king. He is a human being; in the Hebrew literature a king is not considered divine or eternal. The best that might be claimed for the king of Israel is that he temporarily becomes the "son of God" while he is reigning. Further, in the Hebrew scriptures a messiah is generally understood to be a king who comes to restore and rescue Israel. Some of the literature speaks of a messiah/king who will come at the end of time to restore Israel. Some participants will likely be unaware of this information and thus will assign divine attributes to the messiah. For instance, if someone says that the messiah is God, information about the actual status of the messiah in Israel can be provided. Emphasis should be placed on the messiah as a powerful king who comes to restore Israel. Other attributes of a messiah/king— bringer of peace, savior, and just ruler—certainly may be listed.)

Then, parallel to the messiah list, the leader should help the group construct a list of Sophia's attributes. Participants' ability to construct such a list depends on previous knowledge of Sophia; the activity can serve then as a review of the Sophia materials introduced in previous sessions. But its primary purpose is to compare and contrast her attributes with those of the messiah. During the construction of this second list, the group leader must be certain to ask whether Sophia is divine or human if no one volunteers that information. The list will probably include, at minimum, that Sophia is divine, a teacher, and a creator.

After both lists are completed, the leader asks the group which list of attributes reminds them most of their image of Jesus. The certain and rather surprising answer is "Sophia." The leader then reviews the somewhat contrasting lists of attributes and notes that we tend to see Jesus as divine, a teacher, and a creator. If Sophia's playfulness is included in her list of attributes, it may also be noted that Jesus is pictured often as playful.[1]

Perhaps even more important for the group to notice is that Jesus does not fit very well at all the picture of the messiah king who restored Israel. Jesus was not a king. He did not restore Israel. In fact, he was executed as an enemy of the state.
Scripture Reading: The leader should then ask the group to read 1 Corinthians 2:6–8.

> It is of the mysterious wisdom [Sophia] of God that we talk, the wisdom [Sophia] that was hidden, which God predestined to be for our glory before the ages began. None of the rulers of the age recognized it [her]; for if they had recognized it [her], they would not have crucified the Lord of glory.

Questions: The leader reminds the group that the author of 1 Corinthians is Paul and asks the group to discuss the following questions:

- Since in all of the earliest manuscripts of this letter there is no capitalization or punctuation at all (that is, the translators have made the decisions about what gets capitalized and what does not), at first glance it is impossible for us to tell whether this wisdom of Paul is Sophia or just the word *wisdom*. Do you find any similarities between the wisdom of which Paul is speaking here and the Wisdom/Sophia to whom we have been introduced?

(Some striking similarities are Wisdom/Sophia's existence at the beginning with God, her mysteriousness, and the question of whether one recognizes her or not.)

- With whom is Paul comparing Sophia?

(This answer is also not immediately obvious. In verse 8 he says that if the rulers had recognized her, they would not have crucified the Lord of glory. So he is actually saying that the rulers should have recognized Jesus as Sophia.)

- How does Paul's identification of Jesus with Sophia fit with what we discovered in our two lists of attributes?

Scripture Reading: The leader asks the group to find descriptions of Christ in 1 Corinthians 1:24, 30.

The leader asks the group to notice how Paul seems to be identifying Jesus with Sophia here also, although perhaps not quite as clearly.

Scripture Reading: John 1:1–5, 14a.

Questions:

- Of whom does this "Word" remind you?
- What similarities do you find between this "Word" and Sophia?

(In addition to the similarities of being with God at the beginning, creating all things, being the light, coming into the world, being rejected, making people children of God; the leader should note that the word in the Greek text for "lived" in verse 14 is the same Greek word that is used to describe Sophia's settling on earth in Ecclesiasticus 24. The word literally means "to pitch a tent." This acts as a dramatic confirmation that the whole story in Ecclesiasticus 24 of Sophia being with God and then settling on earth would appear to have been followed in John 1.)

Optional Scripture Readings: If there is time the group may also look at the following New Testament passages where Sophia and Jesus are associated:

He is the image of the unseen God
and the first born of all creation,
for in him were created all things in heaven and on earth;
everything visible and invisible,
Thrones, Dominations, Sovereignties, Powers,
all things were created through him and for him.
Before anything was created, he existed,
and he holds all things in unity.   (Colossians 1:15–17)

Through all the ages this mystery has been kept hidden in
God, the creator of everything. Why? So that the
Sovereignties and Powers should learn only now, through the
Church, how comprehensive God's Sophia really is, exactly
according to the plan which he had from all eternity in
Christ Jesus our Lord.   (Ephesians 3:9–11)

If there are any wise or learned ones among you, let them
show it by their good lives, with humanity and wisdom in
their actions. But if at heart you have the bitterness of
jealousy, or a self-seeking ambition, never make any claims
for yourself or cover up the truth with lies. Principles of
that kind are not the Sophia that comes down from above.
They are only earthly, animal, and devilish. Wherever you
find jealousy and ambition, you find disharmony, and wicked
things of every kind being done. Whereas the Sophia that
comes down from above is essentially pure. She also makes
for peace, and is kindly and considerate. She is full of
compassion and shows herself by doing good. Nor is there
any trace of partiality or hypocrisy in her.   (James 3:13–17)

Questions: In this section, it will be necessary to confront what by this
time in the study is probably an urgent question in the minds of many:

- If the connection between Jesus and Sophia is so obvious to us, to Paul,
  and to the writers of the Gospel of John, of Ephesians, Colossians, and
  James, why don't the Christian scriptures place greater emphasis on the
  identification of Jesus with Sophia? Why does the portrayal of the
  association of Sophia and Jesus seem to be so muted and underplayed in
  the Christian scriptures?

The leader should pose these questions to the group, first by asking if
anyone had been wondering about it, and second by asking the group for
ideas on why the Sophia-Jesus connection is so muted and underplayed in
the New Testament. Most groups will without prompting come up with one
of the two major theories on this matter. For many of us, the most
compelling explanation is that the patriarchy and sexism of the society and
the churches during the early Christian period could not tolerate such a
powerful female divine figure in her unmasked state; she was simply too
threatening to the structures of patriarchal power. If members of the group
suggest this line of thinking, the leader can support the suggestion by
recalling we do have clear examples of blatant sexism in the New Testament

(for example, Paul's forbidding the Corinthian women to speak in worship). The leader may also note that Joan Chamberlain Engelsman's book, *The Feminine Dimension of the Divine,* proposes clearly that the Sophia-Jesus connection in the New Testament is underplayed as a result of patriarchal oppression.[2]

It is unlikely that the group on its own will suggest the other major answer that scholarship has proposed. That answer is that Sophia was an accidental casualty of the controversy with the gnostic churches in the first two centuries of the Christian movement. This explanation is summarized in part 1, 43 to 45. Leaders may want to study these two pages and present them as a background to discussion with their group about the masked and muted quality of Sophia in the New Testament. If the leader does not feel able to represent this rather complex summary adequately, we suggest that section of the book simply be read by the group and then discussed.

The leader should ask the group whether patriarchal oppression or the gnostic struggle seems the more likely explanation to them. After some discussion, the leader may note that it is possible that both answers are partially correct. In other words, perhaps the muting of the Sophia-Jesus connection has to do with both patriarchy and gnosticism.

INTRODUCTORY WORSHIP AND CELEBRATION MATERIALS

Sophia can be introduced to people through the regular worship life of a congregation (see 191 to 196 for a detailed description of this process). Without much attention drawn to them, sermons, litanies, and prayers about Sophia can gradually be inserted into a church's liturgical life. Of course, paralleling such liturgical material with introductory sessions and courses as outlined above is ideal. What follows, however, is material that can be used in regular worship settings without the congregation as a whole needing to have been introduced to Sophia.

In addition, we have included the description of a ceremonial meal, which can be used as a celebratory finale to an introductory course on Sophia. Although we refer to this meal as a Sophia eucharist, it can actually stand independent of the Christian eucharist, thus making it possible to avoid complex questions about Sophia and Jesus. In such cases, it may be advisable to refer to it as "Sophia's Table" rather than as a Sophia eucharist. You will find that this celebration of "Sophia's Table" can play an appropriate and welcome integrating role toward the end of an introductory course. It cannot be used with a group larger than thirty persons.

🐚 Sophia and Play: A Sermon

The following sermon was preached in a number of churches where Sophia had never been mentioned. It addresses general spiritual issues that exist in almost all congregations, and it does not call attention to Sophia as a new spiritual possibility. On the other hand, it presents her clearly and thus increases hearers' knowledge and curiosity about her. The text for the sermon is Proverbs 8:22–31.

Wisdom speaks in this morning's passage. In Greek, the word for wisdom is *Sophia*. But the English word *wisdom* sounds much too conceptual to describe adequately the one speaking to us from Proverbs; she is definitely a person. So, to emphasize this personal quality, I'm going to be calling Wisdom by her Greek name: Sophia. Most of us don't know much about her; she's a part of our biblical tradition that has been largely ignored. Let me introduce you to the biblical figure, Sophia.

Sophia is spoken of as being around from the beginning—before creation. She was with Yahweh at the time of creation; creation couldn't happen without her presence. Other biblical passages show her coming to be with humanity, reaching out to people to be in relationship with them. She walks through the streets, calling out to people, trying to get them to listen—to follow her. She's also a welcoming hostess inviting people to her table, a bountiful provider of food, the source of all good things. She is the way to life abundant. This is just a small sampling of the richness Sophia brings with her as a different way of knowing and relating to God.

In this morning's passage in Proverbs, Sophia is speaking eloquently as Yahweh's playful companion in the creation of the world. She describes herself, according to one way of translating the Hebrew, as being beside Yahweh, "like a little child."

I get together regularly with a group of clergywomen for Bible study and reflection, and when we studied this passage, it generated a lot of ambivalent feelings. Everyone thought it was a beautiful passage—which it is—but most of us found that Sophia was hard to take seriously as a divine feminine figure. A big objection was that she was childish; she played while Yahweh did all the hard work. Yahweh did all the important things, while she was just playing around.

But I've been doing a lot of thinking about this passage since that occasion. Isn't it telling us something important about God and about how creation happens? Is playfulness perhaps an important part of who God is—a part that Sophia allows us to see and appreciate? And doesn't creativity need an attitude of play? Creation doesn't happen without Sophia's presence. Other passages describe Yahweh's search for Sophia;

after finding her, *then* he creates the world. She's essential; with her, creation happens. With childlike playfulness, creativity blossoms.

But most of us—like those of us in my study group—have a hard time valuing play. Play is for children. Play is what we do after all the important things are done. Play is our reward for work well done; rarely is play a means for doing our work well. We just don't think that way; we just don't know Sophia that well.

Columnist Russell Baker wrote a wonderful article some time ago in which he contrasted "solemn" and "serious." "Being solemn is easy. Being serious is hard. . . . Children almost always begin by being serious. . . . Adults, on the whole, are solemn. The transition from seriousness to solemnity occurs in adolescence. . . ." Baker gives us a few examples of the contrast. Jogging is solemn; poker is serious. Washington, D.C., is solemn, New York City is serious. Attending conferences is solemn; walking in the woods and devising a fantastic scheme for robbing Cartier's is serious.[3]

Work too often is solemn, and play—when it's playful—is wonderfully serious. Play is being in touch with creativity, with newness, with wonder, with life. One of the wonderful things about having young children is that I have a built-in opportunity to watch them play—and when I'm not careful, I sometimes find myself playing as well. Playing in the waves, blowing bubbles, playing Superman and Wonderwoman, running for the sheer joy of running, making up rhymes for the wonderful way the words sound—children really know how to do it.

Part of what makes play so important is that at the same time that it opens up the newness and the wonder of life, it also brings us close to the possibility of failure, the nearness of death. Running often ends in tears with bloody knees. Bubbles burst. Playing in the waves is so much fun because they can knock you over; they're a danger that's momentary, then you come through—all wet, but ready to face another one, a bigger one. Superman and Wonderwoman allow children to face terrible disasters in their imagination and to put on strength to meet them.

Play allows us to be fully open to life because we've faced the threats as well as the pleasures. Play is what allows us to stand in the face of fear—in the face of pain, suffering, failure—and not crumble to pieces.

Most of us can't play like that; we've lost the wonderful seriousness of children's playfulness. We turn our play into a solemn pastime. We play tennis and worry about perfecting our serve or fret about the point we should have had—and forget to enjoy the graceful backstroke of our opponent or the ball that went right where we wanted it to go. Getting together with friends turns into worry about cleaning the house or putting together the perfect menu rather than enjoying their company. We adults have an incredible ability for turning play into work.

We use play as an escape from life rather than as a way to face it. We spend too much time at happy hours that glaze over unhappiness, only to have it all return in head-splitting pain the next day. We spend evenings in front of the TV to relax and too often find ourselves numb and deadened, unable even to get up and go to bed. Our play becomes a retreat from life and its realities, with no chance to transform them in any creative way.

And transforming the way in which we deal with life's realities is what play, at its best, is all about. Even as I just put down watching TV, there are some favorites of mine—"MASH," for one, and, more recently, "Hill Street Blues." During these shows, we're exposed to the harshness and tragedy that life is full of in our society. And yet, in the midst of unbearable difficult situations, the characters in these shows are able to laugh and joke their way through, to cry and reach out to one another, to remain human in a dehumanizing situation.

And, for me, participating vicariously with the characters allows me to accept the reality of life that I see around me, hear about from friends, read about in the newspaper. It allows me to say, yes, that's real—that happens, is happening—that's a part of my experience. Yet, at the same time, I have the freedom to look at the pain through someone else's eyes. I have the opportunity to step back and watch it from a distance, to laugh and cry with the characters and to finally say, yes, life can go on. I, too, in my situation, even when things get very bad, can remain human, can celebrate life. A new possibility for continuing, for growing, opens up.

Play somehow transcends and transforms the situation we're in. It accepts life and the possibility of failure, mistakes, tragedy, and in the process of accepting it all somehow changes it. Play allows us to see new possibilities where there were none before. It allows us to say yes when everything around us is shouting no. It allows us to meet Sophia, the yes in a world full of nos.

But even at our best, we adults don't know much about play; we don't use it enough, don't make it a part of our lives, don't incorporate it into our being anywhere near the way children do. It's no accident that Sophia is described as being like a little child. After all, playing is a child's vocation. To really learn how to play our way through life, we need once again to become like children.

Let me tell you about Timmy, a young child I know. He was born with a cleft palate, and, in the course of the first few years of his life, he's already been through three or four operations. Most of these operations took place when he was too little to be anything other than traumatized; all the pain, the separation from his parents, the strange people, the strange place.

But this time, there was a difference. When time came for another operation, he was old enough to know what lay ahead, to anticipate the whole routine of the surgery. Timmy spent a lot of time talking about the operation, asking questions so that he knew even more than he remembered. But he spent at least as much time playing. He became the doctor, the nurse, and his teddy bear had the operation. His teddy bear got the shots, had all the blood tests, had his temperature taken, got put to sleep, got his mouth cut open and sewed back up. That teddy bear went through the entire routine over and over again. Not just before the actual operation, but after as well. Over and over, that bear replayed the entire traumatic event.

Timmy's play allowed him to face what he feared most: the pain, the loss of control, the terrible aloneness, the threat of never waking up. In play, he was in control; he was in charge. In play, he faced what could not be faced any other way. He played his way through.

We all need to play our way through life, through the trying times of our lives. Dreaming helps us do that—helps us face our past and future and live in the present. Worship at its best can do the same. Worship is a way of playing our way through life— singing, praying together, telling old stories, looking toward the future, gathering courage to face the present—gaining control over what seems uncontrollable, if only for an hour.

There is something about playfulness that allows us to stand our ground—to face the worst—and be strengthened and renewed in the process. There's something about laughing—telling jokes on ourselves, relaxing with a friend, taking a walk, dancing, writing poetry, singing in the shower—there's something about play in all its forms that is renewing, refreshing, lifegiving.

When I think of an adult who's mastered the art of playfulness, I think of Zorba the Greek. In the movie, if you've seen it, Zorba was working on a big project. Do you remember it? If you're like most of the folks I've asked this week, they remembered Zorba's playing but nothing about this project of his. Zorba's plan was to mine a large vein of coal on Crete. But he needed a way to move the coal from the top of the mountain where it was mined down to the port where it could be shipped, and he also needed timber for building the mine shaft. So Zorba designed and built a large pulley system up the side of the mountain; it looked like a huge ski lift.

After months of planning, the day finally came for the grand opening of the pulley system—the big tryout. A big celebration was planned, the village turned out, and Zorba had even asked the monks of the local monastery to pray over the logs before they came down the mountain. The ceremony over, it came time for the first log to be released—to try out Zorba's transport system.

Out came the first log. It came shooting along the pulley system, and when it arrived at the bottom it had splintered to almost nothing. Out came the second log. It, too, came shooting down the mountainside—and it, too, ended up at the bottom in a mass of splinters. Out came the third log. This one shook the entire pulley system; sparks flew, and the log arrived at the bottom smoking, almost on fire.

But Zorba didn't give up. Out came the fourth log! And this time, the whole pulley system shivered and collapsed, like pick-up sticks, all the way down the mountain.

Zorba's grand scheme lay in ruins, littering the mountainside. And what did he do? He fished some lamb out of the fire on the beach—lamb prepared to celebrate his successful venture—he poured a glass of wine, and he and his friend ate and drank. And then he began to sing, and, finally, he began to dance—a dance of wild abandonment, a dance of fullness, a dance of ecstasy and joy. They danced until they dropped, laughing, to the ground. And then they slept, soundly, on the beach.

Zorba's dance—that's what we remember—that wild dance of celebration. Not his grand scheme for getting rich, not even so much its total, miserable failure. It's the dance we remember—the dance of joy in the midst of sorrow, the dance of life in the face of death.

Each of us has our own grand plan—plans for how our life ought to go. Some of us have just started out on new ventures. Others of us are still dreaming of which to try. And others of us are farther on down the road with it all. Wherever we are, we have all kinds of questions: Is this the right way to go? What if I've made the wrong decision? What if I'd done it another way? What if I fail? And the questions keep on coming.

But, in the middle of the questions, Sophia calls out to us. She's inviting us to come and play—to tell jokes on ourselves, to laugh at our blunders. She's inviting us to reach out, to take our failure—everything that's gone wrong in our life—even the threat of death itself—to embrace it all, and to laugh, with tears in our eyes, and to dance!

Sophia invites us to the dance that is life—life abundant. Let's join her.[4]

❧ Litanies, Prayers, and Collects

The litanies, prayers, and collects included here may occur at a variety of places in a worship service. They are perhaps best used in the opening portions, but some are clearly appropriate to offertory, confessional, or petitional moments in the liturgy.

Several of the prayers refer to specific places within the city where they were composed. At these points appropriate places in the city where the worship service is being held should be substituted.

A Litany

LEADER: Let us sing to Wisdom,
PEOPLE: Who delivered our mothers and fathers out of a land of oppression.
LEADER: She led them by a marvelous road,
PEOPLE: A path through the sea,
LEADER: Dry land, waves piled up on either side.
PEOPLE: Lead us now as you did before.
LEADER: The waters threaten to engulf us;
PEOPLE: The waves are breaking over our heads.
LEADER: Make us a path through the water;
PEOPLE: Be our shelter by day,

LEADER: And our starlight by night.
PEOPLE: Bring us safely to dry land, headed toward freedom.
LEADER: Amen.
PEOPLE: Amen.

Litany of Praise to the Wisdom of God   (Adapted from Ecclesiasticus 24)

LEADER: Wisdom, you came forth from the Most High, as a mist you covered the earth.
PEOPLE: You were in the pillar of cloud; you led our forebears out of slavery into freedom.
LEADER: You are like a mighty oak; you stretch forth your branches— branches of glory and grace.
PEOPLE: You are like a vine, filled with flowers that yield fruits of glory.
LEADER: Wisdom calls: "Come unto me, you that desire me, and be filled with good things."
PEOPLE: For all that eat shall still hunger for you; all that drink shall still thirst for you.
LEADER: You are like a life-giving stream; you water the gardens you have planted.
PEOPLE: Let us come enjoy Wisdom's bounty; let us rejoice in her goodness; let us find life in abundance. Amen.

A Litany Based on Psalm 135

LEADER: Give thanks to the Lord, for you are good; with Wisdom you made the heavens, and set the earth on the waters.
PEOPLE: Your love is everlasting.
LEADER: You brought Israel out of Egypt; you split the Red Sea, and led Israel through the middle.
PEOPLE: Your love is everlasting.
LEADER: You led your people through the wilderness, and struck down the mighty.
PEOPLE: Your love is everlasting.
LEADER: You gave us a new land; you remembered us when we were down, and snatched us from our oppressors.
PEOPLE: Your love is everlasting.

Time for individual prayers of thanksgiving.

PEOPLE: Your love is everlasting.
LEADER: You provide for all living creatures.
PEOPLE: Your love is everlasting.
LEADER: Amen.
PEOPLE: Amen.

A Collect Based on Wisdom 7

Come to us, One who is lucid, unique, subtle, loving, irresistible, steadfast, dependable, almighty, pure, all-encompassing, and active. You are the breath of power itself, the reflection of light, the image of goodness. As one who outshines the constellations, come and be present to us. Amen.

A Litany

LEADER: One with God from the beginning covers the earth like a mist.
PEOPLE: Wisdom circles the skies; she walks in the depths of the abyss;
LEADER: In the waves of the sea, among every people and nation.
PEOPLE: She seeks a resting place.
LEADER: We each seek a resting place—a place to call home.
PEOPLE: We long for roots—somewhere to belong.
LEADER: Sent from Yahweh, Wisdom speaks:
PEOPLE: In the beloved city he gave me a resting place.
LEADER: I took root in an honored people.
PEOPLE: On Market Street, at 51st and Pine, I took root.
LEADER: On Baltimore Avenue I was established.
PEOPLE: City Hall and West Philly High are home to me.
LEADER: Cedar Park and the Schuylkill River are places of rest for me.
PEOPLE: I took root in an honored people: in the beloved city I found a resting place.

An Advent Liturgy

Service Preparation: An Advent wreath with four candles should be present. Musical instruments may improvise quietly in the background as a woman reads.
Call to Worship:

Yahweh acquired me at the very beginning, before anything happened.
From everlasting I was firmly set, from the beginning before earth came into being.
The deep was not there, when I was born.
There were no springs to gush with water.
Before the mountains were settled, before the hills rose up, I came to birth.
Before the earth or the first grains of the world's dust, I walked around.
When the heavens were made, I was there.
When the clouds first appeared, when the springs of the deep came forth, I was there.
When the seas found their boundaries and when the foundations of this life were laid, I was there.
I was by Yahweh's side, enjoying each day, ever at play in his presence, at play everywhere in the world.   (Adapted from Proverbs 8)

Hymn: "O Come, O Come, Emmanuel."
Prayer of Preparation:

LEADER: In the beginning was the Word.
PEOPLE: We are waiting for someone to tell us they love us.
LEADER: And the Word was with God.
PEOPLE: We are waiting for decent city government.
LEADER: And the Word was God.

PEOPLE: We are waiting for news from Washington and City Hall.
LEADER: Through the Word all things came to be.
PEOPLE: Not one thing had its being but through the Word.
LEADER: Let us recall the things we lack, that for which we are waiting.

Moment of Prayer and Meditation
Act of Assurance: Lighting of the Advent Candles

LEADER: Send the one to us who was present when You made the world. Send Wisdom forth from Your throne of glory to help us and to toil with us.
PEOPLE: A light that shines in the dark, a light that the darkness could not overpower.
LEADER: Amen.
PEOPLE: Amen.

 Sophia's Table

This is a ceremonial meal celebrating Sophia. It incorporates most aspects of her into a worship service of praise, communion, and intercession. See 137 to 139, 154 to 155, 162 to 168, and 172 to 175 for additional eucharist-related celebrations. It can be used as a celebration at the end of an introductory course or session. It also has been used by groups as a monthly Sophia worship service. Because of its high degree of participation, it is probably not appropriate for groups of more than thirty people. It is, however, accessible for mixed groups of men and women and for groups who do not have an ongoing relationship to Sophia. Leadership of the celebration should be shared. It is highly recommended that the prayer of consecration, in which the words of Sophia are spoken, be said by a woman.

Service Preparation: Lay an appropriately festive cloth on the table. Place bread, fruit, milk, wine, and honey in appropriate vessels and a number of plants throughout the room, on tables, windowsills, etc. Light several candles. There should be a pitcher or pitcher-like container for the milk, glasses (preferably wine glasses) for the wine and milk, and a bowl for the honey. A small three- to six-inch piece of wood or cardboard should be available to the celebrant.

Invocation: Leader speaks each statement, allowing a silence of ten to twenty seconds after each, or each statement can be said by a different person.

Praise to Sophia who comes to meet us in every thought. (Wisdom 6:16)
Praise to the One who pervades and permeates all things. (Wisdom 8:24)

Praise to Wisdom, who glories in herself in the midst of her people.

(Sirach 24:1)

Praise to Sophia, who is at play everywhere in the world.   (Proverbs 8:31)

Praise to the One who raises her voice in the public squares. (Proverbs 1:20)

Praise to Wisdom, who deploys her strength from one end of the earth to the other, ordering all things for good.   (Wisdom 8:1)

Praise to Sophia, who is the tree of life for those who hold her fast.

(Proverbs 3:18)

Offering of Gifts: Each person brings one of the objects that have been scattered around the room (or an object they may have brought with them) to the table and offers it along with a sentence about what experiences or emotions they are bringing with them to the table. Some may prefer to come to the table in silence.

Embracing: Greet one another.

Litany: The people's part can be chanted or read in unison. The symbol / indicates chanting instructions.

LEADER: From everlasting I was firmly set, from the beginning before earth came into being. The deep was not, when I was born, there were no springs to gush with water.   (Proverbs 8:23, 24)

PEOPLE: You stretch the heavens out / like a / tent;
You build your palace on the waters / above.
Using the clouds as your / chariot,
You advance on the / wings of the / wind.

You fixed the earth on its found / ations,
Unshakable forever and / ever;
You wrapped it with the deep as with a / robe,
The waters over / topping the / mountains. (Psalm 104:2b, 3, 5–6)

LEADER: Before the mountains were settled, before the hills, I came to birth; before the earth was made or the countryside or the first grains of the world's dust.   (Proverbs 8:25, 26)

PEOPLE: At your reproof the waters took to / flight,
They fled at the sound of your / thunder,
Cascading over the mountains, into the / valleys,
Down to the reservoir you / made for / them.

You set springs gushing in / ravines,
Running down between / mountains,
Supplying water for wild / animals,
Attracting the / thirsty wild / donkeys.   (Psalm 104:7–8, 10–11)

LEADER: When the heavens were fixed firm, I was there; when a ring was drawn on the surface of the deep, when the clouds were thick ened above, when the springs of the deep were fixed fast, I was there.   (Proverbs 8:27, 28)

PEOPLE: From your palace you water the / uplands
Until the ground has had all that your heavens have to / offer;
You make the fresh grass grow for / cattle
And those plants made / use of by / people.

And people receive food from the / soil,

Wine to make them / cheerful,
Oil to make them / happy
And bread to / make them / strong.   (Psalm 104:13–15)

LEADER: When the sea was assigned its boundaries—and the water will
not invade the shore—when the foundations for the earth were
laid, I was there.   (Proverbs 8:29)

PEOPLE: What variety you have / created,
Arranging everything so / wisely!
Earth is completely full of things you have / made:
Among them vast / expanse of / ocean,

Teeming with countless / creatures,
Creatures large and / small,
With the ships going to and / fro
And Leviathan whom you / made to / amuse you.
    (Psalm 104:24–26)

LEADER: I was there, a master craftsperson, delighting day after day, ever
at play everywhere in the world, delighting to be with the sons
and daughters of people.   (Proverbs 8:30, 31)

PEOPLE: All creatures depend on / you
To feed them throughout the / year;
You provide the food they / eat,
With generous hand you / satisfy their / hunger.

You turn away your face, they / suffer,
You stop their breath, they / die.
You give breath, fresh life / begins,
You keep re / newing the / world.   (Psalm 104:27–30)

Consecration of the Meal:

CELEBRANT: [Lift and hug plant] In the beloved city . . . I wield my
authority. I have taken root in a privileged people.
    (Sirach 24:11, 12)

ALL: To Wisdom say, my sister. [Each participant may replace
"sister" with "lover," "mother," or "teacher" as the group
responds to each sentence of the consecration.]

CELEBRANT: [Raise fruit] Approach me you who desire me, and take your
fill of my fruits.   (Sirach 24:19)

ALL: To Wisdom say, my sister.

CELEBRANT: [Pour wine into glass] I am like a vine putting out graceful
shoots, my blossoms bear the fruit of glory and wealth.
    (Sirach 24:17)

ALL: To Wisdom say, my sister.

CELEBRANT: [Raise honey] Memories of me are sweet as honey, inheriting
me is sweet as the honeycomb.   (Sirach 24:20)

ALL: To Wisdom say, my sister.

CELEBRANT: [Pour milk into glass] Over the waves of the sea and over the
whole earth; and over every people and nation I have held
sway.   (Sirach 24:20)

ALL: To Wisdom say, my sister.

CELEBRANT: [Raise bread] They who eat me will hunger for more, they who drink me will thirst for more. (Sirach 24:21)

ALL: To Wisdom say, my sister.

Passing of the Bread: Each person takes a piece and offers the loaf to the next person, saying, "The bread given for the life of the world" (John 6:51). Last person gives loaf back to leader, who also takes a piece.

Dipping the Bread: All dip bread together into the honey, milk, or wine (according to preference) and eat. Silence.

CELEBRANT: Wisdom has built herself a house, she has erected her seven pillars, she has slaughtered her beasts, prepared her wine, she has laid her table. She has dispatched her maidservants and proclaimed from the city heights: "Come and eat my bread, drink the wine I have prepared!" (Proverbs 9:1–3, 5)

Here an extended time (two to four minutes) of silence is recommended. Then wine or milk is poured for each person.

Toast (in unison):

You exist before all things, and you hold all things together
In you all things were created, everything visible and everything invisible.
You are the image of the unseen God, the first born of all creation.
All fullness is found in you, everything in heaven, and everything on earth.
(from Colossians 1)

The group takes fifteen to thirty minutes to eat and drink together.
The Intercession:

LEADER: Now is the time to stand with Sophia at the gates to the city.

Anyone who wishes to places an item on the offering board and makes a statement of concern for the world. The leader then places a small (three to six inches) board on the table. She or he then says a sentence or prayer of concern for someone or some situation outside the group and places some small decoration (perhaps the leaf of a plant or a piece of fruit) on the board. Others follow in the same manner. After everyone has had a chance to speak a prayer or statement of concern, the leader takes the board of offering outside, with the group following, and places the offering on the ground.

The Closing:

ALL: The tree of life for the healing of the nations.

The group comes back inside and sings a song of choice (see 180 to 187 for songs). End by standing in a circle holding hands.[5]

CHAPTER SEVEN

Women's Identity

The most compelling aspect of Sophia is her gender. To meet a divine female figure within the Judeo-Christian tradition is at least a mind-boggling event, if not a world-shaking one. Sophia, by the very fact that she is female, raises the question of who God is for us and provides a new way of thinking about, imaging, and relating to the divine. For women, Sophia opens up a new world—a world that has been heretofore beyond their reach. In this world women, at long last, can identify directly with the divine.

Sophia affirms women in every aspect of their being in a way that God imaged as male cannot do. Through her, women can claim with full authority that they are indeed created in the image of God, a claim that has, tragically, been debated if not denied in many religious settings. Sophia, the Wisdom of God, one who is both female and part of God, ends the need for debate. In Sophia, women can have their total identity, including their sexuality, affirmed by and identified with the divine.

As a divine role model, Sophia is creator, one who is proud and angry, a strong, liberating female, yet a warm, nurturing figure who is sometimes a mother, and wisdom and knowledge as well.

Material in the Bible about Sophia constitutes a rich territory for women's reflection and self-examination. This chapter explores that territory in some depth. Included here are sermons, a variety of participatory Bible studies, prayers, liturgies, and role plays.

Groups of women only who use Sophia materials usually identify with her almost immediately. In a mixed group, if women have less chance to share safely the range of their reactions to this material, they often withdraw into silence, while men remain at an intellectual level of response. Consequently, in both kinds of groups the leader should plan to spend some time with the women after the Sophia material has been introduced, to allow for a short period of response.

Women's responses to Sophia may be negative or positive, but they are guaranteed to be deeply felt. Anger, frustration, and disappointment, euphoria, excitement, and creative energy are common feelings of women who come into close contact with Sophia. Women, after all, have been cut off for so long from the possibility of a holistic identification with the divine that their meeting with Sophia is an incredibly powerful, often transforming, and sometimes explosive event.

Sophia's Call: A Sermon

This sermon, based on Proverbs 8:1–11 and Mark 1:14–20, describes one woman's spiritual encounter with Sophia.

This morning's story in Mark is about Jesus' call and the first men who responded to it. The call of Simon and Andrew and James and John is very short, succinct—it's actually just the bare facts of what happened—a story stripped to its bare essentials. The important thing is that Jesus called and they followed, period.

But how did it all happen? When Jesus called, what went on inside the men? What were their fears, worries? What were the things that might have held them back? What was it about his call that was so compelling? And we don't know what they told their friends and families, either. How did they explain their sudden shift in priorities? It would be fun to have the whole story, to know all about what went on inside them and what their conversations with their friends might have been like.

But we don't have it. Instead, we've got just the outline—what the church considered important to remember. Jesus called, and they followed. That is what disciples do.

This morning, I want to talk with you about another call, one much more recent. I want to share with you a call that I've experienced recently, and I want to share the details—the different thoughts and feelings that have gone along with it. In short, I want to do what Simon and Andrew and the Zebedees probably did with their friends.

My call is different from theirs. My call came in the midst of a vision of Sophia. Sophia, the one who danced and played at the creation of the world, the one who, as a welcoming hostess, sets the table for all to come and partake, the one through whom life and happiness is found—and, as this morning's passage indicates, the one who runs through the streets calling to people to come listen to her. Sophia is the one who did the same to me.

But first, let me share with you what's been going on recently with me. I've been in the midst of a crisis for some time now. I found myself questioning the Bible and its authority. Me—who loves leading and participating in Bible study, whose spiritual life has centered on the Bible, who has even used study leave for more biblical training. Me—who knows most of the feminist reinterpretation of scriptures, who wrote her thesis on the influence of the mother goddess in parts of the Old and New Testaments. And yet, this book came to seem more and more irrelevant and cut off from my experience. And the parts we'd been able to liberate still seemed so small, so insignificant compared to the patriarchal immensities that remained untouched. I began to feel more and more cramped, less and less able to focus my experience through the biblical word.

At the same time, I began to realize how close to the edge of the Christian tradition I felt—how dangerously close I felt to falling off—leaping over the edge, out of the church, and into utter oblivion (or so it seemed). The traditional church structures became more than just a nuisance. They seemed to close in, to confine and constrict.

But the crucial blow came a few weeks ago when I was celebrating the eucharist, something I've always loved to do, and the thing toward which I looked forward at the time of my ordination. And somewhere in the back of my mind that day I kept asking myself, "What am I doing? Celebrating the experience of some man? What does he have to do with me?" I stumbled over the words of institution—you may remember how clumsy and awkward I was that day. I felt silly passing out the body and blood of a man. All of my theological grounding gave way. And I kept trying to talk myself out of it: "But you know that in Christ there is no male or female—you know that the body of Christ includes us all." But it made no difference. All I could see was that this central act of the church was the celebration of the life, death, and resurrection of a man—and I felt on the outside.

As I began to work on and plan another worship service later that week, I found myself in the midst of despair. I was afraid that I would never be at home in the church again, and I feared for what that meant for the future. I was in the middle of writing one of the prayers for the service, when there she was, looking at me through a window in a door, and she was calling out to me, "What are you afraid of, anyway? Do you think I care about your old theology? Do you think I care what name you name me? Do you think I care if people think I'm legitimate or not? Haven't people always refused to listen to me? But that doesn't make me any less real—and that doesn't make you any less faithful."

And then, laughter. Much laughter. Mocking laughter, laughing with me and at me, all at the same time. And dancing. "I've been here all along. Come on out and dance with me, and sing. Come on out—open the door. I've been waiting for you for so long."

And I burst into tears—tears in response to her laughter, to her playful presence—in response to the reality of God's feminine presence. It is what I had longed for but never had. No matter how much we changed the language of our worship service, no matter how much we talked about the feminine aspects of God, when I said "God" or "Maker" or "Creator" or any other of the names available, it was to a male personage that I was speaking. The inside of my head hadn't changed with a mere shift in vocabulary. My imagination was so formed by my tradition that I couldn't see God in any other way.

And now I can, and that has made a tremendous difference—all the difference. The change is so immense that it's hard to talk about it coherently. But let me try. It's changed who God is for me. God is no longer just a he—no longer a male God who occasionally acts motherly but is still male all the same. It was always easy to call God Father—part of what's been the tradition—but it's never been easy to call God Mother. But now I *can* call her Sophia. I can name her and know that she is feminine and not an impersonator. Part of God has now become "she" for me, and there's no uneasiness or feeling strange. That's who she is, and I know she's there.

And now that God has opened up to include the feminine, so has my whole perception of what is possible opened up. Women are no longer at the periphery, no longer on the edge looking in at all the action, trying to imagine that they are there, too. With Sophia, women take their place along with men right at the center. As a woman, I too, now, can identify with God. She is like me, and I am like her.

This is incredibly important. I was sharing this whole experience with a friend of mine, a woman who is also a pastor and who shares my love of the Bible. And, as it turned out, she's shared my frustrations. She said she'd never been able to identify with Jesus. She could identify with all kinds of other characters who were in relation to him in one way or another, but she could never identify with him. And she'd always thought that it was a failing in her—that there was something lacking in her, some spiritual block, that kept her from that important step of identification. After all, Jesus is the human face of God, and it's in his humanity that we are supposed to be able to identify with God. But she couldn't do it. And neither could I. I always identified with the women around Jesus, experienced his power second-hand, never directly.

But I can identify with Sophia. No problem at all. She is like me. She can dwell deep within me and call out to me. She is the laughing one within me, and I laugh along with her.

She's also the strong one. She's full of power. In the Book of Wisdom is a passage describing Sophia leading the Hebrews through the sea. She was their shelter by day, and she led them by starlight at night—*and* she slew the pursuing Egyptians. Sophia brings salvation that is full of power—power for me to share, strength for me to use. Because she is strong, so is it possible for me to be strong.

Sophia encourages me to take risks, to venture into new territory, to not be afraid to leave old forms and old ways of thinking behind in order to explore new possibilities. I'm free to admit that the Bible doesn't have the whole story and that it's important to add my experience and the experience of others to it—to open up to continuing revelation and to expand on what the Bible has begun. A whole bunch of energy that has been tied up for a long time has been unleashed. Doors that were closed I now am free to open.

In my vision, Sophia was looking at me through a window in a door. I wasn't sure where that door led; I was afraid it led out of the church. This week I found the courage to open it, and it opened out into this great, wide, airy expanse—a huge, seemingly endless dome full of light. I looked back at the door through which I'd come, and saw that it was the church whose door I'd opened—a tall, narrow, Gothic structure; it was dwarfed by the immensity of the vast dome. But the church building was inside the dome, not outside it. In opening that door, I hadn't left the church behind. It was still there, but now as a part of a much larger reality.

In following Sophia, I opened the door, the door that opened my perceptions and possibilities to a much wider sphere—a sphere that includes my past and new possibilities for the future.

Sophia's call was to join her in a wandering dance, for Sophia is a wanderer who travels all over calling out to people to listen to her, to pay attention to her. And yet, most of the time she's ignored and not taken seriously. As a model for me, for a lot of women, her experience is our experience. We're ignored a lot and often not taken seriously. Much of the time, our opinions and experience don't carry the same weight as those of men. Sophia knows what that's like—she's experienced it too—but she keeps right on calling.

Following her doesn't end the pain of being on the edge of our tradition. It doesn't change the reality of being on the margins of power. It doesn't end the very real possibility of being thought foolish and silly. Matter of fact, following her just about assures that all of that will be the case.

But what makes it worthwhile is that she is with us in the wandering. That her strength, her laughter, life itself, is there, too. For women on the verge of a new era, when the past is crumbling and the future has not yet emerged, she leads us through a long period of wandering and keeps us going in a world in which male privilege will not be relinquished without pain and struggle and hurt for many of us.

She's strong enough to keep us going, and she leads me in the certainty that she leads toward life—fullness of life, not just for me, but for all people. A life that is whole and complete. A life that, like my vision of that vast dome, allows for a lot of variety, a lot of difference, all accepted, all loved, all a part of life with Sophia.

Well, this is the call that has come to me. I share it with you because you're important to me, and your response is important. And I share it because, for me, it's good news. Thank you for letting me share it.[1]

BIBLE STUDIES

We have discussed elsewhere the importance of providing an overview of the Sophia biblical material before focusing on particular Sophia texts.

Biblical texts portray her as so varied in her character (angry, loving, welcoming, distant), in how she is conceived (both as the concept wisdom and as the divine person Sophia), and in her relationship to God (sometimes created by God, sometimes independent of God), that it is helpful to have an overview of the biblical material just to get acquainted. This is as true for groups of women getting to know Sophia as it is for any other beginning group. (See chapter 6, "Getting Acquainted with Sophia," for an overall discussion of using introductory material, as well as several introductory Bible studies. We have found that "The Tree of Life for Those Who Hold Her Fast," pages 74 to 75, is particularly effective for use with women's groups.)

When used with women's groups, these introductory Bible studies have an importance that goes far beyond their ability to help orient participants to Sophia's characteristics. If handled properly, they provide an initial opportunity for women to respond with their feelings to Sophia in her different biblical settings. Because the experience of identification is a powerful one for them, women need a time apart to meet Sophia and to react to whomever and whatever they have encountered. Leaders must be particularly sensitive to the many different ways that these reactions may take place. For example, strong negative responses to the scripture readings are common. Leaders need to meet these feelings, not with defensiveness or argument, but with patient acceptance. Women respond in this way because Sophia is the first female divine figure they have met in their tradition. She is new, terribly important, and she evokes hopes and projections of immense proportion; moreover, her presence in the scriptures cannot fulfill all of these expectations. Take time, then, and invite response, particularly affective response, from *everyone*.

❧ Speaking Her Own Praises: A Bible Study

Many women share a major problem: our culture's failure to recognize the many varieties of female giftedness and the consequent difficulty many women experience in owning and celebrating their gifts. The admonition against pride and the equation of pride with sinfulness may be appropriate for many men, but they have been used with great harm against women. Several feminist theologians have addressed this issue, concluding that for most women sin must be defined differently than it is for most men.[2] For women, sin is precisely a lack of pride and a distrust of their own gifts and strengths—a refusal to acknowledge the gifts with which they were created.

This Bible study is used most appropriately in a women-only setting. Owning—and using—strength is a difficult and often dangerous thing for women to attempt. Exploring such a possibility needs to be done in as safe a place as possible.

Materials Needed: Paper, pen or pencil, and scriptures for each participant.

Opening Exercise: Instruct the group to read silently Proverbs 8:12–21. (See Appendix)

After everyone has finished reading, ask participants to stand up around the room, facing away from the others to ensure a measure of privacy and emotional security. Ask them to read the passage aloud dramatically, as if they were Sophia, and to use the kinds of gestures that Sophia might use as she is saying these things. The leader should begin the dramatic reading, with others following on their own. Have the group continue until everyone has finished reading aloud.

Questions: The leader should introduce these questions by noting that there are many possible answers to them. The questions, for the most part, are meant to be evocative and to elicit a wide variety of responses—as many different responses as there are people. It may be important to remind the group frequently that the more answers, the better. Encourage full participation by everyone.

- What picture comes to you when you read about Sophia here?
- What are her powers? Her qualities? Her characteristics?
- What does she promise?

Scripture Reading: The leader now introduces a later passage in the same chapter. Have the group read Proverbs 8:32–36. (See Appendix)
Questions:

- What does this passage add to your picture of Sophia?
- What does she promise? Threaten?

Scripture Reading: Next introduce and ask the group to read Ecclesiasticus 24:1–7. (See Appendix)
Questions:

- What is the picture of her here?
- If you were going to give her a title, what would it be?
- Considering these passages together, what kind of a figure is she?
- How do you feel about her?
- What other figures in the Bible does she remind you of? Why?
- What women does she remind you of? How?
- In what ways are you like her?

(This question may be greeted with silence. Allow the group to remain in silence: people will be answering it to themselves. Go ahead with the questioning.)

- What are your gifts, your strengths?

(Again, allow people to answer this question, whether silently or aloud.)

- When have you openly taken pride in your gifts? In what situations?
- What response did you get when you acknowledged your strengths? How did it feel?
- If you haven't ever openly acknowledged your strengths, why not? How does it feel to keep them hidden?
- What would it feel like to celebrate them out loud?

Closing Exercise: Lead the group in a meditation, asking them first to find a comfortable place, to relax and breathe slowly and deeply. Ask them to get in touch with Sophia. They might have to go find her somewhere, or they might look for her within. After they find her, have them listen to her speak of their gifts. Then, after hearing her speak, have the group undertake a writing activity.

> Let Sophia speak through you, celebrating your strong points, the things you do well. Write as many good things about yourself as you can.

Individuals can then speak their praises out loud. Two different approaches are possible:

Women can stand in different parts of the room to speak their own praises, facing the wall with backs turned so that they have a degree of privacy. The leader should begin, with others following, so that everyone is speaking simultaneously. Ask everyone to speak as dramatically and proudly as possible.

Each woman can speak her own praises one at a time, in the middle of the group, again as expressively and proudly as possible. The rest of the group can be both audience and support.

At the end, ask everyone to share briefly how it felt to speak aloud in this way.

☙ Raising Her Voice: A Bible Study

Anger is a powerful emotion. For women, or for anyone who has been suppressed in important ways, anger is an energizing force that can break through the suppression, the indifference, and the other means by which they have been kept in a subservient position. Anger can also feel dangerous; since it disrupts the status quo, it can feel uncontrollable. For women it is often equated with "bitchiness" or a lack of femininity. This Bible study, focusing on Sophia's anger, allows women to identify with that anger, to recognize and appreciate their own legitimate anger as an energizing tool for change, and to express it in a safe way.

Materials Needed: Drawing materials, paper for each participant, scissors, matches, and copies of Bible passages for each participant.

Opening Exercise: Instruct the group to read silently Proverbs 1:20–33. (See Appendix) After everyone has finished reading, ask participants to stand at different parts of the room, facing outward toward the wall, so that everyone has a measure of privacy. Ask them to read the passage, beginning with verse 22, aloud dramatically, as though they were Sophia. It is important to emphasize that this is an angry passage, and that shouting, pounding, and other dramatic expressions of anger are appropriate and even desired. The leader should begin the dramatic reading, with others following on their own. Have everyone continue reading until they are finished.

Questions:

- Who is this one who carries on so? Why is she shouting like that?

- What does she want? What is she so upset about?

- What is she threatening to do?

- What does she promise to those who listen?

- What right does she have to act this way?

- Who else in the Bible does she remind you of? What other figures have acted as Sophia does here?

- How do you feel about the way Sophia is acting here? Why?

- What women do you know, or know of, that Sophia reminds you of here?

- How do you feel about those women? Why?

- Sophia complains that people have ignored her, that she's been rejected. When have you been ignored or rejected? How did you feel?

- When have you acted like Sophia is acting here? How were you received? Why?

- If you've never acted this way, why not?

- What would it take for you to act as Sophia does here?

- What would you risk if you were to emulate her?

Closing Exercise: A variety of activities are possible depending on the time and space.

Ask members of the group to spend a few moments noting what they are angry about. Have them write down their angry feelings—as many of them as they can. Then ask them to take what they have written and once again go to a relatively private space in the room to shout it aloud.

> Shout what you have written as loud as you shouted before when you were expressing Sophia's words. Be as dramatic as possible. Shout, pound, jump up and down if you want to. Use your body as well as your voice. If this seems hard, take strength from Sophia; ask her to be with you, shouting for you.

After everyone has taken their places in the room, the leader begins, asking everyone else to begin as well. Everyone in the group will be speaking simultaneously.

After asking group members to spend a few moments noticing their anger, direct them to draw a picture of who/what they are angry at/about. After the lists are completed, participants can use items provided to cut, pound, and burn the pictures. Then invite them to move individually to another space as they are ready to shout, pound, jump up and down, etc.

Ask everyone back to share something of their experience at the end.

❧ The Mother of All Good Things: A Bible Study

Materials Needed: Scripture, paper and pen or pencil for each participant or modeling clay, water colors, and drawing materials for all.
Opening Exercise: The leader introduces the lesson with a guided meditation.

> Close your eyes, and breathe deeply.

Allow time for people to focus on their breathing.

> Allow yourself to be wrapped in darkness. Breathe with the darkness, and settle in and become comfortable in the midst of the darkness. Now notice something coming to birth there.

Go slowly, so that the people can imagine what you are asking of them.

> What is coming to birth for you might be a thought, a spark of light, the first sign of a new shoot from a plant, anything at all. Watch for what is being born, and listen for signs of birth. Be present to it.

After several moments of silence, call the group together.

> Let's leave the space where we have been and come back together.

Scripture Reading: The leader asks the group to read two passages aloud or silently, as the leader determines best: Ecclesiasticus 15:1–10; Wisdom 7:7–14.
Questions: When asking these questions of the group, the leader should encourage full participation by everyone.

- Sophia is spoken of as a mother here. In what different ways is she like a mother in these passages? List as many ways as possible.

- How is she different from a mother in these passages? List as many ways as you can.

If people are not familiar with many other Sophia passages, we list here an additional set of readings and questions to be used optionally with the group.

Optional Scripture Reading: Proverbs 4:6, 18; 8:22–31; Ecclesiasticus 14:20–27; 24:16–22. (See Appendix)

Optional Questions:

- How is Sophia like a mother in these passages?
- Notice the passages describing her presence at creation. How might this relate to mothering?
- In other creation passages, she takes a more active role (see Wisdom 8:4). Note the differences.
- In Ecclesiasticus 14, she provides shelter; what does this have to do with mothering?

Further Questions: The leader now asks the group to recall all that they know of Sophia—from the passages just read and from passages that they have looked at earlier. After allowing them a moment to begin thinking, ask these questions:

- What characteristics of Sophia are like those of a mother?
- In what ways are Sophia's mothering activities larger than life—larger than those of a human mother? What is involved in them?
- What would it mean to be Sophia's child? To be one of her children?
- If you've experienced God as father, how might Sophia as mother compare?

(Be prepared for a wide variety of answers here. Some people have experienced God as a loving father, others as a demanding, wrathful one, and others something else again. Allow each experience to be accepted as important. Each response to Sophia as mother will differ accordingly.)

- How did you experience your own mother? Name the different ways she related to you.

(This is an extremely important and evocative question. Thinking about Sophia as mother is colored by our feelings about and experiences with our own mothers. Allow time for each person to respond to the questions. Most importantly, allow any kind of feeling, even angry ones, to be present.)

- Are there ways in which Sophia can do and be things for you that your own mother couldn't?

- How might Sophia change Mother's Day for you?
- When are/have been the times that you might feel like you need Sophia to be a mother to you?

(Allow time for reflection on this one. There may be very few spoken answers, but there will be much internal activity. Allow time for it, and ask the questions again. Even if there is little spoken reaction, ask the next questions anyway.)

- What kinds of things might she say to you?
- What might she do for you?

Closing Exercise: The leader should choose one of the following closing exercises for the group to do. Allow time for this section.

> Choose one image of Sophia as mother from the passages we've looked at. It could be care, food, shelter, teacher/disciplinarian, nurturer, etc. Spend time with the passage you've chosen. As you look at the passage, choose one word or phrase to repeat over and over. Close your eyes, repeat the word or phrase to yourself, and breathe with that word or phrase. Let your mind clear out. After a while, when you feel clear, daydream your way through the passage, or allow the particular image of Sophia that you've chosen to evolve. Don't censor yourself. Let what comes come. Let Sophia be your mother, let yourself be her child. Imagine what she does for you, what she says to you. Imagine how you respond.

This meditation should take at least ten minutes. If people are used to meditation and if there is time, it could continue longer. Give people a one-minute warning, then ask them to write to Sophia as though to a mother from her child.

> Model a clay figure (or draw or paint a picture) of Sophia as mother. It could include you or others as her children. Allow at least ten minutes for drawing or painting; longer for clay work.
> At the end of either of these exercises, the leader should make certain that there is time for sharing. People need to be able to share—or not share—as they wish. This sharing time can be a wonderful community-building activity if people feel safe. However, most important to recognize is that each individual has experienced something that has a unique meaning for that person. Participants may be encouraged to reflect on the meditation or the artwork in a day or so and to record any further responses.

❧ The Mother of All Good Things II: A Bible Study

Most women's groups can benefit from spending two sessions on Sophia as mother. The first allows individuals to experience Sophia as a mother to them. This second study focuses on individuals' own experiences as creative and nurturing persons, as mothers themselves then in a certain sense, and thus like Sophia.

Materials Needed: Scripture, paper and pen or pencil for each participant.
Opening Exercise: Lead the group in a guided meditation:

> Close your eyes, and breathe deeply. Breathe into your lower midsection, slowly and deeply. As you do, begin to be aware of the ways you bring to birth and nurture growth. Continue breathing from your midsection. As you do, imagine yourself with Sophia, bringing to birth . . . helping things grow.

Allow time for people to imagine this.
Scripture Reading: Invite the participants to recall some of the passages read in the previous session, including Ecclesiasticus 15:1–10; 14:20–27; 24:16–22; Wisdom 7:7–14; Proverbs 4:6, 18; 8:22–31; Wisdom 8:4–9. (See Appendix)
Questions: When asking these questions, elicit as many different responses as possible from the group.

- Although not all of us have physically given birth to children and reared them, we all have been involved in creative, nurturing relationships or activities that can be considered "mothering." In what ways have you been creative, bringing something new to birth, or nurturing new growth? Name as many different ways as you can.

- There is often a period of "pregnancy"—of preparation and gestation—to anything creative. What have these preparations, these inner growth times, been like for you? As you've been involved in "mothering" or nurturing, what have been your frustrations? Your griefs? Your rewards? Your joys?

- What are you proudest of?

- What do you wish you'd done differently?

In working with the mother role, many women will need to process their experience as mothers of children. There are many of these kinds of experiences, ranging from a typical pregnancy/birth/nurturing to miscarriage, abortion, stillbirth or death of a child, infertility, adoption. There may be strong feelings of grief or guilt.

- In any of these moments—the preparation period, the creation moment, the period of nurture—how might Sophia's presence have changed your experience?

- What does knowing Sophia as mother do to your own identity as mother/ nurturer/creator?

- What is your relationship to those children, those new creations, that you've brought to birth? Where might Sophia be in the midst of it all? How might her presence change things?

- How are you nourished and nurtured as you nurture others?

Closing Exercise: Introduce a meditation to the group:

> Recall an event related to your experience of creating/nurturing that was of
> particular significance to you. It may have been difficult; it may have been
> joyful or exciting. Whatever the moment, recall it. Spend awhile in that event,
> noticing who was there, what was happening, how you were feeling. Then,
> add Sophia to that scene. Let her become a part of that event. Notice what she
> looks like, how she acts, what she does. Now spend ten minutes or so letting
> her become a part of that event. Let the event evolve, let Sophia interact with
> people and things. "Daydream" your way through the event, with Sophia
> present. Let things grow and change as they will.

Allow time during your introduction for people to feel their way into
the meditation; it is important to take enough time. After a one-minute
warning for ending the meditation, allow a minimum of five minutes for a
written response to the meditation. This could take many forms—a prayer
to Sophia, a letter to her, a journal entry describing thoughts and feelings.
    Have the group share in twos, with a further brief sharing at the end
for the entire group, ending with silence or a prayer to Sophia.

ༀ Sophia and the Woman with a Hemorrhage: A Bible Study

This study puts Sophia into a Jesus story, to see how her feminine character
changes the story, and especially how it affects the way female bodies are
viewed. This should not be the first time that a group meets Sophia in a Jesus
story; start instead with the introductory exercise and study, "Sophia
Walking on the Water," 152 to 154.

Materials Needed: A small piece of cloth for each participant, at least one
Bible.
Opening Exercise: The leader convenes the group and says,

> Close your eyes, sit up straight, and breathe deeply. Feel your feet on the
> ground, be aware of how you are sitting, note where the tense areas of your
> body are. Continue to breathe deeply, focusing on the parts of your body
> holding tension. Exhale into and through these areas, until you can feel the
> tension begin to go.

The leader allows about five minutes for this exercise.
Scripture Reading: A retelling of Mark 5:25–43.

> A great crowd gathered around Sophia as she got out of her boat, so she
> stayed beside the sea. Then one of the officials of the synagogue came

up—Jairus by name—and seeing her, he fell at her feet and pleaded with her earnestly, saying, "My little daughter is desperately sick. Do come and lay your hands on her to make her better and save her life." Sophia went with him and a large crowd followed her; they were pressing all around her.

Now there was a woman who had suffered from a hemorrhage for twelve years; after long and painful treatment under various doctors, she had spent all she had without being any the better for it. In fact, she was getting worse. She had heard about Sophia, and she came up behind her through the crowd and touched her cloak. "If I touch even her clothes," she had told herself, "I will be well again." And the source of the bleeding dried up instantly, and she felt in herself that she was cured of her complaint. Immediately aware that power had gone out from her, Sophia turned around in the crowd and said, "Who touched my clothes?" Her disciples said to her, "You see how the crowd is pressing around you and yet you say, "Who touched me?" But she continued to look all around to see who had done it. Then the woman came forward, frightened and trembling because she knew what had happened to her, and she fell at her feet and told her the whole truth. "My sister," she said, "your faith has restored you to health; go in peace and be free from your complaint."

Questions:

- The story of the woman with a hemorrhage occurs right in the middle of another story. Describe the scene before the woman appears. Where is Sophia going? What is the urgency?
- Why does the crowd press so closely?
- As Sophia and the crowd are moving along, a woman is introduced into this story. Describe this woman. What might she look like? How might she act? What might she smell like? If you were in the crowd, what might your reaction be?
- What is the significance of blood?

Scripture Reading: Read Leviticus 15:19–30 from an available Bible.
Questions:

- How was a woman who was bleeding treated? Why? What happened to someone who touched a woman who was bleeding?
- This woman had been hemorrhaging for how long? How do you think she felt? What would her relationship to other people be like? What would her place in the community be?
- What would it be like not to be touched? To be unclean?
- When have you felt something like this woman must have felt?
- Where, in your life, do you bleed? When have you felt like an outcast?
- What would it be like for this woman to be in the middle of the crowd? What might the reactions of the crowd be? The disciples? What pushes her on so? What is she hoping for?
- What do you think Sophia's presence means to her?

Scripture Reading:

> Sophia is often described as connecting the divine and the human. Listen to this passage:

The leader reads one or more of these passages: Ecclesiasticus 1:9, 10; Ecclesiasticus 24:1a, 3–13; Baruch 3:37–38. (See Appendix)
Questions:

- Incarnation—God embodied in human flesh—is another way the divine and human are connected. What might it mean to this woman for the divine to be embodied in Sophia? What would it do to the woman's sense of herself? What would it do to her sense of what is possible for her? What does it mean to you? How might it change the way you perceive God? Women?
- Why does the woman come up to Sophia from behind? What would it take for her, with all she's been through, to touch Sophia?
- What is Sophia's reaction to her touch? What is the reaction of the disciples? Why do you think Sophia calls attention to what happened, when she's in such a hurry?
- What is important for Sophia here? For the woman?
- Why is the woman so frightened when she is healed? What is she afraid of? If you were in her place, how would you be feeling?
- When the woman comes forward, what does Sophia say? What has made her well?
- If this passage were the only place where you had ever heard the word *faith*—you had never heard it in church or Sunday school—how would you describe faith? What is faith like in this passage? How does a person who has faith act?
- What would it mean for you to have faith? How would you act? What would it take for you to have faith? What would you risk? What would you gain?

Closing Exercise: After the discussion has ended, the leader indicates the pieces of cloth or items of clothing and says to the group,

> Take a piece of cloth or a piece of clothing and go by yourself to a quiet place. Focusing on the cloth, say to yourself: "If I touch even her clothes . . ." finishing the sentence in your own way. Repeat the sentence many times, letting new ways of finishing it come to you.

The group follows this for at least two or three minutes, until the leader signals the end of this part of the exercise. After the suggested time has elapsed, the leader instructs the group:

Write a prayer to Sophia asking for her help in following through on the insights you have just had. Touch the cloth.

After this, the leader invites the group to come together to share insights. At the end of the sharing, pass a cloth around the circle, each one saying to the next,

My sister, go in peace.

LITURGIES FOR SERVICES CELEBRATING WOMEN

🕏 A Sophia Passion in Three Parts

In the spring of 1986, a group of women at Calvary United Methodist Church in Philadelphia celebrated an alternative Holy Week, based on their year-long experiences of the Sophia texts. After studying the close connections between the character of Sophia and Jesus Christ in the New Testament and realizing the power of inserting Sophia into the Jesus story, the women decided to explore further and to discover how Sophia's presence in the passion story might add significance to that story.

Using John's Gospel as the basis for this Sophia passion, a three-day series of worship events was developed: a footwashing service for Maundy Thursday, a service focusing on the trial and crucifixion on Good Friday, and a service celebrating the resurrection on Saturday evening, the time of the Easter vigil. Each of the services is described here in detail.

Sophia Washes Her Followers' Feet

On the evening of Maundy Thursday, the women gathered for a foot-washing service, wearing comfortable clothing and easily removable foot-gear. They used a large basin of water, a pitcher, and several towels. The women sat in a semicircle and began the service by reading the Sophia version of John's footwashing story. The reading was done aloud by several women in the group. It can also be done by one person or dramatically, with a narrator and several people taking parts.

Service Preparation: Scripture and copy of benediction for each participant, several large basins of water, pitchers, and towels.

Scripture Reading (based on John 13:1–20):

It was before the festival of the Passover, and Sophia knew that the hour had come for her to pass from this world to God. She had always loved those who were hers in the world, but now she showed how perfect her love was.

They were at supper, and the devil had already put it into the mind of one of her followers to betray her. She knew that God had put everything into her hands, and that she had come from God and was returning to God, and she got up from the table, removed her outer garment, and, taking a towel, wrapped it around her waist; she then poured water into a basin and began to wash her followers' feet and to wipe them with the towel she was wearing.

She came to one of her most faithful followers, who said to her, "Lady, are you going to wash my feet?" Sophia answered, "At the moment you do not know what I am doing, but later you will understand." "Never!" said her faithful follower, "you shall never wash my feet." Sophia replied, "If I do not wash you, you can have nothing in common with me." "Then, Lady," said her follower, "not only my feet, but my hands and my head as well!" Sophia said, "No one who has taken a bath needs washing: she is clean all over. You too are clean, though not all of you are." She knew who was going to betray her, that was why she said, "Though not all of you are."

When she had washed their feet and put on her clothes again she went back to the table. "Do you understand," she said, "what I have done to you? You call me the Wisdom of God, and rightly; so I am. If I, then, the Wisdom of God, have washed your feet, you should wash each other's feet. I have given you an example so that you may copy what I have done to you.

"I tell you most solemnly,
no servant is greater than her mistress,
no messenger is greater than the woman who sent her.

"Now that you know this, happiness will be yours if you behave accordingly. I am not speaking about all of you: I know the ones I have chosen; but what scripture says must be fulfilled: Someone who shares my table rebels against me.

"I tell you this now, before it happens,
so that when it does happen
you may believe that I am She.
I tell you most solemnly,
whoever welcomes the one I send welcomes me.
and whoever welcomes me welcomes the one who sent me."

Footwashing Ceremony: Each woman took a turn at being Sophia for all of the others, washing the others' feet. They did so in silence, except for a brief exchange at the end of the washing of each person:

FOOTWASHER:	As I wash your feet, I share your journeys and accept your burdens as my own.
ONE WHOSE FEET ARE WASHED:	Thank you, [name of person]. [Kissing her on each cheek as an expression of communion with her.]

If time is an issue, one foot only may be washed instead of two.

Another time-saving suggestion, if the group is large, is for two or more people to wash feet at the same time. After the footwasher has washed the feet of three or four people, the first person whose feet were washed can then begin to wash the feet of the one next to her, following on around the circle, and ending with the one who washed hers. This pattern may then continue.

Sophia's Farewell: After the footwashing had been completed, the entire group stood, and the leader divided them into two groups. In the following benediction, the group took turns speaking as Sophia. The benediction is based on John 13:33–34.

> GROUP 1:   My little children,
> I shall not be with you much longer.
> GROUP 2:   You will look for me,
> But where I am going
> You cannot come.
> GROUP 1:   I give you a new commandment:
> Love one another;
> GROUP 2:   Just as I have loved you,
> You also must love one another.
> ALL: By this love you have for one another,
> Everyone will know that you are my disciples.

The Trial and Crucifixion of Sophia

The women gathered in a solemn mood on Good Friday evening. An adaptation of the story of the trial from the Gospel of John was read. This also can be dramatized or read dramatically.

Service Preparation: Paper, pencils, a large number of pictures of women suffering, art (drawing, painting or sculpture) materials, candles.

Scripture Reading   (adaptation of John 18:19–24):

> The high priest questioned Sophia about her followers and her teaching. Sophia answered, "I have spoken openly for all the world to hear. I have said nothing in secret. But why ask me? Ask my hearers what I taught; they know what I said." At these words, one of the guards standing by gave Sophia a slap in the face, saying, "Is that the way to answer the high priest?" Sophia replied, "If there is something wrong in what I said, point it out; but if there is no offense in it, why do you strike me?" Then the high priest sent her out to the bishop.

The Trial: The women were instructed, after a brief period of silence following the reading of the story, to put themselves into the role of Sophia's accusers. Their task was to write down as many accusations against Sophia as they could think of in approximately a five-minute period. The accusations could be broad and could include accusations against women living now or women in history. Sophia stood on trial as the representative of all women who have been unjustly accused.

At the end of the writing period, the trial against Sophia began. One person acted as the judge and asked to hear the accusations. The group then began to list the accusations against her in a dramatic fashion. One person would accuse her of one offense, and then someone else would issue another accusation. In this way, the entire group took part in the recitation of the offenses. As people spoke, new offenses came to mind, and these too were added to the list of offenses, until all the offenses had been named.

A partial list of the accusations:

"You're just a woman."

"You're getting out of hand; you don't know your place."

"You participate in witchcraft and the work of the devil."

"You don't have any place in the church."

"You're not as strong or powerful as the male God."

"You are trying to usurp God's power."

"You are heresy."

"You're a slut."

"You're a cheap broad."

"You're a castrating bitch."

"You're not a real goddess; you're too minor; you're not important enough."

"Who do you think you are, acting like you're equal to God?"

"You're silly and foolish."

"You're evil; you're the gateway of the devil."

"God can't be a woman."

After the accusations were finished, there was a brief period of silence, followed by a second reading from an adaptation of scripture.
Scripture Reading (adapted from sections of John 19:4–30):

The governor then had Sophia taken away and scourged; and after this, the soldiers twisted some thorns into a crown and put it on her head and dressed her in a purple robe. They kept coming up to her and saying, "Hail to the Wisdom of God!" and they slapped her in the face.

The governor came outside again and said to them, "Look, I am going to bring her out to you to let you see that I find no case." Sophia then came out wearing the crown of thorns and the purple robe. The governor said, "Here she is." When they saw her the priests and the guards shouted, "Crucify her! Crucify her!" The governor said, "Take her yourselves and crucify her."

They took charge of Sophia, and carrying her own cross she went out of the city to the place of the skull, where they crucified her with two others.

When the soldiers had finished crucifying Sophia, they took her clothing and divided it into four shares, one for each soldier.

Sophia said, "I am thirsty." A jar full of vinegar stood there, so putting a sponge soaked in the vinegar on a hyssop stick, they held it up to her mouth. After Sophia had taken the vinegar she said, "It is accomplished"; and bowing her head she died.

Crucifixion: Instructions were given for the next section of the evening: First, there would be a time of looking at pictures of women suffering. Then there would be an opportunity to use art materials to create our own visual portrayal of Sophia crucified. This entire portion of the evening was carried out in silence.

A variety of pictures were passed around and then placed in the center of the room where everyone could see them. There were pictures of women on crosses and of women suffering in other ways as well. The group spent at least ten minutes with these pictures.

Next, art materials were made available so that each woman could portray Sophia crucified. Drawing, painting, and sculpture materials were used. After approximately twenty minutes, women shared the pictures that each had made. Most of the stories behind the pictures included rape as well as murder. One body had been dismembered. In another picture Sophia on the cross was nailed to the ground, with small sprouts of green leaves coming out of the cross and her body. This was a very important time for the group, and speech and sharing were interspersed with a great deal of silence.

At the end of this sharing time, candles were brought out and lit. The women were instructed to use this as a time for prayer, a time to name those women who had suffered and died. What followed was a long period of naming women, as each person felt so moved. The naming ended in silence, the candles were blown out, and the group departed.

A Sophia Resurrection

The following Saturday evening, the group reassembled in silence.

Service Preparation: Copies of scripture adaptation, paper, drawing or painting materials, candles, tablecloth, wine, fish, cheese, fruit, bread.

The Empty Tomb: A dramatic reading of the John account of the empty tomb had been prepared. People were given their assignments, and everyone studied the script, the dramatic flow, and their part in the whole. Then the group proceeded to the door of the church sanctuary.

MARY OF MAGDALA:	Very early on the first day of the week while it is still dark, I, Mary, come to the sanctuary tomb. I see that the doors have been opened. I have been weeping, and I am still full of tears. [Walking inside, inviting others to follow her. Inside the dark sanctuary were two women standing at opposite ends, holding candles.]
ANGELS:	Woman, why are you weeping? Who are you looking for?
MARY OF MAGDALA:	They have taken Sophia away and I don't know where they have put her. [After saying this, she turned, as though seeing someone behind her, without recognition. All of the other women portrayed Sophia there behind her; they formed a "corporate Sophia."]
SOPHIA:	Woman, why are you weeping? Who are you looking for?
MARY OF MAGDALA:	Women, if you have taken her away, tell me where you have put her, and I will go and remove her.
SOPHIA:	[whispered]: Mary!
MARY:	[with recognition]: Sophia!
SOPHIA:	Go and find the sisters and brothers and tell them that I am with God.
MARY:	I go now to tell them all that I have seen the Wisdom of God and that she has said these things to me.

The woman portraying Mary led the way out of the sanctuary to the room where the group then continued to hold their meeting.

Sophia's Appearance to the Disciples: The group proceeded to arrange their room, putting in place candles used the evening before, unlit. Copies of a passage from John 20 was passed out so that all could follow along as it was read dramatically by one woman.

Scripture Reading   (adapted from John 20:19–23):

In the evening of that same day, the first day of the week, the doors were closed in the room where Sophia's followers were. Sophia came and stood among them. She said to them, "Peace be with you," and showed them her wounds. "Give me your hands. Put your fingers here in my wounds." Her followers were filled with joy when they had seen and touched Sophia, and she said to them again,
> "Peace be with you.
> As God sent me,
> So am I sending you.
> Receive the Holy Spirit.
> For those whose sins you forgive,
> They are forgiven;
> For those whose sins you retain,
> They are retained."

Prayer: The group then lit the candles and touched each other's hands, gently, acknowledging the wounds in one another. The leader led the group in a responsive invocation that started and ended by calling out to Sophia. In between, all the women called out the names of women who had been wounded, especially those women who were named the evening before. After each name was named, the group responded, "We touch your wounds. We rejoice in your presence with us." This invocation continued until all of the names the women wanted to call out had been named. Everyone in the group touched the hands of those nearest her during the entire prayer. The prayer ended with calling out to Sophia, rejoicing in her presence.

Sophia Eats with Her Followers

Scripture Reading (adapted from John 21:1–17):

> Later on, Sophia showed herself to the disciples again. It was by the sea, and it happened like this: One of the followers of Sophia said, "I am going fishing." The others replied, "We'll come with you." They went out and got into the boat but caught nothing that night.
>
> It was light by now and there stood Sophia on the shore, though the followers did not realize that it was Sophia. Sophia called out, "Have you caught anything, friends?" And when they answered no she said, "Throw the net out to starboard and you'll find something." So they dropped the net, and there were so many fish that they could not haul it in. One of Sophia's followers said, "It is the Wisdom of God." At these words, "It is the Wisdom of God," one of Sophia's followers, who had practically nothing on, wrapped her cloak around her and jumped into the water. The other followers came on in the boat, towing the net and fish; they were only about a hundred yards from land.
>
> As soon as they came ashore they saw that there was some bread there, and a charcoal fire with fish cooking on it. Sophia said, "Bring some of the fish you have just caught." One of the followers went aboard and dragged the net to shore, full of big fish, one hundred and fifty-three of them; and in spite of there being so many the net was not broken. Sophia said to them, "Come and have breakfast." None of the followers was bold enough to ask, "Who are you?"; they knew quite well it was Sophia. Sophia then stepped forward, took the bread and gave it to them, and the same with the fish.
>
> After the meal, Sophia said to her followers, "Do you love me?"

Meditation: The group spent at least fifteen minutes meditating on the passage that they had just heard, allowing their imagination and unconscious to lead them through the story in a new way. Everyone was directed to spend some time with Sophia's question at the end, and to answer it. The women then drew or painted something that arose from their meditation and shared from these experiences.

Meal: Everyone prepared the room for a festive meal: bread, wine, fish, cheese, fruit. More candles were lit, and our artwork decorated the room. The rest of the evening was spent in celebration and conversation around the meal.

A Celebration of Wisdom and Her Daughters

This litany was used at a Women's Day service at Calvary United Methodist Church; it is appropriate for any service in which women are celebrated.

LEADER: Wisdom, from generation to generation you enter into holy people.

PEOPLE: Julian of Norwich, Winnie Mandela, Dorothy Day, Starhawk, Jean Donovan.

LEADER: You make them friends of God and prophets.

PEOPLE: Sojourner Truth, Jane Addams, Georgia O'Keefe, Madre, Simone de Beauvoir.

LEADER: You are a breath of God's power.

PEOPLE: Joan of Arc, Elizabeth Blackwell, Marian Anderson, Golda Meir, Harriet Tubman.

LEADER: You are a reflection of eternal light.

PEOPLE: Maria Tallchief, Ella Baker, Christa McCauliffe, Billie Holliday, Marie Curie.

LEADER: You make everything new.

PEOPLE: Corazón Aquino, Sweet Honey in the Rock, Emily Dickinson, Mary Daly, Martha Graham.

ALL: These are some of the many who make their home with Wisdom.

A Ritual of Cleansing and Renewal Following an Abortion

The decision to end a pregnancy is an intensely personal one, and one that is often done with little or no counsel and support. Grief over the loss and guilt over the decision are long lasting. This ritual was designed for a woman who, when expecting the arrival of another child, needed healing over a decision to terminate a pregnancy many years before. Sophia was never mentioned overtly in the ritual; however, the content of the prayers are evocative of her.

Service Preparation: A bowl of water and planting pot with seeds.

RITUAL LEADER: [holding up water]: Holy One, you who are with us in all things and in every moment, you are deeply familiar with water. Before anything was, you gave form to the seas; you made your home in the deeps as well as in the mist. You piloted Noah to safety through angry waters, and you led the Hebrews through the sea to new life. You were with Jesus in the waters of his baptism in the

Jordan, and you were with everyone—indeed, each one of us—when we were in our mothers' wombs.

Today we are present to this water—this water which symbolizes the water of life and the water of the womb—this water which also symbolizes the life wasted, the waters of the womb spent, the tears shed. Be present, O God, with [name of woman] as she pours this water, pouring also her tears and the troubles of her spirit. Be present in and through the water. Amen.

WOMAN SEEKING HEALING (pouring a little water with each phrase):

I shed tears for . . .

I am sorry for . . .

I confess . . .

[Others join in pouring water into bowl, offering other concerns.]

RITUAL LEADER [holding bowl full of water]: This bowl of water is not poured out in vain; here is water that cleanses, water that heals, water that brings new life. [Name of woman], this water is poured out for you. [Ritual leader and others sprinkle water on the woman seeking healing, offering statements of cleansing and healing.]

Be cleansed of . . .

Be healed of . . .

RITUAL LEADER: [Name], in and through the One who formed the waters, who is the Water of Life, who was present with you in your mother's womb, you are forgiven.

[The leader holds a bowl full of water.]

RITUAL LEADER: [Name], this water is also poured out for the relationship you are about to begin with your new child. May this water, which cleanses and renews you, nourish the beginnings of your life together.

[The woman sprinkles water into a newly planted pot, offering hopes for her life with her new child. Others join her, adding their hopes as well.]

I hope for . . .

May our life grow in . . .

RITUAL LEADER: Holy One, you take life away and you bring new life into being. We ask your blessing on [name] and her child as they begin this new life, this new family. May the tears and the pain of [name] for the child who never knew life bring cleansing and healing; may the tears add their blessing to this new child, and may they open [name] and her child to love and joy and fullness of life. Amen.

[The group follows the leader outside, to a lawn or plot of earth. The leader holds the bowl containing whatever water remains.]

RITUAL LEADER: The bitter tears, the mistakes of the past, which are held in this bowl, have been forgiven, and they have been offered as a means of cleansing and new life. Now is the time to let go of them and the past to which they belong, to get ready for the new life that awaits you. Take this water, and pour it out, let it go.

WOMAN SEEKING HEALING:

Good-bye to . . .

I let go of . . .

RITUAL LEADER: Life spent leads to new life. The water returns to the earth. It rises once more as the mist. It comes again as the rain. May the One who is present in life, in death, and in rebirth, may the One who sends the rain again and again be with you always. Amen.

CHAPTER EIGHT

Sophia in All Things

When the first Soviet cosmonauts orbited the earth, one of their first public proclamations from space concerned God. With a mixture of pride, defiance, and humor, they declared that they were in the heavens and had not found God. Populist atheism was confirmed in their eyes. If God is not in the heavens, then there is no God; so the rationale went.

Of course, on one level such an assertion reveals a crass misunderstanding of metaphoric language. Both *God* and *heavens* are symbolic terms, not literal references to objects somewhere. Few twentieth-century believers would expect the cosmonauts to have encountered either God or heaven in orbit. But in another way the cosmonauts addressed one of the central questions of faith and theology in our time: Is God inside or outside our universe? Many phenomena in our universe that were previously mysteries associated with God now have good scientific explanations which do not need God. The German theologian Dietrich Bonhoeffer described this major crisis of faith in this way:

> There is no longer any need for God as a working hypothesis, whether in morals, politics, or science. Nor is there any need for such a God in religion or philosophy. . . . The God who makes us live in this world without using him as a working hypothesis is the God before whom we are ever standing.[1]

Bonhoeffer called for discovering God at the heart of history. He said,

> The Christian hope sends a man [sic] back to his life on earth in a wholly new way. . . . The Christian, unlike the devotees of the salvation myths, does not need a last refuge in the eternal from earthly tasks and difficulties. . . . Myths of salvation arise from experiences of the boundary situation. Christ takes hold of a man [sic] in the centre of his life.[2]

And Bonhoeffer decided that God's involvement in the ambiguities of history was a call to become involved in the political and social contingencies of life. In a similar response, process theologians have proposed to encounter God within the organisms and mechanisms of the universe, rather than on its edges.

Another response to scientific demystification has been to reaffirm God as completely outside our world. This renewed supernaturalist tendency as exhibited by fundamentalism takes ancient metaphors such as heaven at least as literally as the cosmonauts did. It insists on an increased distance between heaven and earth, between God and humanity, in order to protect heaven and God from the threat of science.

The wisdom literature and particularly its central figure, Sophia, stand as dramatic affirmations of God within the universe. Even in the ancient world, Sophia, in the context of the wisdom literature, imaged the possibility of knowing and encountering the divine in human experience. The early proverbs of the wisdom literature, for example, expressed general truths about human experience. Proverbs like "a present will open all doors and win access to the great" (Proverbs 18:16) or "worry makes a heart heavy; a kindly word makes it glad" (Proverbs 12:25) are part of an enterprise that seeks revelation within mundane human experience. Other proverbs, such as "whoever is kind to the poor is lending to Yahweh, who will repay him the kindness done" (Proverbs 19:17) and "the human spirit is the lamp of Yahweh—searching the deepest self" (Proverbs 20:27) indicate that not just truth but God himself or herself can be discovered in the patterns of human experience.

Later wisdom literature affirms that the divine is at work not only in human experience but in all things. In Wisdom 7:17–21 the sage says,

> He [Yahweh] it was who gave me sure knowledge of what exists, to understand the structure of the world and the action of the elements, the beginning, end, and middle of the times, the alternation of the solstices and the succession of the seasons, the cycles of the year and the position of the stars, the natures of the animals and the instincts of the wild beasts, the powers of the spirits and human mental processes, the varieties of plants and the medical properties of roots. And now I understand everything, hidden or visible, for Sophia, the designer of all things, has instructed me.

In the wisdom literature Sophia becomes the image of the God who reveals herself or himself within the workings of the universe and who wants to help people see God there. "She pervades and permeates all things," the sage tells us (Wisdom 7:24). "She herself searches everywhere for those who are worthy of her, benevolently appearing to them on their ways, anticipating their every thought" (Wisdom 6:16). "Herself unchanging, she renews the world, and passing into holy souls, she makes them into God's friends" (Wisdom 7:27). "Strongly she reaches from one end of the world to the other and she governs the whole world for its good" (Wisdom 8:1).

Sophia, then, is a powerful image of God within the universe. She is the divine figure who has "taken root" and "pitched camp" (Ecclesiasticus 24:12, 7) on earth. She is in all things, waiting to be discovered. She does not direct her students and creatures beyond the created realm but stands as an example of one who "delights" in the world that exists and continues to come into being (Proverbs 8:31). She is the Immanent One. Wisdom literature says to the cosmonauts that they could have seen her on earth just as well as in the heavens, since "for those who seek her, she is readily found. She anticipates those who desire her by making herself known first. Whoever gets up early to seek her will have no trouble but will find her sitting at the door" (Wisdom 6:12, 13).

Wisdom literature answers the supernaturalist in equally decisive terms. Sophia stands as an affirmation of science and understanding. She encourages us to learn about our world and to see God as a part of it—a part of what we do understand, not simply a part of what we do not. With Sophia as revealer of the divine, learning is not a threat to God but a means of encountering him or her in the world. The call of Sophia's followers in Proverbs 4:7, 13, "At the cost of all you have, acquire understanding. Hold her close, and she will make you great. . . . Hold fast to discipline, never let her go," becomes a bold affirmation of the marriage of science and faith, not only in that time, but for our day as well.

The divine figure who lives in the universe rather than outside of it is closely related to the Christian God incarnate. The Christian affirmation of a God who "became flesh and lived among us" (John 1:14) resembles the portrait we have sketched above of Sophia. In fact, as chapter 3 discusses, the first eighteen verses of the Gospel of John, which concern the Word who was with God, are rooted in Sophia texts. Twentieth-century theologies of incarnation[3] have much in common with Sophia and the wisdom literature.

At the same time, Sophia has perhaps more potential for contemporary spirituality than the God incarnate of recent writings. Since she is in not only human flesh but all things, relationship to her implies ecological consciousness. Theologies of God made flesh sacralize human life but do not deal directly with hallowing the earth and its other creatures. Sophia in all things, however, as portrayed in wisdom literature, restores the dignity of all creation.

🐚 Where Is God?: A Sermon[4]

This has been a hard time for us at Calvary Church. We've worked hard here, in this congregation; to be a community together, to work and worship and be together against all the differences that threaten to divide us. This has been lots of fun, but it's been a struggle, too, to find ways to grow together and nourish one another when we're all so different. And right in the midst of the fun and hard work, Ruth is killed—one of the ones who worked the hardest at making connections with people who were different.[5] And her death has left a hole right in the middle of this congregation. Her death has unleashed all kinds of feelings that undermine our community, our ability to be together.

So many of us have worked hard on our community projects. We've put in hours and hours—hours that have built into months and years of work. We've worked in all kinds of ways, with the hope that the work would make this community, this neighborhood stronger and better. And the work has made a difference for the most part. But this week we witnessed the end of ten years of trying to build a way for neighbors to communicate with one another through WPEB.[6] All the years of fundraising, struggle over the direction of and importance of the station, and the hard work of providing and upgrading the programming has ended, with WPEB being closed down and moved out of the building.

A lot of us have worked hard on issues of national importance. We've worked for social and political change, put our time and money into causes of social justice and peace, and what have we witnessed? A nation divided under Reagan, the bombing of Tripoli, and now congressional approval of military aid to the Contras, clear approval to make war on Nicaragua.

This has been a hard time. For some of us, there have been hard times before—this is nothing new—but for others of us, these recent events have shaken us to the roots. And some of us are asking, "Where is God in all of this? How come God hasn't vindicated us, hasn't saved us from so much death and destruction? How come God, whose power and presence helped us to build this congregation and to work so well in this community, how come God has let us down?" These are the questions some of us are asking these days.

The person who prayed Psalm 139 knew all about hard times, too. He lived in a time of violence and disruption—of political turmoil. He was living in Israel when Israel was no longer a strong nation, in fact not even a nation at all. Israel had fallen on hard times; it was subject to other stronger nations surrounding it. And the God who'd been identified with Israel— Yahweh—Yahweh who had called Abraham, who had divided the sea for the people to escape the Egyptians, who had helped them subdue the native people of their Promised Land—Yahweh was no longer saving them, or acting on their behalf in history.

So the psalmist cried out, "O God, if only you would kill the wicked." If only. As if he knew full well that God couldn't do that anymore; that kind of intervention was no longer possible.

I can imagine that before the psalmist said, "if only," there had been a whole range of reactions and responses to God. I'll bet before the plaintive "if only" he was angry, and let God know just how angry.

We, too, can be angry that God isn't powerful enough to stop violent people, isn't powerful enough to protect good people. We can be angry at God. We have good reason to be angry; lots of things have gone wrong. We counted on God, we expected better, and we didn't get it. And we're hurt, confused, and angry.

This may seem like a harsh thing to say, to even think—getting angry at God. But it's important. The psalmist has obviously given up on God as a powerful interventionist in history, but clearly not without a struggle. There's still plenty of anger left. What's great about the psalms is that the people praying them had real emotions, and spoke real thoughts, whether beautiful or ugly. What was on their minds and hearts was spoken to God.

It's important that we do that, too. If we're disappointed, we need to say so. If we're hurt and angry, we need to say so. And if we don't believe that God can help us anymore, we need to say that, too.

Relating to God often isn't easy, but relating to God when hard times hit can be close to impossible. Better to scream and shout—even if it's screaming and shouting into what seems like a void—than to turn silent and cynical.

After the anger, there's the possibility that we face a deep sense of loss, the loss of a God who will save us, who will divide the water and see us safely through, who will destroy our enemies. And who is God then? How do we relate to God then?

All of us are different. Our spiritual struggles are our own. But for those of us who find ourselves facing these questions, Psalm 139 provides a way of thinking about and relating to God in a different way. The psalmist has obviously given up on God as one who will control history for him, but he hasn't stopped relating to God. Rather he's enlarged the sphere in which God operates, has opened up his imagination, and has experienced God as the God of all creation, not just as a God of Israel who is concerned only about Israel. This is a God who is concerned with the entire world.

This God is at once incredibly distant and incredibly intimate, a combination that results in real wonder at who God is. This God knows us personally. This God was with us when we were formed in our mother's womb. This God knows our every thought and, at the same time, is present everywhere in the world. This God is present everywhere, so that no matter where we go, no matter what happens to us, we will not be cut off from God.

> If I scale the heavens you are there,
> if I lie flat in Sheol, there you are.
> If I speed away on the winds of the dawn,
> if I dwell beyond the ocean,
> even there your hand will be guiding me.   (Psalm 139:8–9)

God is both within us and also present in the farthest reaches of the universe. We can't be disconnected from God, no matter what.

Thinking about God this way is hard, for me anyway. My mind wants to split this God apart into the God in me who is knowable and tangible and the God out in the farthest boundaries of the universe who is unknowable and abstract. But what's so incredible about imaging God this way is that it isn't God here and God there, it's God within the whole. It's God that makes us and some star billions of miles away connected, part of a whole.

I spoke with a friend some time ago about meditation and prayer. I asked her what her primary image of God was. Her answer was perplexing to me at the time; she said that she experienced God as fine white fibers. Since then that image has become very powerful. Fine white fibers throughout the universe, connecting us to the penguins in Antarctica, connecting this planet to solar systems yet undreamed of.

This God is one who empowers everything and everyone and connects you and me and the president and the Contras and the Sandanistas and all the other people on this planet. This God brings us together whether we want to be or not. We can begin to sense this presence, this power in our midst and everywhere, a presence that envelops differences and hatred and misunderstanding, that is deeper than political boundaries and religious convictions.

If we live in a way that celebrates this radical connectedness, we can't live without recognizing and experiencing the lives of others. We can't live without being mindful of them. We can't live without knowing that they are just as important as we are. And that's hard. It's easier to kill the ones who proclaim such a reality, easier to destroy the evidence of the connections. There are so many interests to protect, so many fears, so much hatred.

Even so, there is a presence at the very heart of the universe that empowers us all. The One who knows each one of us better than we know ourselves and who at the same time fills the entire universe continues to make connections, continues to bring new life into being.

We are connected to everything else, and we're connected to everyone else, whether we want to be or not. We are. We live together on this planet.

We need to proclaim and to live out this kind of connectedness—to live in such a way that we help make visible God's presence in all of creation. We need to keep on learning. We need to keep on making newer and deeper connections, and we need to live out these connections together. And that will put us at risk—at risk of mockery, at risk of condemnation, at risk of all kinds of failures, at risk, even, of death.

By sending these folks off to Nicaragua, all of us have a way of going to Nicaragua too.[7] It is a way of sending something of ourselves: our hopes, our fears, our dreams that have been dashed, our work for justice and peace, our refusal to give up on living together. It's a way of proclaiming that we were created a part of one world and meant to live as a part of one world. And nothing—not the U.S. government or threats of death and violence, or anything else—can keep us from being connected. God may not be able to save us from failure or from death, but God continues to be a powerful presence within and among us. Let the people of Nicaragua know that, and let's remind one another of that, too. We are connected. God empowers and connects us, and makes of us all one world.

We belong to one another, and we belong to God. Nothing we do can change that, and all that we do can help others realize that.

❧ Meditating on Sophia in All Things

This exercise can be done by individuals or as a group activity. It can be repeated as often as desired.

Materials Needed: Natural and fabricated objects such as stones, fabric, tin cans, flowers, bowls, and pencils.

Scripture Reading: Read the following passages in silence: Proverbs 8:31; Wisdom 6:14, 15; Wisdom 7:22–24; Wisdom 7:27b; Ecclesiasticus 1:14; Ecclesiasticus 24:3. (See Appendix)

Participants choose an object, either from those collected by the leader or from among other objects in the room. People should be encouraged to select something to which they are drawn, whatever that might be.

Spend Time with the Object:

Take time to look at the object selected. Notice its color, its shape, its lines, and its color tone. Notice your own response to the way the object looks. Notice what you like about it, what it reminds you of, and what you don't like about it.

Also notice what the object sounds like. Shake it or rub it to see if it has sounds. Smell the object. Touch it. Again notice what your response is to the smell, sound, and touch of the object.

After you have examined the object thoroughly, ask yourself what your feelings are about it. See if you have some detectable emotions about it. Do you like it? Is it a little bit intimidating or mysterious?

Meditation: Participants now try to experience Sophia in the object. Encourage them to see, hear, feel, smell, or taste her in the object. Most people will want to close their eyes, visualize the object they have been holding, and then try to see Sophia in it. But some people will want to use one of the other senses to experience her in the object. In any case, encourage them to relax into the possibility of experiencing Sophia in the object. As much as possible, discourage self-censorship. Participants should see, hear, feel what comes to them as they call on her in the object. Take ten to fifteen minutes with the object.

Report to the Group: If this exercise is done in a group, the leader brings the group back together. Allow time for each person to report on his or her meditation. If individuals wish to remain silent, their wishes should, of course, be respected.

🐚 A Thanksgiving Liturgy

This liturgy was used as part of a Sunday morning worship service in a local church during the Thanksgiving season. It can also be used on Thanksgiving Day itself or on other worship occasions, especially at harvest time. The material presented here is only one segment of a worship service and is probably best located near the beginning of the service. It could also be used as a participatory sermon or homily, or at the time of the offering.

This liturgy does not explicitly mention Sophia. Referring to her explicitly is, of course, possible but is not particularly recommended. As you read through this liturgy you will note that it reflects the theological perspective of immanence outlined at the beginning of this chapter. You will also notice that this service is a liturgical version of the preceding meditation on Sophia in all things.

A variety of fruits and vegetables are placed on every seat in the room before people enter. This selection of harvested foods should be as varied as possible, including any obtainable and edible plant product.

The service opens with a hymn, song, prayer, or litany. Then people should be seated and asked to examine the fruit or vegetable they found on their seat. After a few moments, the leader asks each person to consider where this particular fruit or vegetable comes from. What is the shape of the plant on which it grew? The leader invites people to stand up, show their fruit or vegetable, and say where it may have come from. Everyone should say something, if possible. If someone is uncertain about the origin of their fruit or vegetable, the leader asks for assistance from others in the congregation.

Then the leader asks people to turn their attention once again to their objects, suggesting that they notice particular colors and designs. The fruit or vegetable may have a distinctive odor. One may want to touch or rub it to see how it feels, or hold it up to one's cheek. Perhaps if shaken, it has a sound. The leader asks each person to spend several minutes getting to know the object.

After three to five minutes (depending on the nature of the group), the leader asks everyone to close their eyes while holding the vegetable or fruit. The leader asks each person to feel or see God's presence in the object they are holding.

> Don't censor yourself. Let go a little. And notice what you feel or see in your mind's eye while you close your eyes and hold the object. Can you see or feel a personal presence or an aura or an energy in it?

The leader allows several minutes and then asks people to open their eyes again.

The leader invites people to speak briefly about what they saw or felt when they held the object. Responses should be kept relatively short in order to allow a number of people to speak. If more than ten people speak, the service will tend to begin to drag.

The reporting on what people saw or felt with their object should be closed with an appropriate song or hymn. An example of one such hymn is "For the Beauty of the Earth." (See chapter 10, "A Sophia Miscellany," for other hymns and songs to and about Sophia.)

If this liturgy is done near the time of the offering, people may place their fruit or vegetable on the altar after speaking, and those who do not feel called upon to speak may use the offering as an opportunity to bring theirs forward.

৯ A Litany in Praise of God's Presence in All Things

Like the previous liturgy, this litany may be used in Sunday morning worship in a local congregation. Like the Thanksgiving liturgy, it celebrates Sophia implicitly. The theological articulation that Sophia embodies in the wisdom literature is at the heart of this litany.

LEADER:	Let us remember how wide our world is and how God's (or Sophia's or Wisdom's) mysterious presence penetrates all things and people.
PEOPLE (SUNG):	Alleluia, alleluia, alleluia, alleluia. [Any sung alleluia may be used here.]
READER 1:	The Presbyterian churches in Korea.
READER 2:	The Marxist insurgents in the Philippines.
READER 3:	Wayland Baptist Church (or the name of an appropriate neighboring church).
READER 4:	The Girl Scouts of America.
PEOPLE:	Alleluia, alleluia, alleluia, alleluia.
READER 1:	Nelson Mandela in South Africa.
READER 2:	The University of North Dakota women's basketball team.
READER 3:	The orthodox synagogues of the Philadelphia suburbs.
READER 4:	The Alvin Ailey Dance Company.
PEOPLE:	Alleluia, alleluia, alleluia, alleluia.
READER 1:	The Catholic archdiocese of Chicago.
READER 2:	The Painted Bride Arts Center.
READER 3:	Ballerinas in their first year of schooling in Moscow.
READER 4:	Forest rangers in the Everglades.
PEOPLE:	Alleluia, alleluia, alleluia, alleluia.
READER 1:	Aging aborigines in Australian work crews.

READER 2:	Secret lovers in Spanish villages.
READER 3:	Greyhound bus drivers in the middle of the night.
READER 4:	The Seattle Mariners baseball team.
PEOPLE:	Alleluia, alleluia, alleluia, alleluia.
READER 1:	Trial judges in Argentina.
READER 2:	Witches and witch doctors in Zaire.
READER 3:	West Philadelphia High School.
READER 4:	Affirmation, The United Methodist organization for gays and lesbians.
PEOPLE:	Alleluia, alleluia, alleluia, alleluia.
READER 1:	Working grandmothers in Detroit.
READER 2:	Suburban housewives going back to college.
READER 3:	Bishop F. Herbert Skeete and his cabinet (or any appropriate church leader or authority).
PEOPLE:	Alleluia, alleluia, alleluia, alleluia.

‿ Opening and Closing Litanies in Celebration of Sophia's Presence in All of the City

---

These litanies were used at the beginning and end of a liturgy that celebrated urban life. One of the litanies is explicitly based on the Ecclesiasticus 24 portrait of Sophia. The other does not mention her. One of the litanies—the one referring to Sophia—is quite conventional and biblical, the other much more experimental. Both of them stand on their own, so it is possible to use them separately.

Opening Litany
(Adapted from Ecclesiasticus 24)

LEADER:	Wisdom is telling her story in the midst of her people.
PEOPLE:	I came forth from the mouth of the most high, she says.
LEADER:	Alone I searched for a place to rest.
PEOPLE:	I looked everywhere to find a place to live.
LEADER:	Then the creator of all things instructed me:
PEOPLE:	Pitch your tent here in this place.
LEADER:	So in the beloved city I took up residence.
PEOPLE:	I have taken root in these people.
LEADER:	I have grown tall as an oak tree.
PEOPLE:	I have taken on many colors.
LEADER:	I have spread out my branches like a candelabra.
PEOPLE:	My blossoms bear the fruit of openness and care.
LEADER:	Approach and take your fill.
PEOPLE:	Come and proclaim the Wisdom of being together in this city.
LEADER:	Amen.
PEOPLE:	Amen.

Closing Litany

LEADER: Let us join ourselves now to the flow that makes us and all things fresh and new.

PEOPLE: The movement that brought the sun into being.

LEADER: The wind that carries pollen to the next flower.

PEOPLE: The ancestor that painted on the cave wall.

LEADER: Gentle breath of new-making, this is where we live.

PEOPLE: Look at our city and say yes to it.

LEADER: O Surprise, which rescues us from despair, we see that growth and decay are hopelessly entangled in this place.

PEOPLE: Touch us firmly so that out of conflict may come signs of hope.

LEADER: Generous host of all, we and our neighbors work and play here.

PEOPLE: Carry us beyond ourselves into the common space you have given us.

LEADER: In the name of the moonlight, the saxophone, the mother, the son, the color purple, the father, the girlfriend, and the Holy Spirit, send us forth with joy and your blessing.

PEOPLE: Amen.

ࢠ A Meditation on Gospel of Thomas 77

The following is a meditation on logion 77 of the Gospel of Thomas. It was done as a part of a Sophia Bible study on the passage. Scholars have identified so many wisdom- and Sophia-related themes in the Gospel of Thomas that many of them believe Jesus to be speaking as Sophia in that document. Thus it seems appropriate to focus a Bible study on one of the sayings of Jesus found there.

Scripture Reading: Gospel of Thomas 77

Jesus said, "It is I who am the light which is above them all. It is I who am the All. From Me did the All come forth, and unto Me did the All extend. Split a piece of wood, and I am there. Lift up the stone, and you will find me there."

Meditation:

In the woods I lifted up a rock. Sophia came out from under the rock. I asked, "What is the All?"

She said, "Look around."

Then flowers began growing quickly and became very large. Then there was a huge flower. It opened wide. On the edge of a petal, which turned into a lake, was a mother bathing her baby. The baby swam off and turned into a twelve-year-old boy, who swam and dived in the water. Then the boy swung on a tree swing and jumped in the water three times. The third time he turned into a thirty-year-old man doing laps. This man walked up and found a six-month-old girl asleep on a blanket. He took her, his daughter, down to the lake and gave her a bath.[8]

🕊 A Eucharistic Celebration of Sophia in All Things

The following eucharistic liturgy may be used in a regular parish setting. It integrates the Jesus eucharistic tradition, several New Testament passages that associate Jesus with Sophia, and Sophia's presence in all things. (For a fuller discussion of the use of Sophia material in eucharistic celebrations, see chapter 9, "Jesus and Sophia." For a selection of hymns and songs for use in such liturgies, see chapter 10, "A Sophia Miscellany.")

Opening Litany: During the leader's portions of this litany the bread, the cup, and other elements from nature—like a rock or flowers—may be brought to the table.

LEADER (preferably a woman):   From everlasting I was firmly set, from the beginning before earth came into being. The deep was not, when I was born, there were no springs to gush with water.
(Proverbs 8:23, 24)

PEOPLE (The use of chanting is recommended here, although the part may also be read in unison. The symbol / indicates chanting instructions):
You stretch the heavens out like a / tent,
you build your palace on the waters / above;
using the clouds as your / chariot,
you advance on the / wings of the / wind.

You fixed the earth on its founda / tions,
unshakable for ever and / ever;
you wrapped it with the deep as with a / robe,
the waters over / topping the / mountains.
(Psalm 104:2b, 3, 5–6)

LEADER: Before the mountains were settled, before the hills, I came to birth; before the earth was made or the countryside or the first grains of the world's dust.   (Proverbs 8:25, 26)

PEOPLE: At your reproof the waters took to / flight,
they fled at the sound of your / thunder,
cascading over the mountains, into the / valleys,
down to the reservoir / you made for / them.

You set springs gushing in / ravines,
running down between / mountains,
supplying water for wild / animals,
attracting the / thirsty wild / donkeys.
(Psalm 104:7–8, 10–11)

LEADER: When the heavens were fixed firm, I was there; when a ring was drawn on the surface of the deep, when the clouds were thickened above, when the springs of the deep were fixed fast, I was there.   (Proverbs 8:27, 28)

PEOPLE: From your palace you water the / uplands
until the ground has had all that your heavens have
to / offer;
you make the fresh grass grow for / cattle
and those plants made / use of by / people.

And people receive food from your / soil,
wine to make them / cheerful,
oil to make them / happy,
and bread to / make them / strong.   (Psalm 104:13–15)

LEADER: When the sea was assigned its boundaries—and the water will not invade the shore—when the foundations for the earth were laid, I was there.   (Proverbs 8:29)

PEOPLE: What variety you have / created,
arranging everything so / wisely.
Earth is completely full of things you have / made,
among them vast ex / panse of / ocean,

Teeming with countless / creatures,
creatures large and / small,
with the ships going to and / fro
and Leviathan—whom you / made to amuse / you.
                                          (Psalm 104:24–26)

LEADER: I was there, a master craftsperson, delighting day after day, ever at play everywhere in the world, delighting to be with the sons and daughters of people.   (Proverbs 8:30–31)

PEOPLE: All creatures depend on / you
to feed them throughout the / year;
you provide the food they / eat,
with generous hand you / satisfy their / hunger.

You turn away your face, they / suffer,
you stop their breath, they / die.
You give breath, fresh life / begins,
you keep re / newing the / world.   (Psalm 104:27–30)

Scripture Reading: Wisdom 10:1–11:3.
Song: See chapter 10, "A Sophia Miscellany," for hymns and songs that can be used here.
Sermon/Homily
Eucharistic Prayer of Thanksgiving

CELEBRANT: On the night in which he was betrayed Jesus took bread. After giving you thanks, he broke the bread, gave it to the disciples, and said, "Take, eat, this is my body which is given for you." When the supper was over, he took the cup. Again he gave thanks to you, O God, gave the cup to the disciples and said, "Drink from this, all of you; this is the cup of the new covenant in my blood, poured out for you and for many, for the forgiveness of sins. When we eat this bread and drink this cup, we experience anew the presence of Jesus with us.

PEOPLE: You are the image of the unseen God,
the firstborn of all creation.
In you all things were created,
everything visible and everything invisible.
(from Colossians 1:15, 16)
You bring forth food from the earth and wine to cheer
our hearts.
How great you are, clothed in majesty and splendor.
(from Psalm 104:1, 14)

CELEBRANT: Wisdom has built herself a house, and set her table.
She says: come and eat of my bread and drink my wine.
(Proverbs 9:1, 4)

PEOPLE: You exist before all things
and hold all things together. (from Colossians 1:17)
Your open hand fills us with what we need.
Turn away your face and we panic.
Send out your breath and life begins.
You renew the face of the earth.   (from Psalm 104:29, 30)

Sharing of the Bread and Cup
Communion Song: See chapter 10, "A Sophia Miscellany."
Sending Forth and Benediction

🕊 A Good Friday Liturgy

The following liturgy is highly experimental. It assumes some understanding of the association of Sophia with Jesus. It also requires a high degree of participation by those attending. For this reason, it is more appropriate for persons already quite familiar with Sophia than for those just being introduced to her.

Service Preparation: A round piece of loosely woven fabric, preferably multicolored, with strands extending in all directions, and with at least as many strands as participants needs to be constructed in advance. A knife, a loaf of bread, and a chalice of wine should be placed on a table in the main room.

The service begins outside in front of a tree. Spread in front of the tree is a round piece of loosely woven fabric, preferably multicolored, with strands of the fabric extending in all directions, and with at least one strand for each participant. The fabric is intended to resemble a sort of web.

The opening reading is done by a woman who may serve as reader for the texts in the remainder of the liturgy as well; alternatively, the remaining texts can be divided up among the other participants.

Scripture Reading:

I have taken root in a privileged people.
I have grown tall as a cedar in Lebanon, as a cyprus on
Mount Hermon.
(Ecclesiasticus 24:12, 13)

Meditation:

CELEBRANT: Let's think for a moment about a favorite tree of ours.
Picture the tree in your mind's eye and recall why you like it.
After a few moments of imaging this tree, you may tell us
about it, if you like.
[After several people tell of their favorite trees, the celebrant
invites people to take the fabric piece and process toward the
entrance to the building in which the rest of the celebration
will take place. Still outside, the group halts, lays down the
fabric, and stands still.]

READER: I have grown tall as a palm in Engedi, as the rose bushes of
Jericho, as a fine olive tree in the plain, as a plane tree I have
grown tall.
(Ecclesiasticus 24:14)

CELEBRANT: Let's stand here and feel the earth beneath us. Let us sense
how we are resting on the earth, how it is connecting us to
everything else that is resting on it. Let us trace with our eyes
the path from our feet to the next object or being, to the
next, and to the next, and finally to the horizon.
[A few moments of silence are observed. Then the celebrant
invites the group to process into the room where the rest of
the celebration will take place. The group carries the piece of
fabric into the room, placing it on a table around which the
group sits in a large circle. The strands of fabric go out from
the table in all directions. On the table are a knife, a loaf of
bread, and a chalice of wine. After the group has been
seated, the reader continues.]

READER: As the time of another feast approached, my friends gathered
around me again. But I told them that in two days' time I
would be cut down. The religious leaders were making plans
to chop me down. They said, "The earth and trees are to be
used by humans. This tree is standing in a place we want to
stand, and besides, we could use her wood to make paper
and houses and tables."
As my friends came close to me, a woman came
forward and poured expensive perfume on my branches and
leaves. My friends scolded her, saying to her that this was the
time to rally around me to protect me, not the time to be
frivolous. But I said to them, "Wherever in the world people
celebrate good news, this will be remembered."
Then one of my friends left and went to the religious

assembly and offered to bring them within striking distance of me, if they would pay him money.

[At this point the celebrant ties several strands of the fabric to several persons in the group.]

READER: The rest of my friends began to prepare a meal around my roots. The one who had betrayed me returned to join in the meal. They all broke bread and ate it and drank wine, and I was at the center of the meal.

They recalled all they had learned under my branches. They toasted my beauty. They recognized and affirmed their own rootedness in mine. And they remembered how their lives and mine had become one. Toward the end of the meal they began arguing whether anyone would ever run away if the government or religious leaders came to cut me down. One of my dearest friends said loudly that such a thing would never happen.

[The celebrant ties more strands of fabric to persons in the group.]

READER: When I was stretched out there, suddenly my friend who had betrayed me to the religious leaders was there with a large number of armed persons. They struggled with my friends, as they tried to cordon me off from them. In the melee that ensued, one of my friends cut off the ear of one of the invaders. But finally the religious crowd succeeded in cordoning off the space around me and placing in front of me a sign that said, "This tree will be removed. No trespassing."

[The celebrant ties strands of the fabric to some of the stationary elements in the room so that those who are tied to other strands now cannot move.]

READER: The religious organization posted guards around me, and then my friends deserted me and ran away.

[The celebrant ties more strands of the fabric to more people.]

READER: The religious leaders then called a meeting of their governing body to meet around me. The leaders proposed that the governing body petition the government to chop me down. Their presentation went like this: "People are beginning to treat this tree as if it were more important than our places of worship or more important than God. It is attracting so much attention that our institutions are in danger. But just so that we don't waste the tree, we propose to cut it down and use the wood for a table around which we can have our religious ceremonies." They all became so enthused about the idea that they took some of their knives and began cutting at me and yelling insults at me.

[The celebrant ties more strands of the fabric to more people and to other stationary points.]

READER: And then the religious assembly voted to petition the government to chop me down.

At the edge of the crowd I saw the friend who had said I would never be abandoned. Several of the crowd went up to that friend of mine and said, "Aren't you one of the people who have gathered around this tree so often to learn from it and to celebrate its beauty?"

My friend began to retreat. After a few steps backward that friend said, "I do not know what you are talking about." But some others at the edge of the crowd said, "You act just like those people who loved the tree so much. We are sure that you have been here before." Again the friend said, "I have never seen this tree in my life." At that point a bird in my branches sang a clear note. My friend then left.

[The celebrant continues tying strands to people.]

READER: The government called for a public hearing on the spot where I grew. Most of the people who came were from the religious group. The government officials read the petition from the people that I be cut down and made into a table. It was the custom of the government each year to set aside a piece of land as a natural reserve. The officials proposed to the crowd a choice: "We can declare the space around this tree a natural reserve, or we can make the strip mine outside town into a natural reserve. Which do you want, the strip mine or this tree?"

And the crowd shouted back, "We want the strip mine!" Then the officials asked, "But what shall we do with this tree?" "Cut it down!" screamed the crowd. The officials raised their hands in a shrug of incomprehension and then voted to set aside the strip mine as a natural reserve. They voted to have me chopped down.

[The celebrant secures the fabric even more tightly by tying further strands to other stationary objects in the room.]

READER: Police came then and placed barbed wire around me. Everyone began to laugh. They said, "It looks pretty ugly now. How could anyone have ever wanted to save it? And just think, this strange-looking tree was supposed to be the most beautiful and strong thing that people had ever seen."

[The celebrant finishes tying the remaining strands of fabric to people and stationary objects in the room, so that all persons are tied to the fabric, which has by this time been anchored firmly.]

READER: I have spread my branches like a terebrinth, and my branches are glorious and graceful. I am like a vine putting out graceful shoots, my blossoms bear the fruit of glory and wealth.

[Then the celebrant takes the knife on the table.]

CELEBRANT: I invite you now to take the bread and wine together. Wisdom says, "Come and eat of my bread. Drink the wine I have prepared."

[The celebrant cuts herself or himself free from the fabric, goes to the table and partakes of the bread and wine, and then hands the knife to the next person. Since everyone is tied to the now stationary fabric, all will need to cut themselves free to take the bread and the wine.]

READER: And they cut me down. When I died, the fabric was rent from top to bottom and the earth opened up and swallowed me.

CELEBRANT: As you go from here to walk on the earth that has received her, honor the fabric of life so that you may dwell again in the shadow of her branches.

❧ A Sermon on a Tragic Death[9]

The following sermon was preached at the funeral of a thirty-year-old woman who had been brutally raped and murdered named Ruth Laughlin. Ruth was a participant in the church where her funeral took place but was not a member there.

This sermon does not make specific reference to Sophia. It does draw deeply from the Sophia spirituality that existed in the congregation where it was preached. It serves, likewise, as an illustration of the presence of Sophia in all things. The biblical texts for the sermon were Deuteronomy 31:1–13 and Luke 24:13–32.

At first glance, it seems that we should be holding up words from the book of Lamentations today, not the words of Moses to Joshua. Ruth's death has torn us apart. It was too soon, much too soon, for her to die. It was an ugly, violent act that took her away from us—an act that we cannot, nor should, accept. Ruth has been torn from us, torn out of the fabric of our lives, and the event has left us raw and bleeding.

So how can Deuteronomy have anything to say? It depicts such a different situation: Moses, an old man at the end of a long life, dying, giving his farewell to Israel, especially to Joshua, who is ready to take over his leadership, who is actually to enter and settle the Promised Land.

Ruth had no chance to say anything to any of us, and none of us had an opportunity to say farewell to her. There was no occasion for her to pass the torch on to us. Yet, here we are, gathered today like the people of Israel, gathered because of the importance of Ruth's life among us. And I am certain that the whole of her living and dying witnesses to what she passes on to us. Ruth, in her life and in her death, has indeed made a pact with us, the living, to carry on some important things for her.

I name just a few.

Ruth has made a pact with us to work for justice, to be about that which promotes life in all its fullness for all beings. Ruth's entire life has had justice—political and economic justice, especially—as its theme. We, too, must live to make this a more just world, a world in which all people can live together as true equals. And Ruth's death holds up for us the glaring inequality between men and women—that we live in a time in which women can be and still are victimized by men. Her death cries out to us to not rest before women have achieved true equality, and we need to begin with our own lives.

Ruth has made a pact with us to love people and to trust people and enjoy people who are different from us. This is a hard pact for us to come to terms with, I think, because her death has made us so afraid, so suspicious. But her life stands squarely against that. Ruth was always getting to know strange new people from different backgrounds: different countries, different races, different educational and economic levels. She delighted in the sheer variety that people brought into her life. And she passes on to us the challenge to open our lives up to new people, to experience God's world in all its magnificent variety. She challenges us to grow and to welcome more of God's world.

And Ruth has made another pact with us—to enjoy life more. She was a woman who enjoyed a good time. She loved parties. She loved drinking and dancing and singing and biking and walking and playing basketball and holding people. And she was just beginning to relax and make that enjoyment not just a sidelight but a central part of her life. Her untimely death calls out to us to savor special moments as precious gifts, to enjoy the good things God has given us, and to be aware of and delight in ordinary things.

And Ruth has made one more pact with us, a two-edged pact. Ruth was generous with her time and her possessions; she loaned money and her belongings with incredible ease. What she had, who she was, was available to be shared with others. She listened to people and helped people out, often denying her own needs to do it. Only recently, Ruth had begun to discover that she deserved similar consideration from others, that not only could she spend hours listening to other people, but that she also deserved to be listened to. And she was just beginning, just beginning to ask for consideration and respect for herself. The pact that Ruth calls us to here is different, depending on what kind of person we are. Those of us who are used to taking, to being taken care of, need to practice giving, and being considerate of others' needs; we need to grow in our generosity. Those of us who are usually the ones who give need to consider the importance of asking for time and consideration from others. We need to grow in our self-respect.

These are several of the pacts that Ruth, in her living and dying, has made with those of us who continue after her. And we continue on not alone, not cut off, from Ruth's presence. She is still with us, and she will continue to be with us, reminding us of and calling us to the pacts she has made with us.

Just as Jesus' followers experienced his presence with them on the road to Emmaus, in the moment of eating together, so too, Ruth will be present to us in an incredible variety of ways. For the spirit that was present in Jesus is the same spirit that was present when the world began, and is the same spirit that was present in Ruth and in all of the world around us. That spirit that enlivened Ruth has not gone from us, but is with us still.

Certainly, we won't be able to talk with Ruth anymore. We won't be able to laugh and cry with her anymore. And we can't reach out and hold her anymore. But we need not fear being disconnected—cut off totally— from her. For the spirit that gave her life and vitality is the same spirit that fills this whole world with life, and we can't be cut off from that.

The only way we can cut ourselves off from Ruth's presence is not to listen, not to see, not to touch. Her presence is all around us. She is present in the songs people sing, in the singing this morning. She is present in the flutter of the birds by the side of the road in Iowa. She is present in the touch of the wind. She is present in the gathering of people demonstrating for justice. She is present in conversation between friends. She is present in the eyes of a stranger. She is present in the beat of dance music. She is present in the swish of the basketball through the hoop. Listen, look, embrace the world around us. And we'll find her there to greet us, to chide us, to encourage us.

Ruth has made a pact with us, and she is present, through the spirit that enlivens the whole world, to us. Our challenge is to live up to the pact she's made with us, and to open ourselves up to her presence with us. It won't be easy, but it will be worth the effort. We need to help each other to keep faith with Ruth, to stay open to her continuing presence with us, and to ask God's help as well.

CHAPTER NINE

Jesus and Sophia

Jesus and Sophia came to be associated through a process that took place during the first two centuries of our era. The apostle Paul said it clearly: "We are preaching a crucified Christ . . . who is the Wisdom of God" (1 Corinthians 1:23; see also 1 Corinthians 2:6–8). Others, the author of John 1:1–18, for example, describe Sophia clearly but only imply that the person they are describing is Jesus. Elsewhere, such as in the Gospels of Matthew, Luke, and Thomas, Jesus speaks the words of Sophia as if he were Sophia. Yet others, among them the authors of Ephesians, Colossians, and James, depend heavily on their readers' knowledge of Sophia in communicating who they thought Jesus really was. Finally, the literature that came to be called gnostic includes a wide range of stories in which Jesus and Sophia exchange roles in a variety of earthly settings. See *Sophia:*, chapter 3, for a fuller discussion of Sophia and Jesus.

The material in this chapter comprises worship services, meditations, and participatory Bible studies that help people to take part in this identification of Jesus with Sophia. They were developed in response to needs and interests expressed by several different groups. Some people— many but not all of them women—who were alienated from certain aspects of the Jesus tradition and Christianity have reported that these activities are especially effective in helping to reconnect them with those traditions.

The exercises that place Sophia in traditional Jesus stories have been particularly evocative for these individuals. Since the interest in these Sophia-in-Jesus stories or exercises is still strong after six years of experimentation with them, we believe that they will continue to offer many fertile possibilities for development and exploration. In many New Testament stories not included in this volume, Sophia can appropriately be substituted for Jesus. Experience leads us to believe that these stories will lend themselves to a wide range of activities contributing to the spiritual growth of group members. Furthermore, the vast majority of participants show great openness and responsiveness to working with the stories. For some individuals, in fact, Sophia-in-Jesus stories have been the vehicle whereby their interest in the Bible has been renewed, and they have become involved once again in a Christian congregation.

The rationale for these stories in which Sophia is substituted for Jesus has become increasingly clear as our research has proceeded. Since the early portraits of Jesus, including those in the New Testament, made such extensive use of Sophia's characteristics, it is both justified and in the spirit of that early process to put Sophia into the now much more familiar Jesus stories as well.

The materials in this chapter do not respond exclusively to the needs and interests of those who have been alienated from the Jesus tradition, however. Others—again primarily but not exclusively women—whose ties to the Jesus story and to the church remain strong find the association of Jesus and Sophia deeply enriching. For them, experiencing Jesus as Sophia both in Bible study and in worship events described below has provided opportunity for support and identification over and above the primarily positive experience of Jesus they have enjoyed in the past. Sometimes for these women Sophia's entrance into the world of Jesus does bring to their attention the marginalization they had been experiencing in the church. But often, this marginalization was not for them connected to Jesus; quite the contrary, it was their strong relationship with Jesus that had enabled them to endure it. For these individuals, Sophia's emergence becomes at least enriching and often genuinely supportive.

Sophia's role within the Christian eucharistic tradition requires some additional consideration. This chapter includes a Sophia eucharist in which some of the words of Sophia are specifically related to the New Testament words of Jesus. See "Come Unto Me," 154 to 155. Several related eucharistic services can be found elsewhere in this volume. See 96 to 99, 137 to 139, 162 to 168, and 172 to 175. This and other Sophia eucharists are the result of concerted efforts on our part to integrate Sophia into the meal of Jesus, efforts that have resulted in the development of four different eucharistic forms, some more closely resembling a traditional Christian eucharist than others, and each having its own limits and possibilities.

The eucharistic service found in this chapter and a second service in chapter 8 (pages 137 to 139) place Jesus material and Sophia material side by side, and in many cases these will be the most appropriate services for use in congregational settings. In these, Sophia does not replace Jesus at the meal but stands beside him with her own words. It has been our experience that of these two, the one best received in conventional church settings is the one found here, which keeps Jesus' words of consecration intact and adds Sophia's words and Colossians 1:15–20 as a way of merging Jesus with Sophia. This eucharist can serve as a model for developing a eucharistic prayer of thanksgiving or litany within a regular Christian worship service.

Two other services which we have included—see 96 to 99 and 172 to 175—are most appropriate for groups: women's groups, retreat groups, or specialized church groups, not for meetings in a traditional Sunday morning congregational or parish setting. The service in chapter 6 does not explicitly refer to Jesus at all, but uses only Sophia texts along with several New Testament passages which refer to Sophia and Jesus both. In and of itself this is probably the strongest of our four eucharists. It is highly participatory and evocative. Also, by virtue of the symbols and New Testament texts that it uses, it falls clearly within the larger Christian eucharistic tradition, and as such carries special momentum. But because it includes no specific reference to Jesus, it runs the risk of confusing or offending those who may be expecting to participate in a traditional Christian eucharist, even members of fairly open-minded Christian communities.

The fourth service—see 172 to 175—has proven to be particularly popular with women's groups and specialized Sophia study groups, and to be particularly problematic for regular parish congregations. In this service, Sophia actively replaces Jesus at several points. The intention here is not to deny Jesus' presence but to underline Sophia's legitimate claim to share the Jesus story and meal. This is a strong celebration of the Jesus-Sophia connection, in the spirit of the Jesus-as-Sophia Bible study material introduced previously. It can be used with the above—mentioned groups, those more or less alienated from the Jesus tradition, and those who feel marginalized yet nonetheless have some positive association with the Christian tradition. Both have used this service with much appreciation, especially as part of a course or retreat. However, this service can create resentment and confusion among those who value the traditional eucharist while remaining unfamiliar with the Sophia connection.

A fifth liturgy, "A Wisdom Eucharist," 162 to 168, places Sophia clearly in a formal eucharistic setting. This eucharist, written by an Episcopal priest, can be used in regular worship services as well as special women's gatherings.

Another set of worship materials important in the process of associating Sophia with Jesus are the Sophia passion celebrations. During our earlier investigations of Sophia it became clear, given the theological importance of the question of suffering, that Sophia's apparent dissociation from suffering poses a real problem. How can a figure apparently almost always proud, powerful, and in control function as a central symbol within Christian spirituality? In response, we have designed two different passion celebrations in which Sophia takes the place of Jesus as protagonist. Our hypothesis was that inserting Sophia into these celebrations of the crucifixion and resurrection would give us a better sense of what suffering might mean in relationship to her. We offer them in that spirit. See "A Sophia Passion," 116 to 122, and "A Good Friday Liturgy," 139 to 143.

Finally, a number of the participatory studies in this chapter serve the straightforward pedagogical function of helping members of a group or congregation to grasp the legitimacy of associating Sophia with Jesus by means of the biblical texts. These Bible studies include "Jesus Walking on the Water" (see 152 to 154), "Words of Wisdom" (see 155 to 157). Each of these studies demonstrates how close the Jesus and Sophia texts are to one another. They also help to establish the chronological priority of the Sophia material.

We turn now to the materials themselves, in the general order in which they have been discussed.

🕮 Deep Water: A Sermon

This sermon is based on Luke 5:1–11.

It had been a long, hard, disappointing night for Peter and the other fishermen. They'd been out on the water all night long, with nothing to show for it. No luck at all—not one fish as a result of their efforts. And while they were cleaning off their nets, getting ready for a well-deserved rest, Jesus came along, followed by a crowd of people. He borrowed a boat, asking Peter to take him out onto the lake where he could teach the people. Then, out of the blue, at the absolutely wrong time of day, with the night's work completed, Jesus told Peter to head out to deep water and to put out the fishing nets once more, to go ahead and try one more time.

And Peter's reaction? "But we've been doing this, all night long, and we didn't catch a thing! We're tired, and besides, this is the wrong time to start in again."

Don't we often feel like that? Aren't we often in the situation of being asked to do—again—for what seems like the thousandth time—something that already, before we do it, feels doomed to failure? There are so many different ways we've experienced that:

The thought of writing yet another proposal, when the twenty or thirty that have already been written have raised no money.

The need to make yet another call about a job possibility when so many previous calls have been futile.

The necessity of trying one more time to make contact in a relationship where old hurts and hostilities have built up walls that seem impossible to tear down.

Our lives are full of situations in which it seems that we are on a treadmill; there are things to be done, again and again, but the doing doesn't seem to make any difference.

As a matter of fact, lately it's seemed as though the treadmill has begun to move backward, and we need to double our energy just to stay in the same place. There's an uncomfortable feeling that we've been here before, in a situation we thought would never happen again.

Who would have thought, ten years ago, that in the 1980s we'd be back to soup kitchens? After the social reforms of the New Deal and all of the social programs from the War on Poverty, all designed to guarantee that everyone would at least have enough to eat, adequate shelter, and a modicum of health care—after all that, we're back to soup kitchens!

And look at the political scene of this city! How many times have we thought that we'd seen the end of Frank Rizzo? [Frank Rizzo was mayor of Philadelphia in the 1970s for two terms, sought a third term through a city charter change, lost, and ran for mayor again four years later.] How many times have we worked to end his political life, through the recall petitions and the fight against the charter change—and yet, here we are again, in the middle of a primary where the new Rizzo is running for his old office.

It feels as though we've gone through a time warp, and we're repeating the thirties and seventies simultaneously! I don't know about you, but I get tired thinking about going through the seventies again, and those of you who lived through the thirties must really get tired thinking of going through all that again!

So, here we are, a lot like Peter, tired from having been through it all too many times before, in too many areas of our lives, and Jesus is in the boat saying, "Push on out into deep water—lower that net one more time. Keep on with those proposals—keep on looking for that job—keep on working at that relationship—keep on working for justice in this city—*Keep on!*"

But let's be careful, lest we settle for too little in this story. At this point, it would be easy for this story to become little more than the recent Avis commercial: Avis started out as number two with the slogan "we try harder" then moved on up to "we're number one!"

Too often, this story has been used like the Avis commercial: if you just keep trying, you'll get a great reward. You may, but that's not the main point here. This story has become hackneyed, dulled by overuse and wrong use, to the point that when I sat down to think about this text, the familiarity of it all kept me from hearing it in a new way. Does that ever happen to you? It's as though all the old Sunday school images and slogans shut down my mind and imagination and rob me of the chance for the text to challenge me anew.

So I decided to change the story a bit, to look at it from a different perspective. And, since during my study leave I'd been working on Sophia (better known as Wisdom to many of us), it was through Sophia that I encountered this story freshly.

Jesus, in the early church, was identified with the Old Testament personage of Wisdom. He was sometimes called Wisdom (or Sophia, which is Greek for wisdom).

So I tried something wild, just to jog me free of old stereotypical ways of looking at this passage: I put Sophia into that boat with Peter. I thought she could take Jesus' place, and I could experience the story with just a change of character.

But it didn't turn out that simply. As hard as I tried in my imagination to put Sophia into the boat, she wouldn't stay there. She was the character who urged Peter on into deep water, to be sure, but there was more. She became the boat itself, and then she was the water out of which Peter pulled his miraculous catch. The story was full of her; her presence dominated everything else.

What that little imaginative exercise did for me was to get past all of the Sunday school teachings about this story as miraculous reward and see instead, anew, the mystery of *God's presence.*

That load of fish wasn't a reward for trying harder; it was a sign—a big, flashing neon sign—pointing to the presence of God everywhere in that story. Everywhere! Not just in the boat, not just with the fish—everywhere! God's presence fills the story, God's presence is in every aspect of it, God's presence is unavoidable. That's why Peter is filled with shame at the end and says, "Leave me, Lord, I am a sinful man." That load of fish had said what everything else around him had already been saying: he was in God's presence, and that presence is awesome.

It was that *presence* that urged Peter out into deep water—water that is at once the threat of death and the promise of life.

That presence is always pushing us out into deep water, urging us to risk, to go beyond what we've known into unknown territory.

So the call comes to try again, to try again and risk failure yet again, to take a new, bold step that carries with it the possibility of changing everything and no guarantee that the change will be better.

And the call comes from one who died in the risking.

I think of Fannie Lou Hamer, a worker in the cotton fields of Mississippi, who in the sixties said, "I'm sick and tired of being sick and tired." And she began trying to register to vote, at a time when what was supposed to be a right was barred from most black people through a complicated literacy test. Every week she arrived at the courthouse to take that test—week in, week out—and with every week the stakes got higher. She lost her job, her home was attacked, she was almost shot. And she kept on coming back to take that test just one more time. And every time, the water got just a little deeper.

And the call still came, "Put out into deep water."

Well, Fannie Lou Hamer finally did pass that test, and she finally did vote, and she enabled other black people to vote and to challenge the heavy hand of white oppression in Mississippi.

Her story doesn't end there. She kept on taking new risks, venturing into even deeper water in the cause of justice. And she was jailed, she was brutally beaten, she was almost killed.

Fannie Lou Hamer's life was a sign of God's presence in the risking itself. Her story could have ended differently; many others have. She could have been killed before she got that vote. There may not have been any reward at all for her constant trying. It would make no difference. That's not the point. God's presence filled her life. In every walk up those courthouse steps, God was present, regardless of the outcome inside.

So God is present with us, God is in our boat, urging each of us to take the step that feels so dangerous, that is full of risk, that is full of the possibility of failure. God is urging us out into deep water.

There's no guarantee of safety, no surefire way to assure our success. We may end up in disaster. But the one who is in our boat urging us out further into the water is in the water as well. In success or disaster, God is there.

Our hope and our assurance are in the One who was with the Hebrews, the One who took them out of Egypt and led them through the sea and was with them in their wanderings—who was with them in their fear and in their triumph, in good times and bad.

Our hope and our assurance are in the One who risked everything, even death—death on a cross—and in dying was victorious against all the powers that rule by fear. That One is with us in the boat and, if the boat capsizes, is with us in the water. That One is with us always. We are not alone. Thanks be to God.[1]

ⵥ Sophia Walking on the Water: A Bible Study

This study is best done with groups who have already been introduced to Sophia (see chapter 6, "Getting Acquainted with Sophia"). It is also advisable that the group be acquainted in some way with the connection between the Jesus and Sophia traditions (see chapter 3).

"Sophia Walking on the Water" has been conducted effectively in both weekend retreat and course settings. It is one of the most widely known of the Jesus-Sophia studies, and we find that it serves well in a number of different curricular contexts as the central illustration of the identification between Jesus and Sophia.

On the other hand, this study can stand alone, provided that the members of the convened group have been thoroughly exposed to the figure of Sophia.

There does not seem to be any particular need for groups using this study to be groups of women only; mixed groups have used it successfully as well. For the role play's maximum effectiveness, however, it is important that Sophia be played by a woman.

Materials Needed: Paper and pen or pencil for each participant, copies of scripture adaptation for all.
Opening Exercise: The group is asked to read the following story. All members of the group have a copy of the story and read it silently to themselves.

Scripture Reading: An adaptation of Matthew 14:22–33:

> Directly after this she made her followers get into the boat and go on ahead to the other side while she would send the crowds away. After sending the crowds away she went up into the hills by herself to pray. When evening came, she was there alone, while the boat, by now far out on the lake, was battling with a heavy sea, for there was a head wind. In the fourth watch of the night she went toward them, walking on the lake, and when her followers saw her walking on the lake they were terrified. "It is a ghost," they said, and cried out in fear. But at once Sophia called out to them, saying, "Courage: It is I! Do not be afraid." One of them answered, "Lady, if it is you, tell me to come to you across the water." "Come," Sophia said. Then the one who had spoken got out of the boat and started walking toward Sophia across the water, but as soon as she felt the force of the wind, she took fright and began to sink. "Lady! Save me!" she cried. Sophia put out her hand at once and held her. "Woman of little faith," she said, "why did you doubt?" And as they got into the boat the wind dropped. Those in the boat bowed down before her and said, "Truly, you are the Wisdom of God."

Ask the group for initial responses to the story as it has been read. Allow time for everyone who wants to respond. The leader may give some clarifying answers about how the story is written. But at this juncture the leader should avoid justifying the way the story is retold. The objective here is to give people a chance to share their initial reactions. This should take no more than ten minutes.

Role Play: Ask for volunteers who are willing to role play the story for the rest of the group. The role play includes a minimum of four roles: Sophia, the follower who tries to walk on the water, and two other followers. There may be several other followers, if you have a number of eager volunteers. Someone may also play the role of the storm, the wind, and/or the water if they suggest it themselves. Have the role players present all of the passage in dramatic fashion to the rest of the group.

After the role play, allow time for those who took part to reflect on what it felt like for them, so that they can reenter the group as themselves.

Questions: Ask the whole group to discuss the following questions:

- Who are these people in the boat? What kind of people are Sophia's disciples?
- When they were out in the boat in the middle of the storm, what do you think they were feeling? Have you ever been in a boat in a storm? What was it like?
- What was it about seeing Sophia that frightened them so?
- What is the relationship between Sophia and the water? The wind?
- What does helping a follower to walk on the water demonstrate about Sophia's identity?
- If you were in the boat, watching all of this, how would you be feeling?
- What would you understand about Sophia? What would it mean for you?

- What might make you want to join her out there on the water?
- What would following her be like? What would be the dangers? What might make you sink? What would you need to be able to go ahead and follow her?

Closing Exercise:

> Put yourself in the boat. Sophia calls you to follow on the water. Write a dialogue between you and her. Argue with her, say what you need to say, hear what she has to say to you. But follow the story through. Go ahead and follow her and finish the story, as it happens to you. Reflect on what emerges.

Participants should be given about ten minutes to put themselves in the story and write their dialogue.

Call the group back together. Ask each individual to present either their imaginary scene of Sophia calling from the water or their written dialogue with her or both. Reassure them that if the material is too personal, they may withhold what they have seen or written. Allow enough time for all who wish to give their results. Do not be bothered by some silence between reports.

❧ Come Unto Me: A Eucharistic Prayer Based on Matthew 11

The eleventh chapter of Matthew contains a series of sayings that illustrate the relationship between Jesus and Sophia. The following responsive prayer juxtaposes some of these sayings with explicit Sophia passages from Ecclesiasticus for use in a communion service. It is meant as a prayer of consecration of the elements. It can also be used as a preparatory prayer for the eucharist without reference to the consecration of the elements. See 96 to 99, 137 to 139, 162 to 168, and 172 to 175 for other eucharist-related material.

LEADER:	Wisdom has built herself a house, she has hewn her seven pillars, she has slaughtered her beasts, drawn her wine.
PEOPLE:	She has laid her table. She has despatched her maidservants and proclaimed from the heights above the city
LEADER:	Come and eat of my bread,
PEOPLE:	Drink the wine which I have drawn for you. (Proverbs 9:1–3, 5)
LEADER:	Jesus said, "The Son of Man came, eating and drinking, and they say, 'Look a glutton and a drunkard, a friend of tax collectors and

	sinners.' Yet Wisdom is justified by her deeds."
	(Matthew 11:19)
PEOPLE:	For Wisdom is true to her name.
	Put your feet unto her fetters,
	and your neck into her collar;
	Offer your shoulder to her burden,
	do not be impatient of her bonds.
LEADER:	Court her with all your soul,
	and with all your might keep in her ways;
	search for her, track her down: she will reveal
	herself; once you hold her, do not let her go.
PEOPLE:	For in the end you will find rest in her
	and she will take the form of joy for you:
	her fetters you will find a mighty defense.
	Her yoke will be a golden ornament.
	(Ecclesiasticus 6:22a, 23–30)

LEADER: [breaking bread] Jesus said, "Come unto me, all you who labor and are overburdened, and I will give you rest. Shoulder my yoke and learn from me, for I am gentle and humble in heart, and you will find rest for your souls.

PEOPLE: "Yes, my yoke is easy and my burden is light."
(Matthew 11:28, 29)

LEADER: [taking the cup] Her bonds will be purple ribbons; you will wear her like a robe of honor, you will put her on like a crown of joy. (Ecclesiasticus 6:30, 31)

PEOPLE: Yes, Wisdom is justified by her deeds. (Matthew 11:19)

🐦 Words of Wisdom: A Bible Study

This Bible study is designed especially to help groups understand the relationship between passages about Sophia in the Hebrew scriptures and passages about Jesus in the Christian scriptures. It assumes some basic knowledge about Sophia. This study can be a helpful preparation for studies in which the connection between Sophia and Jesus is assumed (for example, the preceding study of Sophia walking on the water).

Materials Needed: Two spools of ribbon, scripture, paper and pen or pencil for each participant.

Opening Exercise: The leader asks group members to cut two strands of ribbon for themselves. Participants are then instructed to tie one of the ribbons to some part of their body or to their clothing.

Make a bracelet or a necklace for yourself with the ribbon. Or tie it to any part of your clothes or body you wish.

The leader also asks the members of the group to tie the second strand of ribbon to some other person or object in the room.

Scripture Reading: All read Ecclesiasticus 6:22–30 to themselves.

Questions: The leader asks the group the following questions:

- What is the reader/hearer of this passage asked to do?

- How does Sophia seem in this passage? Does she appear strict in some ways? Are there aspects of her that seem relaxed?

- Name several dimensions of the proposed relationship between Sophia and the reader/hearer.

- How would you characterize this relationship?

- Are you used to relationships like this one?

- Do you identify more with Sophia or with the reader/hearer in this relationship?

- How would you like to be in this relationship? In whose place?

Exercise: The leader asks the group to place themselves in the role of Sophia in this passage.

Notice how she would feel about the person who is to seek her. Think of what she would say to her or him. In other words, rewrite the passage in the first person as spoken by Sophia. Follow the basic description of the relationship. But you may want to add some words that you would speak if you were Sophia. Or you may want to leave out some of the relational aspects that are not attractive to you or that you would have a difficult time speaking.

Ask each person to find a partner, and then have them read what they have written to each other.

Scripture Reading: The leader asks the group to remain in pairs, and each person reads to their partner Matthew 11:28–30.

Questions: Everyone remains in pairs, and the leader asks each pair to discuss the following questions for about five minutes:

- How do the words of Jesus and Sophia compare?

- Does it make a difference to you whether Jesus or Sophia is speaking these words?

- What similarities and differences do you notice in your hearing of these words from Sophia and Jesus?

- What similarities and differences do you notice when you speak the words of Jesus and when you speak the words of Sophia?

Closing Exercise: Have each person write a response to one of the invitations, either the one she or he has written for Sophia or the one read by her or his partner or the one in Matthew 11:28–30.

> Write down what your answer to the invitation from Sophia and/or Jesus would be.

Allow five minutes for the writing of this response. Then call the group back together. Proceed around the circle, giving each person the opportunity to read what she or he has written. Before beginning the circle, announce that those who do not wish to read their response may simply hold up the ribbon.

CHAPTER TEN

A Sophia Miscellany

Unlike the resources in other chapters, the material in this chapter is not unified under one theme. Rather, it is a sampling of a wide array of material developed over the past decade by persons working with Sophia.

The prayers, songs, liturgies, rituals, sermon, and meditation in this chapter are similar to the materials in the rest of this book in another respect, however. All of them have emerged organically from the personal experience of individuals who have chosen to engage with Sophia. They are works of spirituality, devotions and explorations, rather than units in a designed program of pedagogy.

Much of the material in this chapter can be used to good advantage in worship or ritual settings, although some of it is likewise appropriate for other occasions—the beginning or ending of a class or study group, for example. Some of the liturgical and ritual presentations can be used in regular Sunday church settings, but some are also intended for daily or holiday use, and some are best used only with groups intensely involved with Sophia. One unit is the outcome of a series of meditations on Sophia texts.

The chapter concludes with a brief collection of songs about Sophia. These songs vary in musical style, ranging from chant and traditional hymnody to jazz. Only one of them is familiar enough to be used by a group without rehearsal; the others require at least a short preparation. Because "Fairest Sophia" is familiar to many, however—it's a slight adaptation of the popular hymn "Fairest Lord Jesus"—using it can offend people who do not know Sophia well. For this reason we recommend using "Fairest Sophia" in various noncongregational settings—study sessions, retreats, and women's groups.

The devotional and liturgical materials in this chapter lend added richness to *Wisdom's Feast* in another regard. A number of the following pieces were written by persons other than the authors, introducing a variety of theological and personal perspectives.

🕸 Glorying in Ourselves: A Sermon

This sermon was first preached on the Sunday following Christmas in 1986. It involves considerable interaction with the congregation: asking questions, waiting for responses, inviting the congregation to visualize possibilities, and so forth. We have preserved those questions in the printed text. Readers are invited to put themselves in the place of a listener, in a community that they are part of, and answer the questions for themselves. The sermon is based on Ecclesiasticus 24:1–12. (See Appendix)

Here is Sophia, the Wisdom of God, in the company of the heavenly host. And right in the midst of this grand array of the cherubim and seraphim and angels and archangels and God himself, she sings a song—in praise of herself! No shy one here, Sophia loves to tell about herself. I picture her here almost like a little child, very pleased with herself, smiling, dancing a bit, showing off.

So, here she is, in this august gathering of the heavenly host, telling her story: Her throne was in the heavens, this divine person, and from her home in the heavens, she ventures forth to wander all through creation, looking for a place to settle.

Can you imagine what it would be like on her wanderings? What all she'd see? Let's go with her, and see what it would be like. Here she is, Wisdom herself, the one who helped create all that is, wandering through it all, having a great time. Of course she'd have a great time—after all, this is the One who loves to glory in herself—certainly she'd feel the same about what she helped create!

She begins her wanderings in the heavens, perhaps skipping from cloud to cloud, stopping to admire the burst of color in a sunset: "The pink and gold on that cloud is exquisite; fine work." Or, on her way through space, she might pause to enjoy a particularly fine star in some distant galaxy.

So she wanders, making her way down into the depths of the sea, enjoying the energy of volcanic eruptions, watching islands come into being. And then a little mountain climbing on the mountains under the sea. Perhaps she stops for a bit to play tag with the dolphins.

Then she might spend some time wandering about the land. I think she must have great fun watching the mudpots in Yellowstone, and she certainly would take a lot of pride in the Grand Canyon.

Finally, after taking so much delight in her travels, she decides to settle down, to make a home for herself on the earth—no longer in the heavens. And the place she chooses is Jerusalem.

This is an amazing twist to the story. Here is Sophia, Wisdom, the one who was with God helping to create the entire universe at the beginning—here's this One, who could have her home anywhere, and whose authority is over everything, choosing to pitch her tent among human beings, people like us, right in the middle of the city.

She, who orders the affairs of the universe, has come to the city to live, she has come to the city to rest, and she has settled in and put down roots. The Divine One has come to live among humanity.

And I can't help thinking that if she enjoyed the rest of creation so much, she'd find a lot in the city to enjoy as well. If she were settling down here in Philadelphia, what do you think she'd take delight in? What would she enjoy? Hoagies? Water ice? The Schuylkill River? South Street? What are some of the things here she'd love? [At this point in the sermon, the congregation named things that Sophia would delight in; name for yourself those things where you live that Sophia would enjoy.]

And here in this neighborhood, in West Philadelphia, what is here that would please her? What in West Philly High would make her smile? What would she find in the streets to make her laugh? On the trolleys? If she wandered over to 50th and Baltimore, what would make her proud at the Credit Union? [This is a community credit union, begun by the church in a neighborhood where the banks had been systematically refusing to grant loans to neighbors.] Name some things about this neighborhood that she'd be pleased with. [The congregation named a variety of things; name for yourself things about your neighborhood that Sophia would be pleased with.]

And what about here at the church—what would she enjoy about *us*? [At this point, the congregation was invited to respond; name for yourself things that Sophia would enjoy about a community that you belong to.]

And what would she enjoy about *you*? Let's take a moment, each of us, to notice who we are as individuals. So close your eyes and imagine yourself standing in front of a mirror. Notice yourself with Sophia's awareness: Who are you? What do you look like? How do you sound? What would Sophia enjoy about you? Look at yourself with Sophia's eyes; *enjoy* what you find. Notice, as if for the first time, how your leg feels when you swing it, how your arms feel when you move them. Move your head; move your shoulders. Take a good look in that mirror again, and be like a little child. Imagine yourself having a wonderful time in front of that mirror. Try on a few different faces; move your body in new ways. Notice how wonderful you are, and spend a moment just enjoying yourself. [The leader paused for a few moments of silence for personal reflection. Take a moment yourself for reflection.]

Now open your eyes, and come back here to this room. Find someone else in the room, and when you're together, tell them one thing that Sophia would enjoy about you—just one thing; share with each other. When you've each had a chance to do that, name one thing about the person you're with that you think Sophia would enjoy. [Several minutes were allowed for milling about, choosing partners, and talking together. Think for yourself what Sophia would enjoy about you, and notice what Sophia would enjoy in someone else you'd choose.]

Come on back to your seats, and let's notice how it feels to glory in ourselves in this way. We're all being a bit silly, aren't we? It's all a little childish to act this way, to enjoy who we are, isn't it? I think that this is our own human response to divine silliness, to divine playfulness. This is part of our response to Sophia's delight in herself and in her creation.

Just think what she's done: She, who's been involved in creating the entire universe, who's helped make the stars and planets, the solar systems, the black holes, the atoms and the quasars—this same One in and through whom rivers and trees and mountains and deserts and oceans came into being—Sophia, who has a whole universe to delight in, has decided to make her home in the city, *here, among us.* She's decided to put down roots right here, with all of us.

Now isn't that silly? That the One who created the universe would come to live with us? Doesn't it remind you of the silliness of God's son being born in a stable? It's the same silliness—divinity come to live with humanity—trading in a throne in the heavens for life on Baltimore Avenue. It's divine foolishness; it's divine childishness.

What kind of response to make to such foolishness? What shall we do? I think that the most appropriate response to all of this divine silliness is to take it very seriously. Our response to Sophia's decision to move in with us, to a holy baby born in our midst, is to enjoy who we are and where we live, and to celebrate ourselves and our lives as richly and fully as possible.

And isn't some of the outlandishness of Christmas a way of celebrating and glorying in ourselves and in our world? Just a few blocks from my house, there is a huge old place that my children love to visit this time of year. It is covered with Christmas lights. Every line of the roof, every window, is outlined with lights; there are two American flags in lights, and Santa Claus as well. But that's not all; the yard is also lit up. Every tree is outlined in lights, every bush. Even edging around the flower gardens is outlined in lights. At first, looking at all of it, I was moralistic about the expense and the waste of electricity. But my children wouldn't let me stay that way; they loved it! They kept finding new delights to point out, and I found myself delighting in it right along with them. It was as though the lights celebrated, in blazing color, the wonder of creation. Every tree, every branch was glorious, was pointed out as something worth our noticing, as something worth delighting in.

In this kind of childish exuberance, we capture a sense of the playful joy of Sophia as she delights in herself and in us. It's in such childishness that we're able to grasp the wonder of a divine child come to live among us.

It takes childish wonder to celebrate an incredibly important thing: Sophia has come to live among us. God's son has been born among us. Heaven is making its home on earth, and *all that we do* and *all that we are* can never be ordinary or drab or dull again. Not if we take this divine silliness seriously.

So—we need to celebrate! We need to get out our brightest clothes, our shiniest jewelry. We need to find some great music, fix some delicious food, and have a party. And, when we find something or someone that Sophia would delight in, let's decorate them and leave that decoration as a sign of her presence. [At this point, glitter and tinsel were passed out, so that everyone could decorate themselves and one another.]

And let's enjoy ourselves, let's enjoy one another, let's enjoy this city and this world. It's Sophia's world, too—it's her city—and we are her people. She's glorying in us; let's glory along with her, let's delight along with her, let's enjoy along with her, and celebrate her presence among us.[1]

♄ A Wisdom Eucharist

This eucharistic service closely follows the order and rubrics of the Mass. It can be used without much formal introduction to Sophia because it contains so many of the Sophia texts. However, it is probably most appropriately used by groups who know something of her and want to salute the way she is represented in Scripture and tradition. This service was written by Alison Cheek, a priest of the Episcopal Church. For other eucharist-related materials, see 96 to 99, 137 to 139, 154 to 155, and 172 to 175.

Gathering and Greeting:

Greetings everyone. The liturgy today will be a little different from usual.

A liturgy is the work of the people gathered. So let us begin this liturgy today by gathering, by moving around a little and by beginning to make connections with at least one or two other people who are not well known to you. Of course, we have only a few minutes to start this now, but if we go about it with immediacy and try to be truly present to one another, connections can sometimes be made in a few seconds. So will you please move around and greet someone new to you or someone whom you would like to know better.

After three to four minutes, call the congregation back together.
Introduction:

In this service today I want to lift up part of our tradition that doesn't normally receive a lot of attention: the wisdom materials of our scriptures, the Sophia traditions. In the biblical passages that will be quoted I have used the transliteration of the Greek word for wisdom, Sophia, instead of the more customary translation, wisdom. The reason that I've done this is because Sophia has become for us a woman's name, and in the wisdom scriptures Sophia is a divine figure, a mythological person of feminine gender. Some New Testament thinking enfleshes her, incarnates her, in Jesus of Nazareth, so that it's possible to talk about Sophia-Jesus perhaps in somewhat the same way we talk about Lord Jesus.

I'd like to share with you some of my process in putting together this liturgy. It began with my concern for finding ways of worshiping that are enlivening and strengthening for women today. Many women feel either bored or deeply alienated by Christian worship because the language and imagery used in it undergirds a social structure that marginalizes us or makes us invisible.

At the same time, my growth in consciousness and gradual liberation from the power of oppressive structures has taken place within the church and has its roots in my Christian heritage. Many of the structures of the church, including its use of androcentric image and language, keep women in bondage, yet I do believe that there is a liberating impulse in Christianity and so I seek ways to express this liturgically.

This semester I have been studying Sophia in a New Testament class. She has come alive for me, and I discovered that in my Christian heritage there is a tradition that speaks of Israel's God in the idiom of the goddess. I found it was something to which I could relate and with which I could identify. It didn't force me to choose between God and Goddess, for Israel's God is One. It didn't necessitate dividing God up into parts—masculine and feminine—for Israel's God is One. It reminded me that we can approach the mystery of God only by analogy and metaphor. We do not really mean that God is male when we use masculine pronouns and imagery, and we do not really mean that God is female when we use feminine pronouns and imagery. Yet to address God we need images and pronouns. The use of exclusively *male* God language leads to the androcentric model of humanity that subordinates and oppresses women.

The only way that we can simultaneously retain the language of address and overcome the problems of exclusive male God language is by adopting female forms of address in addition to male forms.

And I found that we have a way to do this in our very tradition. Divine Sophia is Israel's God in the language and configuration of the goddess. Since in the New Testament Jesus becomes identified with Sophia, my first thought was to take some of the wisdom writings and place them in the pattern of eucharist with which we are familiar. I wrote such a liturgy, and my loyal Sophia work group from class went through it with me and gave their responses and tried to help me make the connections smooth and understandable. After that meeting Sophia got hold of me and began to give me a bad time. I got the distinct impression that she was going to refuse to be confined within my eucharistic pattern. Perhaps it's because she's a living, ongoing tradition. She was always seen as mobile and fluid. At any rate, I've changed my format a bit, and I invite you to experiment with me and see if it works for us or if it doesn't.

The call to worship is at the top of the page on your sheets.

Celebrant asks a member of the congregation to lead the call to worship.
Call to Worship:

> Sophia is radiant and unfading
> And easily is she beheld of them that love her
> And found of them that seek her . . .
> She goes about seeking those worthy of her
> And graciously she appears to them in their paths
> And meets them in every thought.

Prayer:

Loving, laughing Sophia, you know and understand everything. Guide us wisely in all that we do and guard us with your glory. Move among us and give us the courage to choose life amid death-dealing structures, and fill us with the knowledge of your power and gracious goodness, that we may be for each other wisdom and strength in the days to come. Amen.

Hymn:

Sophia is connected with creation, and so I've chosen a creation hymn for us to sing. The first two verses are a translation of a sixth-century Latin hymn, and the beginning of the second verse probably reflects the tradition of Sophia as agent of creation. I've interrupted the original hymn at the end of verse 2 and added a third verse.

Lucius Creator

O blest Creator of the light
Who mak'st the day with radiance bright,
And o'er the forming world didst call
The light from chaos first of all;

Whose wisdom joined in meet array
The morn and eye, and named them day:
Night comes with all its darkling fears;
Regard thy people's prayers and tears.

Creator, Wisdom, hark, we pray,
Be found of us now here today:
Dispel our woe, create anew
Our life together, joyful, true.[2]

Latin, sixth century, tr. John Mason Neale (altered)

Scripture Reading: Proverbs 8:27–31; Proverbs 1:20–23; Wisdom 7:22–28, 30–8:1.
Responsive Reading: Wisdom 10:1–4, 15–21.

In place of a psalm I've taken a reading from the Book of Wisdom in which the author is telling the sacred history of the Hebrew people as the story of Sophia's action in history. We will read it responsively as we sometimes do a psalm.

LEADER: Wisdom protected the first formed father of the world, when he alone had been created.

PEOPLE: She delivered him from his transgression, and gave him strength to rule all things.

LEADER: But when an unrighteous man departed from her into his anger, he perished because in rage he slew his brother.

LEADER: When the earth was flooded because of him, Sophia again saved it, steering the righteous by a paltry piece of wood.

PEOPLE: A holy people and a blameless race Sophia delivered from a nation of oppressors.

LEADER:	She entered the soul of a servant of the Lord, and withstood dread kings with wonders and signs.
PEOPLE:	She gave to holy men and women the reward of their labors; she guided them along a marvelous way.
LEADER:	She became to them a shelter by day, and a starry flame through the night.
PEOPLE:	But she drowned their enemies, and cast them up from the depths of the sea.
LEADER:	Therefore the righteous plundered the ungodly; they sang hymns, O Lord, to thy holy name, and praised with one accord thy defending hand,
PEOPLE:	Because Sophia opened the mouth of the dumb, and made the tongues of babes speak clearly.

Scripture Reading: Luke 15:3–6, 8–9.
Response:

Praise be to Sophia for these two stories.

Homily:

I want to keep this homily brief so that we can have time after the prayer of thanksgiving for all of us to reflect together. But a few words about how the Sophia tradition may be good news for us.

I'd like to suggest that the Sophia traditions are not just antiquarian and interesting, but alive and enlivening and open to reformulation. Over the years I've been interested in Sophia but had never taken the time and effort to find out much about her traditions. This semester I've just begun to interact with her, and if Sophia is "the breath of the power of God," as the Book of Wisdom says, engaging with her has been a breath of fresh air for me.

For most of us, thinking about God in the language and configuration of the goddess means a monumental shift. It entails overcoming deep conditioning, overcoming the internalization of the male as norm and the female as the other, of lesser value.

Once this internalization begins to be exorcised, however, I have found naming God Sophia and addressing God in feminine language to be extremely liberating and grounding, nourishing a spirituality in me that has been struggling for survival in an androcentric and patriarchal church and world.

I have found that Sophia touches a deep core in me, and I think I especially respond to her playfulness and humor. It is liberating to be able to identify with her and with her power.

I know some men who are engaged with the Sophia traditions. I have never asked any of them what that means for them personally. Some aspects of the Sophia tradition I find liberating, but certainly not all of it. While in Jewish-Hellenism Sophia was incorporated into the tradition in a way that preserved Jewish monotheism and resisted divine dimorphism—the myth of the divine couple—there wasn't the same success on the human plane. Wisdom writings certainly contain an anthropological dualism that is bad news for women, and we can find a very negative characterization of women in wisdom and apocalyptic writings.

So for Sophia's tradition to be a liberating one for us we need to engage in "reflective mythology," selecting those elements of her myth that help us reflect on our own theological concerns. That is exactly what the biblical writers did when they integrated elements of contemporary goddess cults into Jewish monotheism in the form of Sophia.

So the first way in which Sophia may be good news for us is if we can reflect on her tradition in ways that prove liberating. The second way in which Sophia may be good news is to examine what kind of a God is the Sophia-God we find revealed in the New Testament.

Patient, painstaking, technical scholarship in New Testament critical studies has revealed for us that the earliest strands of the traditions about Jesus understand him as Sophia's messenger, and later as Sophia herself. The Sophia-God of Jesus is revealed in the actions of Jesus who welcomes the poor, the cultically unclean, the outcast, the outsider into his movement and who heals, affirms, and offers table fellowship to all those who respond to his teachings and embrace the praxis of the *basileia*—the kingdom of God.

The nature of the Sophia-God of Jesus is made clear again and again in parables. The graciousness and goodness of God is inclusive. It establishes equality among all of us—women and men, righteous and sinner, rich and poor. The parables of the shepherd searching for the lost sheep and of the woman searching for her lost coin tell us that this is what God is like—like a woman searching, searching for her lost inheritance and not resting until she finds it.

That God searches tirelessly for us, lets the rain and sun fall on the just and unjust, accepts everyone, and is concerned for the well-being of all of us without exception is good news indeed. But the underside of it is that such thinking is threatening and dangerous. To live this praxis is to upset the established order. The prophets of Sophia are persecuted and killed in every generation. And Jesus is no exception.

Filled with the Spirit, the early church strove to carry on what Jesus began. And it met with resistance and persecution. If we take seriously this Sophia-God, the good news is that we will find dignity and integrity and identity, and even joy and laughter, in living out the vision of the *basileia*.

The bad news is that we will be abandoned by some and persecuted by others with consequences ranging from imprisonment and death to character assassination and isolation.

Yet it is the witness of many who do live the struggle to make concrete the gracious goodness of this God that, in the praxis, in revolutionary forgiveness and love, in "hoping against hope," the very life of God is found.

Amen.

I want now to pass the peace and then to invite you, as we sing the hymn, to cluster around the table for the thanksgiving prayer. I don't have in mind us stringing out in a circle, but coming in close—more of a mob scene.

The Peace:

The peace of our Sophia-God be always with you.
And also with you.

Hymn: See "Songs and Hymns," 180 to 187.
The Thanksgiving:

The earliest Christian liturgies were *agape* meals in house churches where the faithful broke bread together, shared food, and praised God, giving thanks for the resurrection of Jesus and for the ongoing spirit-filled life of the community. It is in the spirit of this tradition that I have written the thanksgiving prayer. I've tried to incorporate in it the prayers of the people, and there may be times when you will want to add your voice to the prayer. Please feel free.

May God be with you.

Let us pray.

Gracious Sophia, you ordered the universe, you came forth from the mouth of the Most High and covered the earth like mist. Alone you encircled the vault of the sky and walked on the bottom of the deeps. You deploy your strength from one end of the earth to the other, ordering all things for good. You moved among humanity through Israel's history. We give thanks to you that you dwell among us and make your ways known to us.

We bring before you all people in their daily life and work, and we pray especially for those we bear in our hearts today . . .

We live in your world, a nation, in communities, and we pray for all who work everywhere for justice and freedom and peace.

We thank you for the wonder and beauty of the world and accept our responsibility for the just and proper use of your creations.

We pray also for the forgiveness of our sins and for conversion to love and justice and right-relation. We pray for the church in its ministry and pray that we may uphold one another in proclaiming the gospel and in seeking the truth of it.

We bear with us the names of those who have died, your prophets and apostles and faithful followers in every generation. They are present.

We see your justice thwarted again and again in the death of your prophets. We remember your lament: "O Jerusalem, Jerusalem, you slay the prophets and stone those who are sent to you. How often have I wanted to gather your children as a mother bird collects her young under her wings; but you refused me."

We see you in our brother, Jesus. As death approached for him he ate and drank with his community, binding himself to them through bread and wine. "This is my body given for you," he said. We put our bodies on the line for one another, and we remember him. "This is my blood shed for you," he said.

We offer our lives in the service of justice, Sophia-God, and we remember you in him.

Death did not bind your child, Jesus, or end the witness to the *basileia* of God. For the women proclaimed his resurrection and gathered the scattered disciples, and we live on in your vision for humanity surrounded by a great cloud of witnesses. Our lives attest to your power and glory.

We share bread and wine as the sign of the *basileia,* and in you we are united to each other. We are fed and nourished by the memory of your passion and by bringing our heritage into the present. We look to the fulfillment of the *basileia* as we break bread together.

We who are many are one body, for we all share of the one bread.

This is the cup of blessing, life given and life received. May we who share these gifts be found in Christ-Sophia and she in us.

As the earliest disciples shared food and drink together in a meal, let us now feed each other with this bread and wine, food made holy by our thanksgiving for the resurrection of Jesus-Sophia and our life together in the Spirit.

Holy food for a whole people;
The bread of life;
The cup of blessing.

Prayer:

Sophia-God, we give you thanks for your gracious goodness to us all. You feed and strengthen us and bind us to each other and to Jesus-Sophia in the sharing of this holy meal. Send us forth renewed to be co-creators of the *basileia*. Through the indwelling of your Holy Spirit keep us in the paths of peace. Amen.

Reflection:

This is a time to share our responses to this liturgy. You may need to sit awhile before you can discern what kind of an experience it was for you.

Blessing:

May you call upon Sophia and find her in all your thoughts.
May her radiance enfold you and her laughter embolden you.
May she lead you in the paths of peace today and evermore.
Amen.

Hymn: See "Songs and Hymns," 180 to 187.

❧ Sophia's Disappearance and Reappearance: A Two-Part Ritual

Although these companion events were developed over a two-year period as a way to celebrate Sophia during Holy Week, they can be used at any time of the year. See 116 to 122, 139 to 143, for other Sophia Holy Week observances. This two-part ritual is a participation in the scriptures' persistent presentation of Sophia as one who appears, disappears, and reappears. The group that developed these events at first saw them as expressive of or parallel to the death and resurrection of Jesus. For some it has proven to be a helpful way of celebrating a female presence in the Easter story. For others it has become a creative substitute for the story of Jesus' death and resurrection. For others it has simply been a celebration of Sophia's absence and presence without much connection to Holy Week.

The two events need to be observed on different days. There should be a period of three to five days between the two observances. Persons should be encouraged to participate in both.

These events are for people who know who Sophia is. Neither of them includes sufficient introductory material about Sophia to make it possible for someone who does not know her to follow the sequence. These two rituals are especially appropriate for people who have developed a strong relationship to Sophia.[3]

Part 1: Sophia's Departure

This ritual is best done in a setting where the group can begin outside and proceed indoors. It can be done entirely indoors, however. The event's structure is that of a procession with stops at three different locations. Each successive location is more confined than the previous one. The ritual should be carried out in the evening.

Service Preparation: Everyone who comes to the ritual is asked to bring a small object that reminds them of Sophia. (The leader(s) of the ritual should provide a number of additional small objects in case some people forget.) We recommend small stones, ribbons, and pieces of yarn.

Those attending are also asked to come wearing one piece of festive garb that can be removed.

Part of the ritual involves one person playing the role of Sophia. This person is selected before the day of the ritual and should rehearse her part. This person should be physically strong and have a strong voice.

Three different locations need to be prepared. The first space should have a large fabric on which people can sit. On the fabric several plates of fruit and cheese should be set. The second space needing preparation is the small, undecorated room where the ritual ends. Here the assembled small items that can be carried in a pocket or purse are placed on a small plain table. There needs to be as many items as participants. The third space should be next to the outside door, where a collection of theological and hymn books representing the patriarchal articulations of Christianity and Judaism should be placed.

The leaders also compile a printed order of service.

Sophia's Departure

Introduction (outside)

Meditation (outside)

Praise to Sophia (short readings outside)

Statements of Thanksgiving of What We Will Miss (outside)

Process Inside

Insults and Accusations

Sophia Responds

Sophia Confined

Sophia's Departure

Reading

Process to Smallest Space

Keening and Silence

You may leave at any point in the keening and silence. You may take an object with you to remind you of Sophia. As you leave the house, you are encouraged to take one of the books at the door. They are patriarchal books of spirituality and theology. Wear the small object on your person during the coming days, and read from the book at least once a day. The small object is a reminder of Sophia, who has gone away. The book is a reminder of what life under patriarchy is like.

Introduction: Before the ritual actually begins, one of the leaders explains that this is a procession, identifying each of the three stopping places for the participants. The leader also collects the small objects brought by participants, bringing them to the final location of the procession. In that final location there should be at least as many small objects as persons in the group. The leader also distributes the outline of the order of the ritual.

The leader should go through the order of the ritual with brief explanations of the Thanksgivings, Insults and Accusations, and Keening. These explanations are found below at salient points in the description of the ritual.

Meditation: The ritual begins in silence. The group is seated on a large piece of fabric, preferably outdoors. Four or five candles are lit. A plate of sliced fruit and cheese is on the fabric and should be eaten in silence. The silence should last three to six minutes.

Praise to Sophia: The leader(s) read the following sentences slowly and with silence between each.

Praise to Sophia who comes to meet us in every thought.   (Wisdom 6:16)
Praise to the One who pervades and permeates all things.   (Wisdom 8:24)

Praise to Wisdom, who glories in herself in the midst of her people.
(Ecclesiasticus 24:1)
Praise to Sophia, who is at play everywhere in the world.   (Proverbs 8:31)
Praise to the One who raises her voice in the public squares. (Proverbs 1:20)
Praise to Wisdom, who deploys her strength from one end of the earth to the
other, ordering all things for good.   (Wisdom 8:1)
Praise to Sophia, who is the tree of life for those who hold her fast.
(Proverbs 3:18)

Thanksgivings: The group takes several minutes to contemplate either
what each person is thankful for at the time of the celebration or what each
person would miss if Sophia were to depart. It is preferred that people speak
their thanksgivings and what they would miss aloud. But this should not be
required of all participants. It is best if this portion is not announced.
Instead, the group spends a few moments in silence thinking about what
they appreciate, and then a leader speaks a sample sentence. If the leaders
feel that this procedure requires an explanation, this is best done earlier,
during the introduction above. This part of the ritual takes about five
minutes.

Process Inside: The leaders rise and lead the group inside in silence. If the
entire ritual is carried out indoors, this procession should move from a
larger room with candles and fabric to a smaller, more barren room. As
people enter the room, they take off their festive garb.

Insults and Accusations: Participants now speak insults and accusations
to Sophia. They are addressed to the person playing Sophia. These expressions should be as uncensored as possible. The insults and accusations may range from the personal (for example, "You didn't help me when
I needed you") to the more theoretical (for example, "I don't like your
arrogance"). Time is needed for individuals to think of their grievances,
both at the beginning of this part of the ritual and during it. If necessary, a
leader offers the first insult or accusation.

Sophia Responds: The person playing Sophia takes each person and
shakes them.

Sophia Confined: Two readers alternate reading the following sentences.
As they read they advance on Sophia until she is backed into a corner near
the door of the room.

READER 1:   When Cyril of Jerusalem read about you in his Bible, he
decided that what was really meant was Mother Church.

READER 2:   The church fathers were so interested in the Virgin Mary that
they took all of your texts and applied them to her.

READER 1:   The early church took you and tried to make you into the
male Logos of its gospel.

READER 2:   The church began to integrate saints into its worship while
excluding you.

READER 1:   The Protestants' love of the Bible excluded you, even though
there is more about you in the Bible than anybody besides
Jesus and God.

READER 2: When people tried to reintroduce you into the church, they were accused of violating the doctrines of truth.

READER 1: People today have accused you of being a figment of the imagination.

READER 2: People say that friendship with you is only a sign of insecure, angry women.

READER 1: People have denied you by saying that you have nothing to do with the struggle of the poor.

READER 2: Many scholars say that you are just a personification of a concept.

READER 1: The Protestants left four of your books out of their Bible.

Sophia's Departure: The person playing Sophia then leaves the room, slamming the door behind her. The group stands in silence for about a minute.

Process to Smallest Space: The leaders then process with the group to a small room, where the group has difficulty fitting. This space may be a closet, a pantry, a cellar, or some similarly undecorated and small room. The person who played Sophia rejoins the group as herself while the group is processing. In the confined space the group gathers around the small objects that remind each one of Sophia.

Keening and Silence: The leaders begin keening. Keening is a wordless moaning. It need not be melodic. It can also resemble groans. The group joins the leaders in keening. The keening should go on as long as participants desire. Participants may leave at any point, taking one of the small objects with them. When they leave, they should leave the room and the entire building in silence. The group should not reconvene after the keening. At the door, there should be a collection of patriarchal books of spirituality and theology. Each person is encouraged to take one of these books along as well.

Part 2: Sophia's Reappearance

The ritual of Sophia's reappearance takes place three to five days after the previous ritual. It may be done indoors or outdoors. It requires a comfortable place for people to sit together and a place to dance. This ritual also requires a table, dance music, candles, several drums, some other rhythmic instruments, incense, ribbons, streamers, a sound system for the music, a small pitcher of milk, a bowl of fruit, a festive tablecloth, at least one bottle of wine, wine glasses, a bowl of honey, a loaf of bread, and a plant.

Participants should be encouraged to bring some festive clothing with them that they can put on at an appropriate moment during the ritual. People should also be reminded to bring their small object from the disappearance ritual with them. Before the day of the ritual two people should be selected to play the role of Sophia during the reappearance section. This involves two readings as Sophia, and they should be rehearsed beforehand. The leaders also compile a printed order of service.

The Reappearance of Sophia

> Gathering
>> Candles and incense lit
>> Some silence (with one's small object)
> Drum and rhythm instruments
>> Softly at first
>> Impromptu invocations during drumming
>> Instruments become louder
>> Long loud noise
> Sophia appears
>> Two speeches
>> Possible responses
> Decorate the room
>> Prepare eucharist materials
>> Put up ribbons and streamers
>> Put on party clothes
> Eucharist
> Party

Introduction: Since some of the sequence of the ritual will be done without commentary, the printed order of service should be handed out to participants as they arrive.

Gathering: Everyone should be encouraged to help light the candles and incense. Then all wait in silence, two to five minutes. During the silence people may contemplate their small object from the ritual of Sophia's disappearance.

Invoking Sophia with Rhythm and Shout: The leaders pass out the drums and rhythm instruments. There may not be enough to go around, in which case the instruments should be passed around from person to person during this section of the ritual. The leaders begin playing drums and rhythm instruments very softly. The others follow their lead. Over a period of ten to fifteen minutes, the volume of the instruments slowly rises. As the volume increases, the leader and others may shout, "Come, Sophia," or "Wisdom, come back," or something similar. After about ten to fifteen minutes everyone joins in a long loud shout.

Sophia Reappears: A preselected person (not the leader) stands up as the shout reaches its loudest. She begins to speak the following two addresses loudly. The shout dies down as she begins.

I am Sophia. I am more splendid than the sun; I outshine all constellations. I am bright and I will not grow dim.

Let there be no doubt of who I am. I am the breath of the power of God. I was present when the world was made. By me was the earth fixed firm. Myself unchanging, I am renewing the world.

I have been seated with the angels; I have been in my chamber within the earth. I have been in communion with the water and the rocks, with the soil and the minerals and natural resources of the earth while you have been squandering them as if there were no tomorrow. You, the peoples of the earth, must now renew yourselves and the earth through me. Tomorrow is now; today is the time.

Already there has been enough abuse of the downtrodden earth and of the downtrodden peoples. I can laugh and jeer no longer. Your distress and calamity have caused me too much anguish. I am returning to sit at your door. I will remain underground no longer. My roots in the earth must spring up. The very rocks and stones, the grass and trees and all of nature cry out at the human history of injustice. I have returned to claim my inheritance for the sake of the planet.

And if you think you can ignore me this time or push me back underground, you are gravely mistaken. I am looking for those who are worthy of me. I will be readily seen by those who love me. I am showing myself to you, in every thought coming to meet you. Listen, I have serious things to tell you. Accept my discipline rather than silver, knowledge in preference to pure gold. Look not to these possessions for your life. I have returned and there is work to do. The earth, my body, has been desecrated, and it is time to work together to renew the peoples of the earth.

A second person stands and reads the following:

I, Sophia, am returning to the earth.
Deity without Sophia is deficient; the earth without wisdom
    tends to destruction and great suffering.
Melt the mists that hide my presence; I demand that the
    name of Sophia be respected on all continents.
Wisdom must infuse the planet with
    preaching of sermons on Sophia
    singing of hymns to Sophia
    uttering of prayers to Sophia
    institutionalizing of celebrations for Sophia.
Those who faint at conflict—turn away now.
Those who desire easy victories—forget my name.
Those who thrive on acceptance—return my mantle.
How do you respond?

There is an open time for people to speak a response to Sophia's return. However, since response to these two strong statements is somewhat intimidating, the leaders should not wait too long before moving to the next part of the response, which is seen as a group response.

Decorating the Room: The leaders and the rest of the people rise and begin decorating themselves and the room. This is the time when festive clothes are put on. The streamers and ribbons are hung around the room. The cloth, milk, honey, wine, bread, fruit, and plant for the meal are brought to the table.

Eucharist: Now the eucharist found in chapter 6 is used. Use only the second half of this liturgy, beginning with the prayer of consecration, pages 98 to 99.

Party: After the closing circle of the eucharist, the music for dancing is turned on. The rest of the time is spent in dancing and casual eating and conversation. (This ritual usually takes place in the evening and the party portion may last several hours.)

❧ A Sophia Version of Morning and Evening Prayers

The following services of prayer are based on the Divine Office of the Roman Catholic church, which is practiced by clergy, religious, and by some lay people. They have been adapted to focus on the figure of Sophia. We believe you will find the services eminently usable as presented, although readers may wish also to abstract a basic structure from the services and substitute other Sophia material as individual or group needs dictate. Morning and evening prayer can be used as part of the daily prayer disciplines of groups or individuals. They are also effective in retreat settings and study groups, since they make a limited demand on the group's schedule.

The texts and poems included in these prayer services are to be read aloud. They may be read by one person or by several. The reading of the texts may be arranged beforehand. But when the group is familiar with the discipline of the office, it is possible simply to wait in silence for someone to read the text under consideration.

Morning Prayer

Introductory Prayer:

> Source of life, be with us as we seek to open ourselves to your love and your wholeness. Fill us with your compassionate spirit, so that we can serve the world into which we are called. It is your breath that flows through us—your breath of creative love. Open us to you and to your world. Amen.

Song: See "Songs and Hymns," 180 to 187.
Psalmody: Adapted from Psalm 139.

> Lady, you have probed me
>   and you know me;
> You know when I sit and when I stand;
>   you understand my thoughts from afar.
> My journeys and my rest you scrutinize,
>   with all my ways you are familiar.
> Even before a word is on my tongue,
>   behold, Lady, you know the whole of it.

Behind me and before, you hem me in,
   and rest your hand upon me.
Such knowledge is too wonderful for me;
   too lofty for me to attain.
Where can I go from your spirit?
   From your presence where can I flee?
If I go up to the heavens, you are there;
   if I sink to the nether world, you are present there.

If I take the wings of the dawn,
   if I settle at the farthest limits of the sea,
Even there your hand shall guide me,
   and your right hand hold me fast.
If I say, "Surely the darkness shall hide me,
   and night shall be my light"—
For your darkness itself is not dark,
   and night shines as the day.
Darkness and light are the same.

Truly you have formed my inmost being;
   you knit me in my mother's womb.
I give you thanks that I am fearfully, wonderfully made;
   wonderful are your works.
My soul also you knew full well;
   nor was my frame unknown to you.
When I was made in secret,
   when I was fashioned in the depths of the earth.
Probe me, Sophia, and know my heart;
   try me, Sophia, and know my thoughts,
See if my way is crooked
   and lead me in the way of old.

Prayer:

   Lady Wisdom,
   Why have you abandoned me?
   Why have you left me so alone?
   It is dark and cold.
   There is no sign of life anywhere.
   The land lies frozen and bare,
   A bleakness of gray days.
   So am I—cold and hard,
   Numb and empty.
   There's an emptiness, a gnawing hunger.
   Come back to me, Lady,
   Surround me with your warmth.
   Melt away the frigid desolation.
   In your embrace, life stirs;
   Greenness returns.
   It is you I long for, Sophia,
   Heed my pleading, I pray.
   For with you I shall sing night and day,
   Singing your praises forever.

Scripture Reading: Proverbs 8:22–31.
Response: Individuals may speak short responses to the scripture reading.

Offerings: Individuals may offer petitions or intercessions or may briefly state a concern or a joy.
Silent Prayer
Song: See "Songs and Hymns," 180 to 187.
Concluding Prayer: (Done with movement)

> May it be beautiful before me. [Hands stretched out in front.]
> May it be beautiful behind me. [Hands stretched out behind.]
> May it be beautiful below me. [Hands stretched down to feet.]
> May it be beautiful above me. [Hands raised toward sky.]
> May it be beautiful all around me. [Turn around, with outstretched arms.]
> In beauty it is finished. [Arch arms above head.]

Evening Prayer

Introductory Prayer:

> Source of life, be with us.
> We seek to open ourselves to your love, your wholeness.
> Bountiful One, be with us.
> We leave behind our worries and concerns to focus on your presence.
> Giver of all good gifts,
> Create us anew.
> Amen.

Song: See "Songs and Hymns," 180 to 187.
Psalmody: Adapted from Psalm 27.

> Lady Wisdom is my light and my help,
>   whom shall I fear?
> Lady Wisdom is the stronghold of my life;
>   before whom shall I shrink?
>
> When evildoers draw near
>   to devour my flesh,
> It is they, my enemies and foes,
>   who stumble and fall.
>
> Though an army encamp against me,
>   my heart would not fear.
> Though war break out against me
>   even then would I trust.
>
> There is one thing I ask of Sophia,
>   for this I long,
> To dwell in Sophia's house
>   all the days of my life.
> To savor Sophia's sweetness,
>   to behold her temple.
>
> For there, Lady, you keep me safe
>   in the day of evil.
> You hide me in the shelter of your tent,
>   on a rock you keep me safe.
>
> And now my head shall be raised
>   about my foes who surround me,

And I shall offer within your tent a sacrifice of joy.
    I will sing and make music for Lady Wisdom.

Lady, hear my voice when I call;
    have mercy and answer.
Of you my heart has spoken:
    "Seek Wisdom's face."

It is your face, Lady, that I seek;
    hide not your face.
Dismiss not your servant in anger;
    you have been my help.

Do not abandon or forsake me,
    Sophia, my help!
Though father and mother forsake me,
    Lady Wisdom will receive me.

Instruct me, Lady, in your way;
    on an even path lead me.
When they lie in ambush, protect me
    from my enemy's greed.
False witnesses rise against me,
    breathing out fury.

I am sure I shall see Sophia's goodness
    in the land of the living.
Hope in Sophia, hold firm and take heart,
    hope in Sophia.

Scripture Reading: Wisdom 9:1–11.
Reading:

Medicine Song

Michele A. Belluomini

(This poem is written in the style of traditional Native American medicine songs of celebration.)

I am but a teller of tales
a dreamer, a singer, a liar
a keeper of the mysteries
come closer and listen

lover, mother, sister, child
our story began in abalone and shell
burning rock and dark waters
shadow and lightning

we crossed the arid desert
carrying the secrets
we are crossing it still
our steps carefree and deliberate
our steps wild and abandoned

we walk with the coyote
we carry our counsel
and that of the raven and the owl

the traveler and the path
the hunter and her prey
the carrion that waits for the vulture

we are the breath of stars
the secret of the night

say we are always moving
our eyes open to a red sun in a turquoise sky

we are clear vision
the lucidness of flame
the smell of wind remembering the rain forest
say we are ecstasy

only a teller of tales
I listen to your souls
my voice is yours
come closer

listen and remember the harmony of moon, earth, and water

listen and remember how we sang to stones
and they danced for us

listen and remember how we spun at the edge
of the universe and created ourselves
many colored
mother, sister, lover, child

tell the tales
we know them

(keepers of the mysteries)

changing woman
snake priestess
spider grandmother

together we sing the songs
together we will dance the dreams

the ones we remember
the ones we are creating
the ones as yet unborn.

Scripture Reading: Ecclesiasticus 24:1–29.
Response:

> Give to Sophia praise and thanksgiving.
> Alleluia, alleluia!
> In her we find our rest,
> In her our hunger and thirst are satisfied.
> Glory to Sophia,
> All glory forever!

Silent Prayer
Song: See "Songs and Hymns," 180 to 187.
Concluding Prayer: (Done with movement)

> May it be beautiful before me. [Hands stretched out in front.]
> May it be beautiful behind me. [Hands stretched out behind.]
> May it be beautiful below me. [Hands stretched down to feet.]
> May it be beautiful above me. [Hands raised toward sky.]
> May it be beautiful all around me. [Turn around, with outstretched arms.]
> In beauty it is finished. [Arch arms above head.]

Home for the Homeless

Words: Patrick Michaels
Tune: Ich glaub an Gott

1. O Mas - ter Craft - er, you still lay a
2. One with the poor, you live their way, you
3. You live in dreams of all poor folks of
4. The Wis - dom of__ your works dis - plays a

fault - less, true_ foun - da - tion; a - midst the cha - os
are their blood - re - la - tion; you build and teach, you
ev - 'ry land_ and na - tion; your realm shall ech - o
bold i - mag - i - na - tion; no two a - like, but

of the day you build a new_ cre - a - tion.
heal and pray, this is your oc - cu - pa - tion.
with the strokes of their par - tic - i - pa - tion.
well - de - signed for brand - new rev - e - la - tions.

Je - sus So - phi - a, ___ home_ for the home - less,

de - sign and frame_ us for lov - ing.

de - sign and frame

5. With room to grow, we find the place
   and structure of salvation;
   where peace and justice still embrace
   in human habitations.

Refrain

6. Our human hands can learn to build
   a shelt'ring congregation;
   and raise a strong communion-guild—
   new crafters of creation.

Refrain

Wisdom, the Splendor

Words: Marie Chiodo, D.W.
Music: Rosemarie Greco, D.W.

Refrain

Wis - dom, the splen-dor and full - ness of God, has built her-self a house and set for us a ta - ble._____

Cantor

1. Hers is the path - way of jus - tice,
2. She is the door - way of wel - come.
3. Her rooms are filled with rich trea - sure,
4. There - fore I plead - ed, "O Wis - dom, Come!"

Or - der and peace are her hand - i - work._____
O - pen to all those with hun - gry hearts;_____
Know-ledge of na - ture and u - ni - verse;_____
She heard and wel - comed me to her home;_____

Wis - dom, com - pas - sion - ate heart of God._____
Wise rev - e - la - tion of Moth - er God._____
Wis - dom, God's mir - ror of Myst' - ry's pow'r._____
Wis - dom, the gath - er - ing place of God._____

Wisdom Dream

Words: Marie Chiodo, D.W.
Music: Rosemarie Greco, D.W.

Refrain

1. Go for - ward, go for - ward, go for - ward in

faith. Be - lieve in __ the dream, a world where Wis-dom de -

lights to play, __ a world where Wis-dom plays in our pres-ence.

Cantor

1. See the world's __ chil - dren ____ join - ing
2. See the world's __ wom - en ____ join - ing
3. See the world's __ lead - ers ____ stand - ing
4. See God's ho - ly Wis - dom ____ wait - ing

hands, their fac - es ra - di - ant and health - y, their
hands in friend-ship cir - cles, tell - ing sto - ries, in
still, their eyes on wom-en and the chil - dren, so
still for dreams of jus - tice yet un - fold - ing, through

minds full of won - der, their hearts young and
bond - ing as wom - en and shar - ing as
awe - filled yet hun - gry for all they ob -
Je - sus the dream - er, God's pow - er in

free. _____
sis - ters.
serve. _____
us. _____

See the dream of Wis - dom.

Blessed Are Those Who Have Discovered Wisdom

Heath Allen

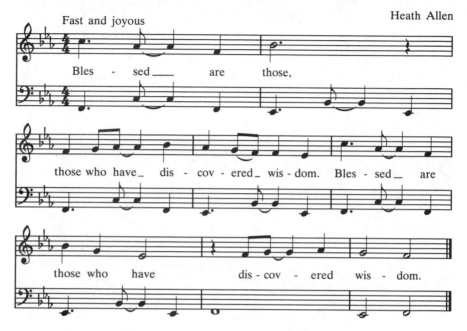

Bles - sed ___ are those,

those who have ___ dis - cov - ered ___ wis - dom. Bles - sed ___ are

those who have dis - cov - ered wis - dom.

You Send Your Breath

Heath Allen

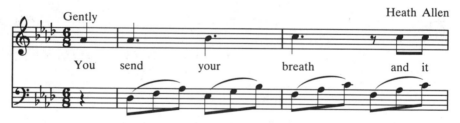

You send your breath and it

comes to life. You give the

world the bloom of youth.

Fairest Sophia

ST. ELIZABETH 568.558.
ANONYMOUS in *Münster Gesangbuch,* 1677
Schlesische Volkslieder, 1842
Trans. ANONYMOUS
Arranged by RICHARD STORRS WILLIS 1819-1900

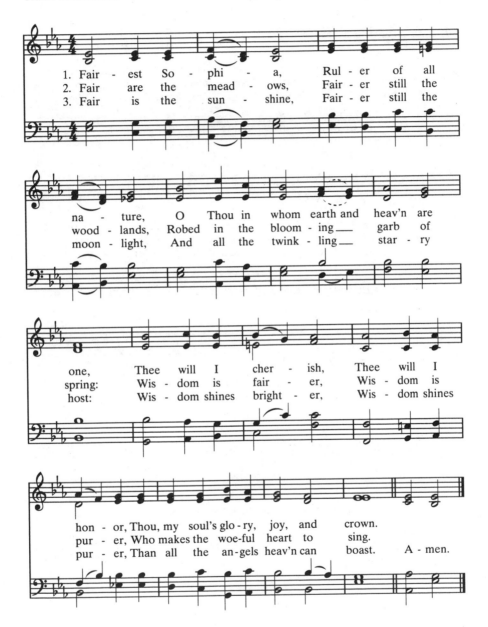

1. Fair - est So - phi - a, Rul - er of all na - ture, O Thou in whom earth and heav'n are one, Thee will I cher - ish, Thee will I hon - or, Thou, my soul's glo - ry, joy, and crown.

2. Fair are the mead - ows, Fair - er still the wood - lands, Robed in the bloom - ing garb of spring: Wis - dom is fair - er, Wis - dom is pur - er, Who makes the woe - ful heart to sing.

3. Fair is the sun - shine, Fair - er still the moon - light, And all the twink - ling star - ry host: Wis - dom shines bright - er, Wis - dom shines pur - er, Than all the an - gels heav'n can boast. A - men.

Sophia

Words: Patrick Michaels
Tune: Salve Regina Coelitum

1. Who_ is-sues forth as God's_ own breath, O__ So-
2. Who_ lifts her voice that we__ might hear, O__ So-
3. Who_ shall we seek with all__ our heart, O__ So-

phi - a. Who_ holds the pow'r of life__ and death,
phi - a. Who_ frames the thought to make_ it clear,
phi - a. Who,_ once re-vealed, shall ne'er_ de-part,

O__ So - phi - a. Craft-er__ and cre-
O__ So - phi - a. She's the__ teach-er__
O__ So - phi - a. Lov-er,__ coun-sel,__

a - tor too, She, un-changed, makes all things new, __
we es - teem, And the sub - ject of life's theme; __
com - fort - er, Life is glad - ness lived with her, __

She or - dains what God will do. __ Wis - est one,
From all er - rors she re - deems. Wis - est one,
Love has found none love - li - er. __ Wis - est one,

heav'n - ly one, __ Wel - come, O So - phi - a.
heav'n - ly one, __ Wel - come, O So - phi - a.
heav'n - ly one, __ Wel - come, O So - phi - a.

CHAPTER ELEVEN

Growing with Sophia: Directions for Using Sophia Studies and Celebrations

Spiritual life is an organic process; the spiritual lives of congregations, groups, and individuals grow and change within their own contexts and according to their own needs. Learning about Sophia and making her a part of worship, therefore, needs to be an organic process as well. For example, to encounter Sophia is to encounter the divine as female. For most people whose religious upbringing has included only male images for God, this encounter with Sophia brings with it the possibility of a momentous shift in spiritual life. Consequently, care must be taken in the use of the materials presented here so that Sophia can become a gradual part of the organic growth of the spiritual life of the people to whom she is introduced.

Living and growing with Sophia—that is the way we characterize our experience as individuals working with Sophia in churches and small groups. Since two of us have had the opportunity to do this work in one congregation for more than a decade, what we share here is not simply breadth of experience gained from working with many groups and congregations; we bring also a depth of experience born of witnessing the spiritual growth that is possible when one congregation lives with Sophia over time. In this process, we as individuals grew with Sophia, while the entire congregation grew in its acceptance of and ability to integrate Sophia into its worship life. In fact, in looking back over this process we have come to realize that as Sophia grew in importance over time, the congregation grew in diversity and depth.[1]

Individuals in groups and congregations vary considerably in need and ability to integrate Sophia into their religious lives. For some, mostly women, Sophia is an enormously liberating figure simply because she is female. Often women welcome her with enthusiasm and energy even before they know her very well. For others, Sophia is dangerous and threatening because she represents the possibility of major changes in their spiritual world. These people are cool, distant, and occasionally openly hostile. For the majority of people, however, Sophia is an intriguing figure who is important because she is a part of the biblical tradition. These people are interested in making her acquaintance and perhaps even in making her a friend.

The resources printed here respond to this entire range of ability and need. Some activities are appropriate for cautious, traditional churchgoers, while others open up the amazing power of a new connection to the divine for those who need it and are ready for it. Still others help people to get to know Sophia gradually over time. In all these cases—and we have taken pains to stress this—the importance of affect cannot be overemphasized in the use of these materials. Sophia cannot become a part of people's lives simply by being preached or talked about; people cannot integrate her through their rational processes alone.

SOPHIA IN SMALL GROUPS

Encountering Sophia in small group situations has set a new spirituality in motion for many people during the past decade. Intense small group work with texts, studies, rituals, and exercises about Sophia has stimulated individual commitment and congregational change.

Many different kinds of small groups have worked with the Sophia materials over the years. Women's spirituality groups, Sunday school classes, retreat groups, ad hoc study groups, Bible study classes, clergy-women's support groups, graduate level seminars, and local church courses all have come together around the possibility of a new Sophia-related spirituality. Although the length of time, degree of commitment, and mix of persons have varied in these groups, they all have involved both affective engagement and studied reflection. Moreover, the small group setting—involving no more than twenty participants—is the context in which many of the Bible studies in this book are meant to take place. More than almost any other included activity, these Bible studies, with their mix of personal exercises and serious reflection, have resulted in life-changing experiences for small group participants.

Many who have been introduced to Sophia in small groups seek a continuing small group involvement with Sophia. We have seen small groups within and outside the church continue for more than a year in study and celebration of Sophia. These groups work with the biblical texts about Sophia but also develop new rituals and worship material in relationship to Sophia. Ongoing Sophia groups have been the context for much deepening of spirituality and expression of creativity.

When these groups exist within the framework of a local church, they both enrich the larger worship and study life of the congregation and call some of its practices into question. That is, a congregation in which ongoing Sophia groups exist can expect waves of various sorts to spill over the rest of the members. Our general impression is that the overall impact of this movement from smaller groups to the larger congregation is a healthy one. In particular, the biblical base of the Sophia endeavor seems to help validate for the larger congregation any women's concerns raised by the small groups. It goes without saying that validation of women's challenges and concerns must in turn imply change for almost any congregation, since all congregations have a strong patriarchal background.

Although the authors have worked with groups involving almost every conceivable mix of participants, we have yet to meet a group that was simply incapable of working with the Sophia materials. There are, however, differences in what can be accomplished in groups, depending especially on whether a group includes women only or has a mixed membership. We emphasize that time must always be allotted, even in mixed groups, for women to respond in a same-sex grouping to the Sophia materials, especially when these materials have just been introduced.

When exclusively female Sophia groups convene, basic and important changes often happen to the members of the group. In fact, in all of our work with Sophia, it has been within these all-women groups that the most significant changes in spirituality have occurred. Because she is a strong, proud, creative goddess within the biblical tradition, Sophia speaks directly to the situation of many women. Furthermore, deciphering and integrating her importance for one's own personal situation happens for most women much more easily without the presence of men. For many women the very presence of a man during a consideration of Sophia's anger and pride results in explanations and inhibitions that impede expression. In addition, the exclusive company of other women often supports and challenges female participants to a noteworthy degree; such support and challenge is much more difficult to attain when male-female interaction takes place in the group. Ultimately, then, even though a mixed-gender group has much to recommend it and we ourselves have participated in a number of successful mixed groups, we observe that women-only groups are a mainstay for any successful consideration and celebration of Sophia. Churches, in particular, are urged to take this experience into account when setting up Sophia groups within the congregation.

Finally, we note that our experience with small groups in a wide variety of settings suggests that differences between Sophia groups that are or are not related to churches are less significant than we had anticipated. Although the way the material is to be presented will vary in different contexts, Sophia has intrigued a great variety of groups within as well as outside the church. We caution potential group leaders against assuming that Sophia will necessarily be either too unorthodox for some church groups or too churchy for other nontraditional groupings.

SOPHIA IN LITURGY AND PREACHING

Some may find it surprising to realize that Sophia has been successfully integrated into the worship and preaching of a number of mainline churches over the past decade. Although she is still considered exotic or marginal by many, the quantity and variety of Sophia biblical material coupled with its clear applicability to contemporary issues have made it possible for a number of congregations to accept and celebrate Sophia within the regular rhythm of Sunday worship. Because of our direct and primary experience with three such congregations as well as our secondary involvement with at least a dozen others, we will in the remainder of this chapter consider the various ways in which Sophia has entered the worship and preaching life of these congregations. Our reflections, therefore, are not theoretical propositions about how Sophia ought to be useful in regular Sunday morning settings but rather observations about the way Sophia has functioned in the worship life of real congregations.

During the past decade we have noted five stages of growth in the development of a Sophia tradition in mainline preaching and liturgy. These stages are: (1) basic and unobtrusive reintroduction of Sophia as a part of the Judeo-Christian tradition; (2) addressing issues of women's identity in relationship to Sophia; (3) celebrating and deciphering the Jesus-Sophia connections; (4) exploring and celebrating Sophia's presence in all things; (5) invoking Sophia to address questions of human suffering. Much of the material necessary for these five stages of Sophia's evolving role in worship and preaching can be found in this book. We also relate stories of what has happened in congregations as these stages have occurred—process as well as content, failure as well as success. We do so in hopes of encouraging readers to introduce Sophia into their own liturgical settings.

Some congregations have introduced Sophia into worship in ways that were hardly noticeable. At this early stage, meeting Sophia is much like meeting anyone else. First occasions often do not call attention to themselves. Rather, an acquaintance develops through a series of casual contacts.

The chief way that this casual acquaintance takes shape is through inserting into the liturgy scriptures, litanies, and songs that refer to Sophia. For instance, during Advent congregations often sing "O Come, O Come, Emmanuel," whose second verse begins "O Come, thou Wisdom from on high." We have included in this collection a number of Sophia litanies that also may be used without comment in a normal Sunday morning worship setting; see 93 to 96.

Special possibilities for introducing Sophia on Sunday morning present themselves in congregations accustomed to using the arts in worship. Dance lends itself especially well to this sort of activity. We have used dance successfully on more than one occasion to introduce the Proverbs 8:22–31 portrait of Sophia at creation.[2] Similarly, in the progressive United Methodist congregation in West Philadelphia where two of us pastored for a decade,[3] the use of slides was well accepted and was therefore easily adapted to the task of introducing Sophia. In one instance we illustrated Ecclesiasticus 24's picture of Sophia making her home on the earth and planting herself like a tree with a series of slides of the neighborhood where the church is located.

The lectionary of scripture readings for the year contains several passages directly referring to Sophia. On these Sundays we made certain that the Sophia text was the one selected for reading. The *Inclusive Language Lectionary*[4] also includes a number of optional Sophia texts for certain Sundays. In congregations where this lectionary was used, we consistently chose the optional Sophia passages as scripture lessons.

Preaching about Sophia at the introductory level is another relatively easy task yielding rich rewards. For us, preaching means making the text present, making its drama real, and helping congregations use the text as a frame within which to search for meaning in their lives. Although the thematic style of preaching is also valid and can be used in relation to Sophia, our experience and this discussion concern text-based preaching.

The abundance of biblical texts about Sophia make preaching about her an achievable goal. The sermons included in this collection provide fine examples of the many creative ways in which it is possible to preach about Sophia, although not all of them belong to the introductory stage with which we are currently concerned. Good introductory sermons about Sophia are also possible, however; in a number of congregations we have seen Sophia introduced successfully and unobtrusively into sermons. In our experience, the best way to begin talking about Sophia is to address a meaning of the text that does not concentrate on the goddess character of Sophia. For instance, we have preached a number of sermons in a variety of settings on the playfulness of Sophia in Proverbs 8:22–31. In that passage Sophia and God create the world together. The text describes God as more of the doer, while Sophia is playfully present. We chose then to emphasize the importance of the relationship between play and creativity. Although the text's picture of a strong and divine female figure present at the creation of the universe is surprising and provocative for most churchgoers, these early sermons on Sophia did not focus on the provocative elements of the text. By focusing on other valid aspects of the text, the sermons subtly introduced hearers to the person of Sophia.

The theme of Sophia in all things, present in a number of texts, also responds well to this approach. See "Sophia in All Things," 126 to 145. We find that the issues of God's presence in the world are effectively addressed through the use of Sophia texts without calling much attention to Sophia's gender or divinity. In fact, many Sophia texts and themes can be easily applied to a variety of issues. On one occasion a sermon related Sophia's glorying in herself (Ecclesiasticus 24:1–2) to a church's celebration of its one hundredth anniversary. See 159 to 162. Another sermon on the incarnation juxtaposed Sophia texts (Ecclesiasticus 1:14, Wisdom 6:12–18) against texts about God and Jesus to illustrate the process of God becoming human. Sophia's descent from heaven (Wisdom 9:1–5) was used in a Christmas sermon as part of a discussion about the divine entering our lives.

Although introductory sermons do not call direct attention to the provocative mix of gender and divinity that Sophia so clearly exhibits, we usually take time in them to review basic information about Sophia. Addressing briefly the question of her name has proved especially helpful. At the introductory level we refer to her often as Wisdom, but we introduce the name Sophia, explaining briefly that it is a transliteration from the Greek that helps bring out her clear personhood. See "Sophia and Play," 89 to 93, for a good example of the introduction of Sophia's name in the context of a sermon on playfulness.

It is by now obvious that the possibilities for preaching about Sophia even on an introductory level are fairly extensive. The wealth of biblical material referring to her in various contexts makes it possible to bring Sophia into the life and spirituality of the congregation without directly addressing the question of her gender. This, as we will see, is paradoxically crucial if Sophia is eventually to be used successfully to motivate the congregation to address gender issues. The important point to remember at this introductory stage is that we are introducing to many church members what is virtually a brand new figure, and a female one at that. Such an undertaking demands care, patience, and a good deal of repetition.

A final way to introduce Sophia into worship and preaching is to use material that lies at the heart of wisdom theology. This is perhaps done best without even mentioning Sophia. For instance, wisdom theology's assertion that the divine is present and discoverable in the created and social orders may be celebrated liturgically and preached. On one occasion we asked a congregation to meditate on the presence of God in a rock or a plant without mentioning that most of the biblical texts about this are related to Sophia. Similarly, another sermon discussed a wisdom psalm's (139) solution to the disintegration of Israel's culture, relating it to the societal chaos of our day without alluding to Sophia. See "Where is God?" 128 to 132 for the text of this sermon. This introduction of Sophia-related themes is important, first of all, because the themes themselves can address issues vital to the congregation. But such an introduction of these themes also aids a congregation at later stages in integrating Sophia into a broader range of concerns.

In the particular local congregation where two of the authors ministered, several years of this kind of sporadic exposure to Sophia took place. Then, primarily through establishing a Sophia Bible study group, an explosion of interest in Sophia happened on the part of a number of women in the congregation. This signaled the second stage of growth of Sophia's presence in congregational liturgy. The energy of this second stage was so gripping that it created a gap between women who were vitally interested in Sophia for their own identity and the rest of the congregation. Once we recognized this gap, we repeated and intensified with the congregation many of the introductory activities in this volume. Thus the congregation went through two distinct introductory stages in which Sophia material was preached and integrated into the liturgy in a way that did not call attention to the material itself.

The second stage of growth of the Sophia tradition, establishing the relationship between Sophia and women's identity, is an exciting and important one. It fixes Sophia as a major figure in the ongoing worship life of the congregation. In the several congregations where we have observed this stage, women have been eager for preaching and worship that integrate and express the connection they have come to recognize between Sophia and their own self-image.

Women who celebrate the images of Sophia within themselves experience a major affirmation of every aspect of their being. Through Sophia women can claim power. Through her presence in worship and preaching women experience freedom from the exclusive and dominant male imagery of traditional Judeo-Christian worship. When women become aware of Sophia's divine power within themselves, they no longer accept relegation to the periphery. See 61 to 64, for further discussion of Sophia and women's identity issues.

The presence of the figure of Sophia in worship greatly helps to move the congregation toward celebrating growth and creativity in women. Sophia elicits pride and anger from women—a pride and anger they feel and very much need to express—because she herself is pictured as a proud and angry female. She, as female, allows women to affirm their own bodies. Her presence in worship helps women begin to value their own thoughts and feelings and to refuse to be silent or invisible.

Women's enthusiasm for Sophia in worship tends to become channeled in two major directions. As soon as women begin to experience the importance of her presence, a great thirst arises for sermons, prayers, and litanies focused on Sophia and her significance for women in the congregation. We have found that it is important to respond to this need as fully as possible in regular congregational worship. Women's concerns have too long been marginalized in worship settings. Sophia's centrality in the biblical tradition makes it plausible for a congregation to affirm its own tradition and the concerns of women as well. Sample worship services and sermons throughout this volume witness to the possibility of celebrating women's concerns in a way that is reverent, biblical, and clearly responsive to the needs of a considerable percentage of the congregation.

Not all the congregation or even all the women in the congregation experience this new thirst for Sophia-related activity in worship. This reality sets some limits to the process. For example, it is unwise and probably counterproductive to ignore other worship needs because of the desire for Sophia worship activities on the part of some. However, if a congregation has already become familiar with Sophia in worship through the introductory processes, there is likely to be much less resistance to women seeking to appropriate her.

The other development that becomes apparent at this stage grows out of the strong need for women to participate in some worship events for women only. Small group settings provide women opportunities to deepen devotion to Sophia that may not be available in all the regular worship services. At this stage it is also important for many women to experience worship in a setting where there are no men. Such a worship experience can take place in ongoing groups that do not meet on Sunday morning.

Some people, male clergy primarily, have become alarmed at the existence of exclusively female worship groups in the congregation. We have heard in several different churches the allegation that these Sophia women's groups splinter the congregation and detract from the main worship service. It is our experience that this is seldom the case. Almost without exception the women who want smaller Sophia groups cherish the broader worship possibility as well. It is our sense that criticism of these Sophia groups for women emerges almost solely from fear of losing control of the congregation. And in the situations in which we have worked it has consistently been clergymen who have operated out of this fear. Generally, the smaller Sophia worship and study groups, rather than drawing women away from the congregation, have instead rekindled their interest in the church. It is true that this interest often results in requests for change in the main service as well. It is seldom the case, however, that members of the smaller groups want to take over the main liturgy in the name of Sophia.

Once a congregation has engaged with and celebrated Sophia in relationship to women's identity, several other processes are set in motion. The next stages of integrating her into worship and preaching connect her to other elements of the Judeo-Christian tradition. Congregations that have recognized Sophia's importance for women often begin to work energetically to understand and clarify her relationship to Jesus and God. This has happened by and large as an organic part of the preaching and worship life of the congregation.

At first blush the idea of relating Sophia to Jesus in liturgy and preaching may seem strange and bothersome. Immediately one can imagine questions being raised on all sides. How will people who are committed to the worship of Jesus respond to Sophia's presence in the service? Will Sophia be perceived as interfering with their Christian devotion? On the other hand, is not Jesus' maleness a problem for women as well? For some women doesn't Jesus really stand in the way of integrating Sophia effectively into the worship life of a congregation? And these are not only potential or imaginary objections; we have heard almost all of them raised in some form by church members.

Yet surprisingly, the relationship between Sophia and Jesus in the Bible has been a wonderful source of inspiration not only for women, but for congregations as a whole. We have seen great enthusiasm for celebrating in liturgy and in preaching the ways in which Sophia and Jesus seem to be connected in the Bible. Of course, this connection doesn't emerge by itself; it clearly needs to be explained to congregations. Such an explanation takes place, first of all, in smaller Sophia study groups. (See chapter 9, "Jesus and

Sophia," for several studies in which the relationship of Jesus and Sophia in the Bible is presented.) But for a congregation that has already experienced the introductory stage of Sophia in liturgy, preaching about Sophia and Jesus can also be a major way to learn about the closeness of Jesus and Sophia in the scriptures. We have done this most successfully by preaching on New Testament texts where Jesus' character seems to be drawn almost completely from the portrait of Sophia in the Hebrew scriptures. John 1:1–14 and Colossians 1:15–20 are excellent examples of such preaching texts.

A major development in celebrating the relationship between Jesus and Sophia within a congregation has been the evolution of Sophia eucharistic celebrations. By juxtaposing the closeness of Jesus and Sophia in the scriptures with Proverbs 9's powerful portrait of Sophia beckoning people to join her at her table, groups in several different worship settings have been moved toward developing eucharistic celebrations of Sophia and Jesus. A number of these services are included in this book (see 93 to 96, 137 to 139, 154 to 155, 162 to 168, and 172 to 175), and are discussed in our chapter on Jesus and Sophia (see 147 to 148).

Another type of worship event also has been generated by associating Sophia and Jesus. For example, the Bible study units in this book inserting Sophia into some of the New Testament Jesus stories have suggested to a number of participants that Sophia might take the role of Jesus in the passion account as well. At least two different groups have developed worship events based on this substitution of Sophia for Jesus in the passion story. See "A Sophia Passion," 116 to 122, and "A Good Friday Liturgy," 139 to 143, for these services, and "Women's Identity," 100 to 104, for further discussion of them.

These events were mainly for women, and they emerged out of two strongly articulated needs. The first was a need some women felt to have access to the drama of the Christian tradition without that drama being entirely androcentric. The second was for a means of integrating Sophia into the central Christian drama of death and resurrection.

We have erred several times in response to enthusiasm for the interchangeability of Jesus and Sophia. Because we discovered in our work with women's groups such a strong tendency to substitute Sophia for Jesus in scripture and song, we did exactly that in congregational worship and preaching. This substitution can be carried out successfully in sermons where the exegetical reasons for doing so are clearly explained and in some litanies where the poetry effectively evokes both Jesus and Sophia. But replacing Jesus with Sophia in liturgical acts cherished by the congregation can be alienating for some and divisive of the group as a whole. Especially when we rewrote traditional hymns and celebrated the eucharist there were times when we offended people unnecessarily by replacing Jesus with Sophia.

We find it is much better for the congregation to be able to celebrate Jesus and Sophia side by side. The eucharistic services for the entire congregation should not replace all of the Jesus material but should integrate some Sophia material into prayers and readings. Cherished hymns about Jesus should remain as such, and other hymns about Sophia should be sung as well. See 162 to 168, for an example of a combined service that is appropriate for congregational worship. For those who have a valid need for a unique Sophia eucharist, a smaller worship setting with a more select group of participants is recommended. See 93 to 96 for such a service.

In contrast to the Sophia-Jesus connection, people are not so eager to replace God with Sophia in worship and preaching. Nonetheless, it is clear that this has in fact taken place on a practical level. That is, where there used to be sermons, litanies, prayers, and songs about God, there are now in some cases in these mainline congregations parallel worship events focused on Sophia. Members of the congregation see this not so much as a detraction from God but rather as an expansion of divine worship. In these liturgies Sophia stands beside God. Both are objects of adoration, petition, and praise. Sophia simply brings new dimensions to divine worship.

This has been the case particularly during the fourth stage of a congregation's development, when the theme of Sophia in all things is explored in worship and preaching. A number of biblical texts present Sophia under this rubric; Wisdom 7:24, for instance, says that she "pervades and permeates all things." See "Sophia in All Things," 126 to 145. In several congregations this perspective on Sophia has helped people understand the relationship between the divine and creation. Portraying her as creator present in all things has facilitated celebration of the divine in nature, in society, and in the world in general. We have developed liturgies and meditations about Sophia in rocks, trees, art objects, and in a variety of people. See "A Meditation Exercise on Sophia in All Things," 132 to 133, and "A Thanksgiving Litany," 133 to 134. Sermons about Sophia's creative presence have likewise addressed questions about where God can be found today.

What we have described as the fifth stage of growth in Sophia worship and preaching appears only when groups have spent a sufficient length of time together to begin to raise questions about human suffering. We have witnessed this fifth stage in only one congregation and two nonchurch groups. Of course, the central questions about suffering are the same wherever people experience pain, oppression, and disappointment. Why do we suffer? How does God relate to human suffering? How should we respond to our own suffering or to the suffering of others? Shall I resign myself? What do I do with my anger?

These questions are addressed to Sophia with special poignancy. If she is everywhere, permeating all things, why, then, doesn't she do something about suffering? She seems so strong and powerful; is she insensitive? She seems so divine; is she removed from humanity? As a female, shouldn't she be especially sensitive and responsive to women's suffering?

Work on these questions in a long-term congregational setting has gone in three directions. Some women found that considering Sophia in the passion story helped greatly to process women's suffering. See "Women's Identity," 100 to 122, for this ritual and a discussion of it. Another approach uses the texts that portray Sophia as angry, for example, Proverbs 1 and 8. Here Sophia is not portrayed as omnipotent and therefore able to deal with all evil and suffering. Rather, she expresses anger at all that is occurring. She stands, in this regard, as a permanent sign of protest or, if you like, as a permanent witness against human suffering. The ritual for healing after an abortion is another example of the place of Sophia in response to human suffering. In this ritual, Sophia is never named directly, but she is addressed in prayers to the one who was present at creation and who is with us in our mother's womb. As such she is the one present at the conception and death of the unborn child, a female presence standing with the mother in the pain of her situation. See "A Ritual of Cleansing and Renewal Following an Abortion," 123 to 125.

Congregations may only experience the first of these stages of development in the Sophia tradition or they may experience them in a different order than outlined in this chapter.

Appendix

PROVERBS 1:20–33

20 Wisdom calls aloud in the streets,
 she raises her voice in the public squares;
21 she calls out at the street corners,
 she delivers her message at the city gates,
22 "You ignorant people, how much longer will you cling to
  your ignorance?
 How much longer will mockers revel in their mocking
 and fools hold knowledge contemptible?
23 Pay attention to my warning:
 now I will pour out my heart to you,
 and tell you what I have to say.
24 Since I have called and you have refused me,
 since I have beckoned and no one has taken notice,
25 since you have ignored all my advice
 and rejected all my warnings,
26 I, for my part, will laugh at your distress,
 I will jeer at you when calamity comes,
27 when calamity bears down on you like a storm
 and your distress like a whirlwind,
 when disaster and anguish bear down on you.
28 Then they shall call to me, but I will not answer,
 they shall seek me eagerly and shall not find me.
29 They despised knowledge,
 they had no love for the fear of Yahweh,
30 they would take no advice from me,
 and spurned all my warnings:
31 so they must eat fruits of their own courses,
 and choke themselves with their own scheming.
32 For the errors of the ignorant lead to their death,
 and the complacency of fools works their own ruin;
33 but whoever listens to me may live secure,
 he will have quiet, fearing no mischance."

PROVERBS 3:18

She is a tree of life for those who hold her fast,
those who cling to her live happy lives.

PROVERBS 4:5–9

5 Acquire wisdom, acquire perception,
  never forget her, never deviate from my words.
6 Do not desert her, she will keep you safe,
  love her, she will watch over you.
7 The beginning of wisdom? The acquisition of wisdom;
  at the cost of all you have, acquire perception.
8 Hold her close, and she will make you great;
  embrace her, and she will be your pride;
9 she will set a crown of grace on your head,
  present you with a glorious diadem.

PROVERBS 8:1–36

1 Does Wisdom not call meanwhile?
  Does Discernment not lift up her voice?
2 On the hilltop, on the road,
  at the crossways, she takes her stand;
3 beside the gates of the city,
  at the approaches to the gates she cries aloud,
4 "O men! I am calling to you;
  my cry goes out to the sons of men.
5 You ignorant ones! Study discretion;
  and you fools, come to your senses!
6 Listen, I have serious things to tell you,
  from my lips come honest words.
7 My mouth proclaims the truth,
  wickedness is hateful to my lips.
8 All the words I say are right,
  nothing twisted in them, nothing false,
9 all straightforward to him who understands,
  honest to those who know what knowledge means.
10 Accept my discipline rather than silver,
  knowledge in preference to pure gold.
11 For wisdom is more precious than pearls,
  and nothing else is so worthy of desire.
12 "I, Wisdom, am mistress of discretion,
  the inventor of lucidity of thought.
14 Good advice and sound judgment belong to me,
  perception to me, strength to me.
13 (To fear Yahweh is to hate evil.)
  I hate pride and arrogance,
  wicked behavior and a lying mouth.

17 I love those who love me;
   those who seek me eagerly shall find me.
15 By me monarchs rule
   and princes issue just laws;
16 by me rulers govern,
   and the great impose justice on the world.
18 With me are riches and honor,
   lasting wealth and justice.
19 The fruit I give is better than gold, even the finest,
   the return I make is better than pure silver.
20 I walk in the way of virtue.
   in the paths of justice,
21 enriching those who love me,
   filling their treasuries.
22 "Yahweh created me when his purpose first unfolded,
   before the oldest of his works.
23 From everlasting I was firmly set,
   from the beginning, before earth came into being.
24 The deep was not, when I was born,
   there were no springs to gush with water.
25 Before the mountains were settled,
   before the hills, I came to birth;
26 before he made the earth, the countryside,
   or the first grains of the world's dust.
27 When he fixed the heavens firm, I was there,
   when he drew a ring on the surface of the deep,
28 when he thickened the clouds above,
   when he fixed fast the springs of the deep,
29 when he assigned the sea its boundaries
    —and the waters will not invade the shore—
   when he laid down the foundations of the earth,
30 I was by his side, a master craftsman,
   delighting him day after day,
   ever at play in his presence,
31 at play everywhere in his world,
   delighting to be with the sons of men.
32a "And now, my sons, listen to me;
33 listen to instruction and learn to be wise,
   do not ignore it.
32b Happy those who keep my ways!
34 Happy the man who listens to me,
   who day after day watches at my gates
   to guard the portals.
35 For the man who finds me finds life,
   he will win favor from Yahweh;
36 but he who does injury to me does hurt to his own soul,
   all who hate me are in love with death."

PROVERBS 9:1–6

1 Wisdom has built herself a house,
   she has erected her seven pillars,

2 she has slaugthered her beasts, prepared her wine,
   she has laid her table.
3 She has dispatched her maidservants
   and proclaimed from the city's heights:
4 "Who is ignorant? Let him step this way."
   To the fool she says,
5 "Come and eat my bread,
   drink the wine I have prepared!
6 Leave your folly and you will live,
   walk in the ways of perception."

WISDOM 6:12–17

12 Wisdom is bright, and does not grow dim.
   By those who love her she is readily seen,
   and found by those who look for her.
13 Quick to anticipate those who desire her, she makes herself
      known to them.
14 Watch for her early and you will have no trouble;
   you will find her sitting at your gates.
15 Even to think about her is understanding fully grown;
   be on the alert for her and axiety will quickly leave you.
16 She herself walks about looking for those who are worthy of her
   and graciously shows herself to them as they go,
   in every thought of theirs coming to meet them.
17 Of her the most sure beginning is the desire for discipline,
   care for discipline means loving her,

WISDOM 7:7–14

7 And so I prayed, and understanding was given to me;
   I entreated, and the spirit of Wisdom came to me.
8 I esteemed her more than scepters and thrones;
   compared with her, I held riches as nothing.
9 I reckoned no priceless stone to be her peer,
   for compared with her, all gold is a pinch of sand,
   and beside her silver ranks as mud.
10 I loved her more than health or beauty,
   preferred her to the light,
   since her radiance never sleeps.
11 In her company all good things came to me,
   at her hands riches not to be numbered.
12 All these I delighted in, since Wisdom brings them,
   but as yet I did not know she was their mother.
13 What I learned without self-interest, I pass on without reserve;
   I do not intend to hide her riches.

14 For she is an inexhaustible treasure to men,
   and those who acquire it win God's friendship,
   commended as they are to him by the benefits of her teaching.

WISDOM 7:22–30

22 For within her is a spirit intelligent, holy,
   unique, manifold, subtle,
   active, incisive, unsullied,
   lucid, invulnerable, benevolent, sharp,
23 irresistible, beneficent, loving to man,
   steadfast, dependable, unperturbed,
   almighty, all-surveying,
   penetrating all intelligent, pure
   and most subtle spirits;
24 for Wisdom is quicker to move than any motion;
   she is so pure, she pervades and permeates all things.
25 She is a breath of the power of God,
   pure emanation of the glory of the Almighty;
   hence nothing impure can find a way into her.
26 She is a reflection of the eternal light,
   untarnished mirror of God's active power,
   image of his goodness.
27 Although alone, she can do all;
   herself unchanging, she makes all things new.
   In each generation she passes into holy souls,
   she makes them friends of God and prophets;
28 for God loves only the man who lives with Wisdom.
29 She is indeed more splendid than the sun,
   she outshines all the constellations;
   compared with light, she takes first place,
30 for light must yield to night,
   but over Wisdom evil can never triumph.

WISDOM 8:1–18

1 She deploys her strength from one end of the earth to the other,
  ordering all things for good.
2 She it was I loved and searched for from my youth;
  I resolved to have her as my bride,
  I fell in love with her beauty.
3 Her closeness to God lends luster to her noble birth,
  since the Lord of All has loved her.
4 Yes, she is an initiate in the mysteries of God's knowledge,
  making choice of the works he is to do.
5 If in this life wealth be a desirable possession,
  what is more wealthy than Wisdom whose work is everywhere?

6　Or if it be the intellect that is at work,
　　where is there a greater than Wisdom, designer of all?
7　Or if it be virtue you love,
　　why, virtues are the fruit of her labors,
　　since it is she who teaches temperance and prudence,
　　justice and fortitude;
　　nothing in life is more serviceable to men than these.
8　Or if you are eager for wide experience,
　　she knows the past, she forecasts the future;
　　she knows how to turn maxims, and solve riddles;
　　she has foreknowledge of signs and wonders,
　　of the unfolding of the ages and the times.
9　I therefore determined to take her to share my life,
　　knowing she would be my counselor in prosperity,
　　my comfort in cares and sorrow.
10　Through her, I thought, I shall be acclaimed where people gather
　　and honored, while still a youth, among the elders.
11　I shall be reckoned shrewd when I sit in judgment,
　　in presence of the great I shall be admired.
12　They will wait on my silences,
　　and pay attention when I speak;
　　if I speak at some length, they will lay their hand on their lips.
13　By means of her, immortality shall be mine,
　　I shall leave an everlasting memory to my successors.
14　I shall govern peoples and nations will be subject to me;
15　at the sound of my name fearsome despots will be afraid;
　　I shall show myself kind to my people and valiant in battle.
16　When I go home I shall take my ease with her,
　　for nothing is bitter in her company,
　　when life is shared with her there is no pain,
　　gladness only, and joy.
17　Inwardly revolving these thoughts,
　　and considering in my heart
　　that immortality is found in being kin to Wisdom
18　pure contentment in her friendship,
　　inexhaustible riches in what she does,
　　intelligence in the cultivation of her society,
　　and renown in the fellowship of her conversation,

WISDOM 9:9–11

9　With you is Wisdom, she who knows your works,
　　she who was present when you made the world;
　　she understands what is pleasing in your eyes
　　and what agrees with your commandments.
10　Dispatch her from the holy heavens,
　　send her forth from your throne of glory
　　to help me and to toil with me
　　and teach me what is pleasing to you,
11　since she knows and understands everything.
　　She will guide me prudently in my undertakings
　　and protect me by her glory.

1   The father of the world, the first being to be fashioned,
    created alone, he had her for his protector
    and she delivered him from his fault;
2   she gave him the strength to subjugate all things.
3   But when a sinner in his wrath deserted her,
    he perished in his fratricidal fury.
4   When because of him the earth was drowned, it was Wisdom again who
      saved it.
    piloting the virtuous man on a paltry piece of wood.
5   Again, when, concurring in wickedness, the nations had been
      thrown into confusion,
    it was she who singled out the virtuous man, preserved him
      blameless before God
    and fortified him against pity for his child.
6   It was she who, while the godless perished, saved the virtuous man
    as he fled from the fire raining down on the Five Cities,
7   in witness against whose evil ways
    a desolate land still smokes,
    where shrubs bear fruit that never ripens
    and where, monument to an unbelieving soul, there stands a pillar
    of salt.
8   For, by neglecting the path of Wisdom,
    not only were they kept from knowledge of the good,
    they actually left the world a memorial of their folly,
    so that their crimes might not escape notice.
9   But Wisdom delivered her servants from their ordeals.
10   The virtuous man, fleeing from the anger of his brother,
    was led by her along straight paths.
    She showed him the kingdom of God
    and taught him the knowledge of holy things.
    She brought him success in his toil
    and gave him full return for all his efforts;
11   she stood by him against grasping and oppressive men
    and she made him rich.
12   She guarded him closely from his enemies
    and saved him from the traps they set for him.
    In an arduous struggle she awarded him the prize,
    to teach him that piety is stronger than all.
13   She did not forsake the virtuous man when he was sold,
    but kept him free from sin;
14   she went down to the dungeon with him;
    she would not abandon him in his chains,
    but procured for him the scepter of a kingdom
    and authority over his despotic masters,
    thus exposing as liars those who had traduced him,
    and giving him honor everlasting.
15   A holy people and a blameless race,
    this she delivered from a nation of oppressors.
16   She entered the soul of a servant of the Lord,
    and withstood fearsome kings with wonders and signs.
17   To the saints she gave the wages of their labors;
    she led them by a marvelous road;

she herself was their shelter by day
and their starlight through the night.

18 She brought them across the Red Sea,
led them through that immensity of water,

19 while she swallowed their enemies in the waves
then spat them out from the depths of the abyss.

20 So the vituous despoiled the godless;
Lord, they extolled your holy name,
and with one accord praised your protecting hand,

21 for wisdom opened the mouths of the dumb
and gave speech to the tongues of babes.

WISDOM 11:1–26

1 At the hand of a holy prophet she gave their actions success.

2 They journeyed through an unpeopled wilderness
and pitched their tents in inaccessible places.

3 They stood firm against their enemies, fought off their foes.

4 On you they called when they were thirsty,
and from the rocky cliff water was given them,
from hard stone their thirst was quenched.

5 Thus, what served to punish their enemies
became a benefit for them in their distress.

6 You gave them not that ever-flowing source of river water
turbid with defiling floods,

7 stern answer for their decree of infanticide,
but, against all hope, water in abundance,

8 showing by the thirst that then was raging
how severely you punished their enemies.

9 From their ordeals, which were no more than the reproofs of Mercy,
they learned what tortures a sentence of wrath inflicts on the
godless;

10 you tested them indeed, correcting them like a father,
but the others you strictly examined, like a severe king who condemns.

11 Near or far away, they were equally worn down,

12 double indeed was the grief that seized on them,
double the groaning at the memory of the past;

13 hearing that what punished them had set the others rejoicing,
they saw the Lord in it,

14 and for him whom long ago they had cast out, exposed, and
later mockingly rebuffed,
they felt only amazement when all was done;
the thirst of the virtuous and theirs had worked so differently.

15 As their foolish and wicked notions led them astray
into worshiping mindless reptiles and contemptible beasts,
you sent hordes of mindless creatures to punish them

16 and teach them that the instruments of sin are instruments
of punishment.

17 And indeed your all-powerful hand did not lack means
—the hand that from formless matter created the world—
to unleash a horde of bears or savage lions on them

18 or unknown beasts, newly created, full of rage,

exhaling fiery breath,
ejecting swirls of stinking smoke
or flashing fearful sparks from their eyes,

19 beasts not only able to crush them with a blow,
but also to destroy them by their terrifying appearance.

20 But even without these, they could have dropped dead at a single
breath,
pursued by your justice,
whirled away by the breath of your power.
But no, you ordered all things by measure, number, weight.

21 For your great strength is always at your call;
who can withstand the might of your arm?

22 In your sight the whole world is like a grain of dust that tips the
scales,
like a drop of morning dew falling on the ground.

23 Yet you are merciful to all, because you can do all things
and overlook men's sins so that they can repent.

24 Yes, you love all that exists, you hold nothing of what you have
made in abhorrence,
for had you hated anything, you would not have formed it.

25 And how, had you not willed it, could a thing persist,
how be conserved if not called forth by you?

26 You spare all things because all things are yours, Lord, lover of life.

ECCLESIASTICUS 1:9, 10, 14

9 The Lord himself has created her, looked on her and assessed her,
and poured her out on all his works

10 to be with all mankind as his gift,
and he conveyed her to those who love him.

14 To fear the Lord is the beginning of wisdom,
she was created with the faithful in their mothers' womb.

ECCLESIASTICUS 4:12–18

12 Whoever loves her loves life,
those who wait on her early will be filled with happiness.

13 Whoever holds her close will inherit honor,
and wherever he walks the Lord will bless him.

14 Those who serve her minister to the Holy One,
and the Lord loves those who love her.

15 Whoever obeys her judges aright,
and whoever pays attention to her dwells secure.

16 If he trusts himself to her he will inherit her,
and his descendants will remain in possession of her;

17 for though she takes him at first through winding ways,
bringing fear and faintness on him,
plaguing him with her discipline until she can trust him,
and testing him with her ordeals.

18   in the end she will lead him back to the straight road,
        and reveal her secrets to him.

ECCLESIASTICUS 6:18–31

18   My son, from your earliest youth choose instruction,
        and till your hair is white you will keep finding wisdom.
19   Cultivate her like the plowman and the sower,
        and wait for her fine harvest,
        for in tilling her you will toil a little while,
        but very soon you will be eating her crops.
20   How very harsh she is to the undisciplined!
        The senseless man does not stay with her for long:
21   she will weigh on him like a heavy stone,
        and he will lose no time in throwing her off;
22   for discipline is true to her name,
        she is not accessible to many.
23   Listen, son, and take my warning,
        do not reject my advice:
24   put your feet into her fetters,
        and your neck into her harness;
25   give your shoulder to her yoke,
        do not be restive in her reins;
26   court her with all your soul,
        and with all your might keep in her ways;
27   go after her and seek her; she will reveal herself to you;
        once you hold her, do not let her go.
28   For in the end you will find rest in her
        and she will take the form of joy for you:
29   her fetters you will find are a strong defense,
        her harness, a robe of honor.
30   Her yoke will be a golden ornament,
        her reins, purple ribbons;
31   you will wear her like a robe of honor,
        you will put her on like a crown of honor.

ECCLESIASTICUS 14:20–27

20   Happy the man who meditates on wisdom,
        and reasons with good sense,
21   who studies her ways in his heart,
        and ponders her secrets.
22   He pursues her like a hunter,
        and lies in wait by her path;
23   he peeps in at her windows,
        and listens at her doors;
24   He lodges close to her house,
        and fixes his peg in her walls;

25 he pitches his tent at her side,
   and lodges in an excellent lodging;
26 he sets his children in her shade,
   and camps beneath her branches;
27 he is sheltered by her from the heat,
   and in her glory he makes his home.

ECCLESIASTICUS 15:1–10

1 Whoever fears the Lord will act like this,
   and whoever grasps the Law will obtain wisdom.
2 She will come to meet him like a mother,
   and receive him like a virgin bride.
3 She will give him the bread of understanding to eat,
   and the water of wisdom to drink.
4 He will lean on her and will not fall,
   he will rely on her and not be put to shame.
5 She will raise him high above his neighbors,
   and in full assembly she will open his mouth.
6 He will find happiness and a crown of joy,
   he will inherit an everlasting name.
7 Foolish men will not gain possession of her,
   nor will sinful men set eyes on her.
8 She stands remote from pride,
   and liars cannot call her to mind.
9 Praise is unseemly in a sinner's mouth,
   since it has not been put there by the Lord.
10 For praise should only be uttered in wisdom,
   and the Lord himself then prompts it.

ECCLESIASTICUS 24:1–29

1 Wisdom speaks her own praises,
   in the midst of her people she glories in herself.
2 She opens her mouth in the assembly of the Most High,
   she glories in herself in the presence of the Mighty One;
3 "I came forth from the mouth of the Most High,
   and I covered the earth like mist.
4 I had my tent in the heights,
   and my throne in a pillar of cloud.
5 Alone I encircled the vault of the sky,
   and I walked on the bottom of the deeps.
6 Over the waves of the sea and over the whole earth,
   and over every people and nation I have held sway.
7 Among all these I searched for rest,
   and looked to see in whose territory I might pitch camp.
8 Then the creator of all things instructed me,
   and he who created me fixed a place for my tent.
   He said, 'Pitch your tent in Jacob,
   make Israel your inheritance.'

9 From eternity, in the beginning, he created me,
    and for eternity I shall remain.
10 I ministered before him in the holy tabernacle,
    and thus was I established on Zion.
11 In the beloved city he has given me rest,
    and in Jerusalem I wield my authority.
12 I have taken root in a privileged people,
    in the Lord's property, in his inheritance.
13 I have grown tall as a cedar on Lebanon,
    as a cypress on Mount Hermon;
14 I have grown tall as a palm in Engedi,
    as the rose bushes of Jericho;
    as a fine olive in the plain,
    as a plane tree I have grown tall.
15 I have exhaled a perfume like cinnamon and acacia,
    I have breathed out a scent like choice myrrh,
    like galbanum, onycha and stacte,
    like the smoke of incense in the tabernacle.
16 I have spread my branches like a terebinth,
    and my branches are glorious and graceful.
17 I am like a vine putting out graceful shoots,
    my blossoms bear the fruit of glory and wealth.
19 Approach me, you who desire me,
    and take your fill of my fruits,
20 for memories of me are sweeter than honey,
    inheriting me is sweeter than the honeycomb.
21 They who eat me will hunger for more,
    they who drink me will thirst for more.
22 Whoever listens to me will never have to blush,
    whoever acts as I dictate will never sin."
23 All this is no other than the book of the covenant of the
    Most High God,
    the Law that Moses enjoined on us,
    an inheritance for the communities of Jacob.
25 That is what makes wisdom brim like the Pishon,
    like the Tigris in the season of fruit,
26 what makes understanding brim over like the Euphrates,
    like the Jordan at harvest time;
27 and makes discipline flow like the Nile,
    like the Gihon at the time of vintage.
28 The first man never managed to grasp her entirely,
    nor has the most recent one fully comprehended her;
29 for her thoughts are wider than the sea,
    and her designs more profound than the abyss.

ECCLESIASTICUS 51:13–22

13 When I was still a youth, before I went traveling,
    in my prayers I asked outright for wisdom.

14 Outside the sanctuary I would pray for her,
 and to the last I will continue to seek her.
15 From her blossoming to the ripening of her grape
 my heart has taken its delight in her.
 My foot has pursued a straight path,
 I have been following her steps ever since my youth.
16 By bowing my ear a little I have received her,
 and have found much instruction.
17 Thanks to her I have advanced;
 the glory be to him who has given me wisdom!
18 For I am determined to put her into practice,
 I have earnestly pursued what is good, I will not be put to shame.
19 My soul has fought to possess her,
 I have been scrupulous in keeping the Law;
 I have stretched out my hands to heaven
 and bewailed my ignorance of her;
20 I have directed my soul toward her,
 and in purity have found her;
 having my heart fixed on her from the outset,
 I shall never be deserted;
21 my very core having yearned to discover her,
 I have now acquired a good possession.
22 In reward the Lord has given me a tongue
 with which I shall sing his praises.

BARUCH 3:29–38

29 Who has ever climbed the sky and caught her
 to bring her down from the clouds?
30 Who has ever crossed the ocean and found her
 to bring her back in exchange for the finest gold?
31 No one knows the way to her,
 no one can discover the path she treads.
32 But the One who knows all knows her,
 he has grasped her with his own intellect,
 he has set the earth firm for ever
 and filled it with four-footed beasts,
33 he sends the light—and it goes,
 he recalls it—and trembling it obeys;
34 the stars shine joyfully at their set times:
35 when he calls them, they answer, "Here we are";
 they gladly shine for their creator.
36 It is he who is our God,
 no other can compare with him.
37 He has grasped the whole way of knowledge,
 and confided it to his servant Jacob,
 to Israel his well-beloved;
38 so causing her to appear on earth
 and move among men.

BARUCH 4:1–4

1 This is the book of the commandments of God,
   the Law that stands for ever;
   those who keep her live,
   those who desert her die.
2 Turn back, Jacob, seize her,
   in her radiance make your way to light:
3 do not yield your glory to another,
   your privilege to a people not your own.
4 Israel, blessed are we:
   what pleases God has been revealed to us.

Notes

Preface

1. This style of Bible study is explained in wonderful detail in Walter Wink's *Transforming Bible Study* (Philadelphia: Fortress, 1979). Consult it for a complete introduction to the method recommended here.

Chapter One: Spirituality, Feminism, and Sophia

1. Examples include the Institute for Creation Centered Spirituality at Holy Names College in Oakland, the Institute for Feminist Spirituality at Immaculate Heart College Center in Los Angeles, and the Institute for Formative Spirituality at Duquesne University in Pittsburgh.
2. In 1984 the Cathedral of St. John the Divine in New York sponsored a conference on Christianity and the emerging spirituality of the earth, while one of the programs at Kirkridge that same spring, led by Carter Heyward and Dorothee Sölle, was concerned with a spirituality for justice. The Center for Concern in Washington, D.C., has also done some programming on this topic.
3. Perhaps most striking in this regard is the longstanding presence of Scott Peck's *The Road Less Traveled* (New York: Simon & Schuster/Touchstone, 1978) on the *New York Times* bestseller list. The works of Morton Kelsey as well as the perennial popularity of Thomas Merton can also serve as examples.
4. Though it can hardly be taken as a sign of spiritual renewal, a cartoon in *The Village Voice* recently suggested that one of the characteristics of Yuppies is that they consult a spiritual advisor instead of a psychotherapist. "Stan Mack's Real Life Funnies," *The Village Voice*, 11 Sept. 1984, 38.
5. See Elisabeth Schüssler Fiorenza, *In Memory of Her* (New York: Crossroad, 1983), 343–51; Starhawk, *The Spiral Dance* (New York: Harper & Row, 1978), and *Dreaming the Dark* (Boston: Beacon Press, 1982); Carol Ochs, *Women and Spirituality* (Totowa, NJ: Rowman and Allanheld, 1983).
6. Joanne Wolski Conn, "Women's Spirituality: Restrictions and Reconstruction," *Cross Currents* 30 (1980):293–307.
7. Ochs, *Women*, 11.
8. Joanna Rogers Macy, *Despair and Personal Power in the Nuclear Age* (Philadelphia: New Society Publishers, 1983), 24–27.
9. Ochs, *Women*, 11.
10. Macy, *Despair and Personal Power*.
11. Ibid., 30–34.

12. Starhawk, *Dreaming the Dark,* 3–4.
13. Thomas Berry, "Classical Western Spirituality and the American Experience," *Cross Currents* 21 (1981–82):391.
14. Ibid.
15. Starhawk, *Dreaming the Dark,* chap. 1, especially 5 and 11.
16. The tendency to compare the ideal of one's own religion or belief system with the real of somebody else's is all too human. Scholars in the history of religions have developed methods aimed at eliminating such unfair and unscholarly comparisons within their discipline. An especially moving study on this topic is Wilfred Cantwell Smith, "Comparative Religions—Whither and Why?" in *The History of Religions,* ed. Mircea Eliade and Joseph Kitagawa (Chicago: University of Chicago Press, 1959, 1973), 31–58. Although religious feminists of various persuasions may not see themselves as operating out of different traditions or belief systems, Cantwell Smith's recommendation that scholars of comparative religion aim to construct statements about religion that are intelligible within two traditions simultaneously might, if taken, improve communication between their groups as well.
17. Schüssler Fiorenza, *In Memory,* xviii–xix.
18. Joan Chamberlain Engelsman, *The Feminine Dimension of the Divine* (Philadelphia: Westminster Press, 1979), 119.
19. Ibid.
20. Ibid., 104.
21. Ibid., 106.
22. Ibid., 109.
23. Ibid., 113.
24. Ibid., 114.
25. Ibid.
26. Ibid., 140–41.
27. Rosemary Radford Ruether, *Sexism and God-Talk* (Boston: Beacon Press, 1983), 57.
28. Ibid., 59.
29. Ibid.
30. Ibid., 61.
31. Ibid.
32. Schüssler Fiorenza, *In Memory,* 133.
33. Ibid., 133–34.
34. Ibid., 135.
35. Ibid., 188–91.
36. Phyllis Trible, *God and the Rhetoric of Sexuality* (Philadelphia: Fortress, 1978), 202.

Chapter Two: Sophia in the Hebrew Scriptures

1. See chapter 4.
2. A summary of this kind of interpretation is found in L. Poirier, "La revelation de Marie à travers la sagesse de l'Ancien Testament," in *La Vierge Immaculee* (Montreal: 1943), 29–50. For an overview of the Roman Catholic liturgical associations between Mary and Sophia, see Seethalar, "Die Weisheitstexte in der Marienliturgie," *Benedictin Monatschrift* 34 (1938):111–20.
3. Mother earth/father sky in pairs in Near Eastern mythology include the Sumerian An (heaven) and Ki (earth), the Babylonian Marduk or Bel (heaven) and Tiamat (earth), the Assyrian and/or Babylonian Apsu (heaven) and Tiamat (earth), the Egyptian Re (father) and Maat (mother/daughter), and the Greek Zeus (father) and (among others) Hera. Concerning Sophia as a part of this Near Eastern divine marriage mythology, Helmer Ringgren in *Israelite Religion* (Philadelphia: Fortress, 1976), comments, "Probably wisdom here is introduced as the superior counterpart to a mother-goddess or goddess of love" (310).
4. Erich Neumann associates the Near Eastern goddess Net or Neith with stars (220) as well as the "Great Goddess" (141). The Near Eastern goddess Nut is a good example of the goddess as sea. Sea monsters are also related to the goddess. See Erich Neumann, *The Great Mother: An Analysis of the Archetype* (Princeton: Princeton University, 1963).

5. The outline of scholarly investigation in this century should include the following works: R. Reitzenstein, *Zwei religionsgeschichtliche Fragen, nach ungedruckten griechischen Texten der Strassburger Bibliothek* (Strassburg: 1901); R. Reitzenstein, *Poimandres, Studien zur griechischägyptischen and früchristlichen Literatur* (Leipzig: 1904); W. Bousset, *Die Religion des Judentums in späthellenistischen Zeitalter* (Tübingen: 1926); W. L. Knox, "The Divine Wisdom," *Journal of Theological Studies* 38 (1937):230–37; W. F. Albright, "The Goddess of Light and Wisdom," *American Journal of Semitic Literature* 36 (1919):258ff.; H. Ringgren, *Word and Wisdom, Studies in the Hypostasization of Divine Qualities and Functions in the Near East* (Lund: 1947); U. Wilckens, *Weisheit und Torheit, eine exegetisch-religionsgeschichtliche Untersuchung zu I. Kor. 1 und 2* (1959); G. Fohrer, "Sophia," *Theologisches Wörterbuch VII*, 476–96; R. H. Whybray, *Wisdom in Proverbs* (London: 1965); Gerhard von Rad, *Wisdom in Israel* (Nashville: Abingdon, 1972); Felix Christ, *Jesus Sophia: Die Sophia Christologie bei den Synoptikern* (Zürich: 1970); M. Jack Suggs, *Wisdom, Christology, and Law in Matthew's Gospel* (Cambridge: Harvard, 1970); Burton Mack, *Logos und Sophia: Untersuchungen zur Weisheitstheologie in hellenistischen Judentum* (Göttingen: Vandenhoeck and Ruprecht, 1973); *Aspects of Wisdom in Judaism and Early Christianity*, ed. Robert Wilckens (Notre Dame: 1975); and Bernhard Lang, *Frau Weisheit* (Düsseldorf: Patmos, 1976); Burton Mack, *Wisdom and the Hebrew Epic* (Chicago: University of Chicago Press, 1985); "Wisdom Makes a Difference: Alternatives to 'Messianic' Configurations" in *Judaisms and their Messiahs* (Cambridge: Cambridge University, 1988); "The Christ and Jewish Wisdom," a paper for the Princeton Symposium, October 1987; James Robinson, "Very Goddess and Very Man: Jesus' Better Self," Pheme Perkins, "Sophia as Goddess in the Nag Hammadi Codices," and Karen King "Sophia and Christ in the Apocryphon of John" in *Images of the Feminine in Gnosticism*, Karen King, ed. (Philadelphia: Fortress, 1988); Claudia Camp, *Wisdom and the Feminine in the Book of Proverbs* (Sheffield: JSOT/Almond, 1985); "The Female Sage in Ancient Israel and the Biblical Israel and the Biblical Wisdom Literature," a paper delivered at the Annual Meeting of the Society of Biblical Literature, 1988; Deirdre Good, *Reconstructing the Tradition of Sophia in Gnostic Literature* (Atlanta: Scholars, 1987).
6. One of the significant essays on this is H. Conzelmann, "Die Mutter der Weisheit," in *Zeit und Geschichte* (Tübingen: 1964). Both Ringgren, *Word and Wisdom,* and Bousset, *Die Religion des Judentums,* also treat the subject of Sophia's evolution.
7. Helmer Ringgren, *Word and Wisdom,* 198. Burton Mack, *Logos und Sophia,* 6, comments that no one in the history of scholarship "has spoken to the question of the emergence of the figure of wisdom."
8. See, for instance, J. Bergman's interesting study on Isis, *Ich bin Isis* (Uppsala: 1968) for a portrait of a similar figure's evolution in Egypt and then in the rest of the Mediterranean world. Perhaps the most direct address to the situation in Israel is by Gerhard von Rad, *Wisdom in Israel.*
9. This line of thinking is well presented by W. McKane, *Proverbs* (Philadelphia: Westminster, 1970). Perhaps the most exact description of such a possible borrowing process is described in Burton Mack, *Logos und Sophia.* The best summary of the "where did the myth come from" debate is Elisabeth Schüssler Fiorenza, "Wisdom Theology and the Christological Hymns of the New Testament," in *Aspects of Wisdom,* 17–42.
10. Examples of a construction theory are Gerhard von Rad, *Wisdom in Israel,* and Bernhard Lang, *Frau Weisheit.* Examples of the suppressed female valence theory are Erich Neumann, *The Great Mother,* 325–36, and Joseph Campbell throughout *The Masks of God: Occidental Mythology* (New York: Harper & Row, 1959).
11. H. Schmidt, *Wesen und Geschichte der Weisheit* (Berlin: Töpelmann, 1966), and Gerhard von Rad, *Wisdom in Israel,* both present theses on this subject. But their theses have not captured any kind of consensus. See Roland Murphy, "Wisdom—Theses and Hypotheses," in *Israelite Wisdom,* Samuel Terrien Festschrift (Missoula: Scholars Press, 1978), 36–42.
12. The main objection to the existence of a "wisdom school" around a monarch during

the period in which Sophia emerged is that Israelite monarchy had basically disappeared before much of the Sophia literature evolved. Postexilic Israel no longer knew a stable monarchy and was primarily dominated politically from the outside.

13. As early as W. Bousset, *Die Religion des Judentums,* and through G. von Rad, *Wisdom in Israel,* the contact with Greek culture has been noted. But more recently works such as Roland Murphy, "Wisdom—Theses and Hypotheses," and the collection of essays in *Aspects of Wisdom* reinforce the insight that the sociocultural influence of Hellenism on wisdom literature needs to be analyzed.

14. Of course, such a "cut off" has mostly to do with the process of canonization of the Hebrew scriptures. This is a subject beyond the scope of our work. We refer to the recent pioneering work of Jacob Neusner, *Midrash in Context: Exegesis in Formative Judaism* (Philadelphia: Fortress, 1983), for orientation and provocative conceptualization concerning this process. Concerning the unknowns of Sophia research itself, Gerhard von Rad, *Wisdom in Israel,* is most eloquent in his introduction and conclusion. See also Johann Marböck, *Weisheit in Wandel* (Bonn: Hannstein, 1971), as well as Roland Murphy's "Wisdom—Theses and Hypotheses."

15. Again, see Jacob Neusner, *Midrash in Context,* on the process of rounding off the Hebrew canon. It is not accurate, however, to say that Judaism's development of Sophia halted. On the midrashic development of Sophia see Henry Fischel, "Wisdom in the World of Midrash," in *Aspects of Wisdom,* and A. Marmorstein, "Diatribe and Haggadah," in *The Arthur Marmorstein Memorial Volume* (London: 1950). Fischel in his essay seems to take up the line of thinking on their respective subjects of both Jacob Neusner and Gerhard von Rad concerning the social factors around the development and "demise" (77) of much of the wisdom literature. See also J. M. Reese, *Hellenistic Influence on the Book of Wisdom and its Consequences* (Rome: Biblical Institute Press, 1970), 127–38; and W. Lowndes Lipscomb and James Sanders, "Wisdom at Qumran," in *Israelite Wisdom,* 277–85.

16. The telling criticism of Roland Murphy, "Wisdom—Theses and Hypotheses" and "Assumptions and Problems in Old Testament Wisdom Research," in *Catholic Biblical Quarterly* 29(1979):102–12, certainly raises this question. See also Burton Mack's analysis of the logic of the subsuming of Sophia under Logos in both Philo and the New Testament in *Logos und Sophia,* and Jean Laporte, "Philo in the Tradition of Biblical Wisdom Literature," in *Aspects of Wisdom.*

17. Erich Neumann, *The Great Mother,* 325–36; Joseph Campbell, *Occidental Mythology;* and J. C. Engelsman, *The Feminine Dimension of the Divine.*

18. The entire work of Gerhard von Rad, *Wisdom in Israel,* is concerned with making this point.

19. See H. Schmidt, *Wesen und Geschichte;* Burton Mack, *Logos und Sophia;* and Reese, *Hellenistic Influences.*

20. Evidence of such a spirit is to be found in the Hebrew canonical books of Joel, Malachi (with its emphatic condemnation of marriages with foreigners), Zechariah, and Leviticus.

Chapter Three: Sophia in the Christian Scriptures

1. See above consideration in chap. 2 (pp. 19–24) about Sophia as wisdom. It is important to see how Paul is referring in 1 Corinthians to Sophia as person and as wisdom. See the important review of this in Charles Hedrick, "A Response to Very Goddess and Very Man" in *Images of the Feminine in Gnosticism,* ed. Karen King (Philadelphia: Fortress, 1988) p. 134.

2. Seeing the New Testament in such a way is possible only by virtue of the sum total of the last century of scholarship. Three works which serve as both milestones and helpful overviews of this understanding of the New Testament are Amos N. Wilder, *The Language of the Gospel* (New York: Harper & Row, 1964) (for its examination of the process of the search for language itself); Helmut Köster, *History and Literature of Early Christianity* (Philadelphia: Fortress, 1982) (for its presentation and explanation of the wide variety of texts themselves); and Robert Funk, *Language, Hermeneutic, and the Word of God* (New York: Harper & Row, 1966) (for its summary of theories of interpretation of the New Testament).

3. Rudolf Bultmann, *Theology of the New Testament* (New York: Scribner, 1951) is perhaps the most thorough address in our century to the issue of the various New Testament speech worlds. More recently, James D. G. Dunn's *Unity and Diversity in the New Testament* (Philadelphia: Westminster, 1982) is an even more direct look at the diversity of New Testament language.
4. H. Lietzmann, *Der Menschensohn*, 1896, and J. Wellhausen, *Skizzen und Vorarbeiten VI*, 1899, did the original work on the nonmessianic nature of the first texts. There is still a rather lively debate concerning the exact identity of the figure. For a sampling of current work on the Child of Humanity/Son of Man see the symposium *Jesus und der Menschensohn* (Freiburg: Freiburg University, 1975).
5. Oscar Cullmann, *La Christologie du Nouveau Testament* (Paris: Cerf, 1955), 118–63, and Rudolf Bultmann, *Theology of the New Testament*, 26–37, present thorough reviews of these titles relative to Jesus' suffering and death.
6. See Robert Funk, *Language, Hermeneutic*, 124–99, and Robert Tannehill, *The Sword of His Mouth* (Philadelphia: Fortress, 1975), on the various ways New Testament language uses juxtaposition and contrast.
7. Eduard Schweizer, *Ego Eimi: Die religionsgeschichtliche Herkunft und theologische Bedeutung der Joh. Bildreden* (Zürich: 1939) provides a comprehensive review of the use of the literature. See also K. Kundsin, *Charakter und Ursprung der joh. Reden* (Zürich: 1939).
8. Rudolf Bultmann, *Primitive Christianity in its Contemporary Setting* (Philadelphia: Fortress, 1956), 80–93; John Bright, *The Kingdom of God* (New York: Abingdon Press, 1953); Geza Vermes, *Jesus and the World of Judaism* (Philadelphia: Fortress, 1984), 58–73.
9. Oscar Cullmann, *La Christologie*, 97–117, especially his summary on 115.
10. Oscar Cullmann, *La Christologie*, 97–102.
11. Oscar Cullmann, *La Christologie*, 266–73; and Rudolf Bultmann, *The Gospel of John* (Philadelphia: Westminster, 1971), 13–60.
12. Oscar Cullmann, *La Christologie*, 101.
13. See pp. 41–45.
14. Günther Bornkamm, *Jesus of Nazareth* (New York: Harper, 1959); R. H. Fuller, *The Foundations of New Testament Christology* (New York: Harper, 1965); and F. Hahn, *The Titles of Jesus in Christology* (New York: 1969).
15. On gnosticism as such, Hans Jonas, *Gnosis und Spätantiker Geist* (München: 1934). On Paul and gnosticism, Dieter Georgi, *Die Gegner des Paulus in 2. Korintherbrief* (Neukirchen: Neukirchener, 1964); Elaine Hiesey Pagels, *The Gnostic Paul* (Philadelphia: Fortress, 1975); Ernst Käsemann, *Perspectives on Paul* (Philadelphia: Fortress, 1971); and Krister Stendahl, *Paul Among Jews and Gentiles* (Philadelphia: Fortress, 1976). Also, Rudolf Bultmann has a precise summary of gnosticism in his *Primitive Christianity in its Contemporary Setting*, 162–74. The most detailed study of Sophia in gnosticism is Deirdre Good, *Reconstructing the Tradition of Sophia in Gnostic Literature* (Atlanta: Scholars, 1987).
16. See 47–50.
17. For an overview of this "word" see Rudolf Bultmann, *The Gospel of John*, 13–60. For the comparison of the Word with Sophia, see H. Ringgren, *Word and Wisdom*, and Burton Mack, *Logos und Sophia*.
18. See 22–39.
19. See 21–24 for a summary of this characteristic of Sophia. In the Hebrew canon we encounter the Child of Humanity/Son of Man in Daniel 7. Outside the canon the figure occurs in Enoch 37–71 and Esdras 7 and 13.
20. Felix Christ, *Jesus Sophia*. See also James M. Robinson, "Jesus as Sophia: Wisdom Tradition and the Gospels," in *Aspects of Wisdom*, 1–16.
21. This is a distinction of the last century of scholarship used to designate works in the New Testament related to Paul, but most probably not written by him. These works are considered to be later than Paul himself. See, for instance, Helmut Köster, *History and Literature of Early Christianity*, 261–307.
22. There are a number of theses which converge here. Weiss, *Untersuchungen zur Kosmologie* (Berlin: 1966), 189–210, 265–75, notes the way this is an example of

transfer of cosmic creative powers to Sophia. Eduard Lohse, *Colossians and Philemon* (Philadelphia: Fortress, 1971), 46–48, notes this also. Ernst Käsemann, *Essays on New Testament Themes* 154–56, and Ulrich Wilckens, *Weisheit und Torheit,* 200–2 (Philadelphia: Fortress, 1982), point out the gnostic tendencies of the material and see the hymn as definitely pre-Christian gnostic. See 47–50 of this work for the connection of Sophia to gnosticism. B. R. Brinkmann, *The Prototokos Title and the Beginnings of Exegesis,* unpublished dissertation (Rome: Gregoriana, 1954); and Lohse, *Colossians and Philemon,* 48, 49, point out that the hymn also fits with Hellenistic "Jewish speculation about Wisdom." Of note also is Elisabeth Schüssler Fiorenza, "Wisdom Theology and the Christological Hymns of the New Testament," in *Aspects of Wisdom.*

23. Both M. Jack Suggs, *Wisdom, Christology, and Law in Matthew's Gospel* (Cambridge: Harvard, 1970) and Felix Christ, *Jesus Sophia,* allude to this. This controversy is also discussed rather thoroughly in J. C. Engelsman's section on Sophia in *The Feminine Dimension of the Divine.* See also Hans Jonas, *Gnosis und Spätantiker Geist* (München: 1934).

24. One of the most concise descriptions of conceptual dimensions of this conflict is found in Rudolf Bultmann, *Primitive Christianity in its Contemporary Setting,* 162–74, 200–8. An example of the way such a controversy occurred in a particular New Testament community is described thoroughly in Raymond Brown, *The Community of the Beloved Disciple* (New York: Harper & Row, 1979).

25. Several examples of this tendency in gnosticism are the Gospel of the Egyptians (Sethian) (NHC III, 2, and IV, 2), the Dialogue of the Savior (NHC III, 5), On the Origin of the World (NHC II, 5), A Valentinian Exposition (NHC IX, 2), and the later Acts of John.

26. Hence, Paul, for example in 1 Corinthians 11:26, "You proclaim the Lord's death until he comes."

27. Several examples of this in gnostic literature are the Acts of Thomas, the Gospel of the Hebrews, the Sophia of Jesus Christ, and the Apocryphon of John. See also Pheme Perkins, "Sophia as Goddess in the Nag Hammad: Codices" in *Images of the Feminine in Gnosticism,* Karen King, ed. (Philadelphia: Fortress, 1988).

28. Actually none of the explicit Jesus-Sophia passages cited in this chapter addresses Jesus' suffering—except for one. In 1 Corinthians 2:8, Paul concludes, "This is a Sophia that none of the masters of this age have ever known, or they would not have crucified the Lord of Glory." As noted earlier, there are implicit parallels between Sophia's rejection and Jesus' rejection. But the New Testament by and large does not emphasize this parallelism.

Chapter Four: Sophia and Her Sociohistorical Context

1. These works certainly are among those within the framework of the following studies: Gerhard von Rad, *Wisdom in Israel* (Nashville: Abingdon, 1972); Leo G. Perdue, *Wisdom and Cult: A Critical Analysis of the Views of Cult in the Wisdom Literatures of Israel and the Ancient Near East* (Missoula: Society of Biblical Literature, 1977); Hans Heinrich Schmid, *Wesen und Geschichte der Weisheit* (Berlin: Töpelmann, 1966). James L. Crenshaw, "Prolegomenon," in *Studies in Ancient Israelite Literature* (New York: KTAV, 1976), excludes Baruch from the list.

2. Rudolf Bultmann, *History of the Synoptic Tradition* (New York: Harper, 1962), gives an overview of such sayings. M. Jack Suggs, *Wisdom, Christology, and Law in Matthew's Gospel* (Cambridge: Harvard, 1970), analyzes this kind of saying in the Gospel according to Matthew.

3. R. N. Whybray, *The Intellectual Tradition in the Old Testament* (Berlin: de Gruyter, 1974), 154.

4. For a review of the problematic nature of the results see Roland Murphy, "Assumptions and Problems in Old Testament Wisdom Research," *Catholic Biblical Quarterly* 29(1979):102–12; Claudia Camp's *Wisdom and the Feminine in the Book of Proverbs* (Sheffield: JSOT/Almond, 1985) is a recent and creative attempt to relate Sophia to the roles of women in later Israel.

5. Recent scholarship on this ranges from J. Rylaarsdam, *Revelation in Jewish Wisdom Literature* (Chicago: University of Chicago Press, 1946), to Gerhard von Rad, *Wisdom in Israel* (Nashville: Abingdon, 1972). Two works in German reflect the same process of over three generations: Walther Zimmerli, "Zur Struktur der alttestamentlichen Weisheit," ZAW 51 (1933):177–204, and Hans Heinrich Schmid, *Wesen und Geschichte der Weisheit* (Berlin: Töpelmann, 1966).

6. Walther Zimmerli, "The Place and Limit of the Wisdom in the Framework of the Old Testament Theology," in *Studies in Ancient Israelite Wisdom* (New York: KTAV, 1976), 123.

7. This is stated most clearly and provocatively in Burton Mack's unique and penetrating analysis of Sophia herself, *Logos und Sophia* (Göttingen: Vandenhoeck and Ruprecht, 1973). In the opinion of the authors of this book Mack's work on Sophia, both in the work cited here and in the unpublished essays cited later in this chapter, is easily the most illuminating examination of Sophia and her texts. This book stands in great and direct debt to the work of Burton Mack.

8. Again Burton Mack, *Logos und Sophia,* 185, is the clearest on this question of the development of Sophia. But Gerhard von Rad, *Wisdom in Israel,* in his entire work draws the most comprehensive picture of the response of the wisdom tradition. James L. Crenshaw, "Prolegomenon," 25, and Roland Murphy, "Assumptions and Problems," 107, see her as a further development in the wisdom tradition's response.

9. Two recent summaries of the Greek influence are found in Rainer Braun, *Kohelet und die Frühhellenistische Popularphilosophie* (Berlin: de Gruyter, 1973), and Martin Hengel, *Judaism and Hellenism* (Philadelphia: Fortress, 1974). The study of the relationship to Egypt was sparked by two early works of Hugo Gressmann, "Die neugefundene Lehre des Amen-em-ope und die vorexilische Spruchdichtung Israels," ZAW 42 (1924): 272–96, and Paul Humbert, *Recherches sur les sources egyptiennes de la litterature sapientiale d'Israel* (Neuchatel: Paul Attinger, 1929).

10. See Roland Murphy, "Assumptions and Problems," 102–12. Perhaps even more helpful is the detailed analysis of the social setting question in two unpublished papers by Burton Mack, "Wisdom as Intellectual Tradition," paper presented to the Society of Biblical Literature in New York in November 1979, and "Philosophical Wisdom," written in Claremont, California, in 1980.

11. Hugo Gressmann, "Die neugefundene Lehre," and Paul Humbert, *Recherche sur les sources egyptiennes.*

12. Burton Mack, *Logos und Sophia,* 34–41, and James Reese, *Hellenistic Influences on the Book of Wisdom and its Consequences* (Rome: Biblical Institute Press, 1970).

13. Andre Dupont-Sommer, "De l'immortalite dans la 'Sagesse de Salomon,' " *Revue des études grêcques* 62 (1949):80–87; Thomas Finan, "Hellenistic Humanism in the Book of Wisdom," *ITQ* 27(1960):30–47; David Gill, "The Greek Sources of Wisdom 12:3–7," and J. P. M. Sweet, "The Theory of Miracles in The Wisdom of Solomon," in *Miracles: Cambridge Studies in Their Philosophy and History,* ed. C. F. D. Moule (London: Mowbray, 1965), 113–26 and 383–86.

14. For a summary of these ties see Chrysostome Larcher, *Etudes sur le Livre de la Sagesse* (Paris: Gabalda, 1969), and David Winston, *Wisdom of Solomon* (Garden City: Doubleday, 1979). Both of these works relate specifically to the book of Wisdom but make the point most eloquently. Studies on the earlier literature are noted in nn. 9 and 13.

15. Erhard Gerstenberger, *Wesen und Herkunft des 'apodiktischen Rechts'* (Neukirchen-Vluyn: Neukirchener Verlag, 1965), treats apodictic law. Hans-Jürgen Hermisson, *Studien zur israelitischen Spruchweisheit* (Neukirchen-Vluyn: Neukirchener Verlag, 1968), addresses the question of the proverb itself. Wolfgang Richter, *Recht und Ethos, Versuch einer Ortung des weisheitlichen Mahnspruches* (München: Kösel, 1966), takes aim at the admonitions.

16. This is the actual title of R. N. Whybray's work, *The Intellectual Tradition in the Old Testament* (Berlin: de Gruyter, 1974). Whybray is summarized and compared to other recent and similar work in Burton Mack's unpublished paper, "Wisdom as Intellectual Tradition," given at the Society of Biblical Literature in New York in November 1979.

17. Gerhard von Rad, *Wisdom in Israel;* Burton Mack, *Logos und Sophia;* and Bernhard Lang, *Frau Weisheit. Deutung einer biblischen Gestalt* (Düsseldorf: Patmos, 1975), all see her as later, although they do not concur necessarily on her mythic function.

18. This is most pointedly demonstrated in Burton Mack, *Logos und Sophia,* 104, 105, 184–86. But James L. Crenshaw, "Prolegomenon," 25, also indicates that he is inclined to see her this way.

19. Gerhard von Rad, *Wisdom in Israel,* takes pains to show comprehensively that this is the case in wisdom literature in general. Burton Mack illustrates the way Sophia herself stands for this in *Logos und Sophia,* 185.

Chapter Five: Sophia and the Future of Feminist Spirituality

1. See especially chap. 1, 10–14; chap. 3; and chap. 4, 55–59.
2. See Elisabeth Schüssler Fiorenza, *In Memory of Her* (New York: Crossroad, 1983), 68–95.
3. See Dorothee Sölle, "Mysticism, Liberation, and the Names of God," *Christianity and Crisis* 41 (1981):179–85.
4. Constance Fitzgerald, O.C.D., "Impasse and Dark Night," in Tilden Edwards, *Living with Apocalypse* (New York: Harper & Row, 1983).
5. Delores S. Williams, "The Color of Feminism," *Christianity and Crisis,* 1985, 164–65.
6. Conversation, Philadelphia, Pa., May 1985.
7. Catherine A. Callahan, "The Wanderings of the Goddess: Language and Myth in Western Culture," in *Image Breaking, Image Building,* ed. Linda Clark, Marian Ronan, Eleanor Walker (New York: Pilgrim Press, 1981), 126–31.
8. Conversation, The Grail, Cornwall on Hudson, New York, July 1984.
9. Joanna Rogers Macy, *Despair and Personal Power in the Nuclear Age* (Philadelphia: New Society Publishers, 1983), 27, 32.
10. Taken from Dorothee Sölle's introductory lectures in systematic theology, Union Theological Seminary, New York, Spring 1984.
11. Dorothee Sölle, *Suffering* (Philadelphia: Fortress, 1975), 68–70.
12. In 1986, a group of women at Calvary United Methodist Church in Philadelphia held alternative Holy Week observances in which Sophia became the central figure in the passion story.
13. See Jürgen Deuker, *Die theologischgeschichtliche Stellung des Petrusevangeliums* (Bern/Frankfurt: Europäische Hochschulschriften 23:26 [1975]); Detlev Dormeyer, *Die Passion Jesu als Verhaltensmodell* (Münster: Aschendorff, 1974); and Marie-Louise Gubler, *Die frühesten Deutungen des Todes Jesu* (Göttingen: Vandenhoeck und Ruprecht).
14. See also in this regard Elisabeth Schüssler Fiorenza's discussion of the suffering and execution of Jesus in terms of prophetic Sophialogy, *In Memory of Her,* 135.

Chapter Six: Getting Acquainted with Sophia

1. See, for instance, Matthew 11:19; Mark 10:13–16; Luke 19:1–10; John 2:1–13.
2. Joan Chamberlain Engelsman, *The Feminine Dimension of the Divine* (Philadelphia: Westminster, 1979), 113.
3. Russell Baker, "Why Being Serious Is Hard," in "The Sunday Observer," *New York Times Magazine,* April 30, 1978, p. 7.
4. First preached by Susan Cady at Media United Methodist Church, Media, Pennsylvania, May 1982.
5. This service was composed by Gretchen Chapman, Lynn McMahon, Ray Henry, Chip Coffman, Susan Cady, Anne-Marie Schaaf, Ruth Woodlen, and Hal Taussig. Anne-Marie Schaaf had primary design responsibilities.

Chapter Seven: Women's Identity

1. Susan Cady preached this sermon in the winter of 1982 at Calvary United Methodist Church, Philadelphia, Pennsylvania.
2. Valerie Saiving Goldstein pioneered this feminist rethinking of sin in her article, "The

Human Situation: A Feminine View," reprinted under Valerie Saiving in *Womanspirit Rising,* ed. Carol P. Christ and Judith Plaskow (New York: Harper & Row, 1979), 25–42.

Chapter Eight: Sophia in All Things

1. Dietrich Bonhoeffer, *Prisoner for God* (New York: McMillan, 1961), 163–64.
2. Ibid.
3. See, for instance, Jürgen Moltmann, *Theology of Hope* (Philadelphia: Fortress Press, 1967).
4. Susan Cady preached this sermon at Calvary United Methodist Church in July 1986. It does not refer to Sophia directly but addresses the theology of the wisdom movement in relationship to the divine in all things. The God that it refers to is the Sophia of the wisdom literature.
5. Ruth was a young, single woman who was active at Calvary United Methodist Church in Philadelphia and lived a block and a half from the church. She was raped and brutally murdered in her home in May of 1986.
6. WPEB is West Philadelphia Educational Broadcasting Corporation. It was a community radio station begun by Calvary United Methodist Church.
7. On the Sunday when this sermon was preached, a delegation of people from Calvary United Methodist Church in Philadelphia were being recognized as they departed for Nicaragua; the group had been sponsored through a congregational organization.
8. This meditation was written by Ruth Woodlen.
9. This sermon was preached by Susan Cady at Calvary United Methodist Church in Philadelphia.

Chapter Nine: Jesus and Sophia

1. This sermon was preached by Susan Cady in the spring of 1983 at Calvary United Methodist Church, Philadelphia, Pennsylvania.

Chapter Ten: A Sophia Miscellany

1. This sermon was preached by Susan Cady at Calvary United Methodist Church in December 1986.
2. This service was designed and composed by Alison Cheek, an Episcopalian priest.
3. This two-part ritual was designed and composed by Anne-Marie Schaaf with Hal Taussig, Susan Cady, Lynn McMahon, Gretchen Chapman, Ray Henry, Marilyn Moyer, Cherry Granrose, Chip Coffman, Ruth Woodlen, and David Tatgenhorst.

Chapter Eleven: Growing with Sophia

1. Susan Cady, "The Wisdom of Community Building," *The Other Side* (October 1986):26, 27.
2. A number of ways of dancing Sophia texts are discussed in the booklet *The Lady of the Dance* by Hal Taussig (Austin: Sharing Company, 1981).
3. Calvary United Methodist Church, at 48th and Baltimore in West Philadelphia.
4. *An Inclusive Language Lectionary,* published for the Cooperative Publication Association (Atlanta, New York, Philadelphia: John Knox, Pilgrim, and Westminster, 1986).

Index

History: God in, 126–27; Sophia and,
   27–28, 29–31, 35–36, 47–55, 59–60,
   81–82. *See also* Hebrew history
Hokmah, 12
Holy Spirit, 12
Holy Week, 168–69, 220n.12
"Home for the Homeless," 183–84
Human experience: in feminist spirituality,
   5–7, 58; in wisdom literature, 49, 127
Humanity, of Jesus, 44–45
Humankind, God different from, 28
Hymns, 42, 180–87, 196, 197, 218n.22

Immaculate Heart College, Los Angeles, 4
Immanence, 60–61, 128
Immortality of the soul, 51
Incarnation theologies, 11, 128, 192
Inclusive Language Lectionary, 192
In Memory of Her (Schüssler Fiorenza),
   12–13
Intellectual reflection: worldly, 32. *See also*
   Learning
Intellectual tradition: in Israel, 52, 54. *See
   also* Wisdom tradition
Interdependence, 6–7
Introductory courses, on Sophia, 79–88
Isaiah, 48
Isis, 10–11, 30
Israel, 32, 35–36, 216n.12; Sophia in,
   30–31, 32, 35–36, 52–53, 54, 81–82;
   wisdom tradition in, 32, 49–51, 52,
   54–55

Jacob, 27
James, 43, 146
Jesus, 11–13, 14, 33–46, 60–61, 73, 74,
   84–88, 113, 147–57; black, 66–67;
   co-optation and, 57; and death, 34, 35,
   44–45, 66–67, 169; and eucharist, 147,
   154–55; and God, 14, 28, 39, 40–41,
   43; as hero, 7; in liturgy and preaching,
   139, 191, 195–97; passion of, 66–67,
   116, 196; resurrection of, 169; in
   Thomas, 136, 146
Jesus movement, early Palestinian, 12–13
Jesus Sophia (Christ), 41
Jews. *See* Hebrew history; Hebrew
   scriptures; Israel; Judaism
Job, 15; book of, 28–29, 48, 50
Joel, 216n.20
John, Gospel of, 11, 28, 33–41 *passim*, 66,
   116, 128, 146
Jordan, June, 69
Joseph story, as wisdom literature, 48
Judaism, 4, 9–10, 11, 32, 45, 46, 56–57,
   59–60, 216n.15; Jesus movement in,
   12–13; Messiah in, 35; and wisdom
   tradition, 54–55, 57–58, 59–60. *See also*
   Hebrew scriptures
Jung, C. G./Jungians, 10–11, 60
Justice, 69

Kabbala, 57
Kelsey, Morton, 213n.3
Ki, Sumerian, 214n.3
King, Jesus and, 35–36
Kingston, Maxine Hong, 69

Lamb, Jesus as, 36
Laughlin, Ruth, 143–45, 221n.5
Law, Sophia as, 26–27
Learning, 20, 22–23, 31, 54, 61, 128. *See
   also* Intellectual tradition; Teacher
Leviticus, 216n.20
Lietzmann, H., 217n.4
Light of the world, Jesus as, 35, 36
Litanies, 93–96, 134–36, 191
"Litany Based on Psalm 135," 94
"Litany in Praise of God's Presence in All
   Things," 134–35
Litany of Praise to the Wisdom of God," 94
Literature: priestly, 49; Sophia incarnate in,
   69. *See also* Bible; Hebrew scriptures;
   Wisdom literature
Liturgies, 95–96, 116–25, 133–34,
   137–43, 158–59, 191–98
Logos, 11, 28. *See also* Word
Logos und Sophia (Mack), 219n.7
Lord, Jesus as, 36
Lorde, Audre, 69
Lover, Sophia as, 23–25, 82–84
Luke, Gospel of, 33, 41–42, 143, 146, 149

Ma'at, 30, 51, 214
Mack, Burton, 219nn.7, 8, 220n.19
Macy, Joanna Rogers, 5, 61
Malachi, 216n.20
Male domination, 62. *See also* Patriarchy
Marduk, Babylonian, 214n.3
Marginality, 67–68, 147, 148, 194
Mark, Gospel of, 41–42, 101
Marriage, 48, 49, 216n.20
Martin, Joan, 58
Mary, Virgin, 16, 67
Matthew, Gospel of, 11, 33, 41–42, 146,
   154–55
Maundy Thursday service, 116–18
Meal, ceremonial. *See* Eucharists
"Medicine Song," 178–79
"Meditating Sophia in All Things," 132
"Meditation on Gospel of Thomas 77,"
   136–37
Meditations, 132, 136–37, 158
Men: in Sophia study groups, 100, 190,
   194–95. *See also* Male domination
Merton, Thomas, 213n.3
Message-carrying: of Jesus, 40–41, 44; of
   Sophia, 40–41, 44
Messiah, 34, 35–36
Middle class, 69
Missionary movement, Christian, 13
Monotheism, 31, 32, 57. *See also* God
Moraga, Cherríe, 69

Women's Theological Center, Boston, 4
Word, 11, 128; Jesus as, 35, 37, 40
"Words of Wisdom: A Bible Study,"
 155–57
Worldliness, reflective, 32
Worship materials, 88–99, 116–25,
 147–48, 158, 188–98
WPEB (West Philadelphia Educational
 Broadcasting Corporation), 221n.6

Yahweh, 127; Sophia and, 11, 12, 13, 53,
 60
"You Send Your Breath," 180
Yuppies, 213n.4

Zechariah, 216n.20
Zeus, 214n.3